THROUGH THE YEAR
WITH CHRIST

THROUGH THE YEAR
WITH CHRIST

Sermons on the Church Year

GOSPELS OF THE THIRD SERIES

By

EDWIN C. MUNSON
Pastor of Gustavus Adolphus Lutheran Church
Chicago, Illinois

AUGUSTANA PRESS
ROCK ISLAND, ILLINOIS

THROUGH THE YEAR WITH CHRIST

⟦PRINTED IN U·S·A·⟧

AUGUSTANA BOOK CONCERN
Printers and Binders
ROCK ISLAND, ILLINOIS
1959

Dedicated to
my wife, Hannah

Contents

ix

Preface

A SERMON is a strange and wonderful thing. Like a human being, it is a product of much that has gone before—education, folk-ways, social pressures, and tradition. It is also the product of much that is powerfully present at the moment—temperament, the historical or emotional situation, the deep feelings of the heart of the speaker, and the desire to enter into rapport with other human beings. Like a human being, a sermon must also have the spark of life that God has given, or it is a dead thing.

For this reason, there are those who insist that a sermon is a sermon only during those pulsating minutes when one is sharing with others his experience of that spark of spiritual light and warmth given by God, and that it ceases to be a sermon when it is reduced to black type on white paper.

However, just as imagination must go into the making of a sermon, so imagination should go into the reading of a published sermon. Imagine the point in history at which the sermon was delivered; imagine the type of people who must have been present; imagine the temperament and back-ground of the preacher. For example, until one knows how real the threat of Islam was in Luther's day, one cannot appreciate his repeated references to the Turk, and unless one realizes the crudeness of the era one may not excuse some of the uncouth language that Luther employed to gain rapport with his audiences.

These sermons were preached toward the close of a twenty-three year pastorate to a congregation comprising "town and gown" elements. Professors and students mingled with trades people, professional people, and factory workers. To minister to such a variety of personalities has always been regarded as both privilege and challenge. It is my hope that these published sermons may reach a still wider variety of people than they reached when preached from the pulpit. It is my prayer that the Holy Spirit may work through them to bless many lives.

I am indebted to the following for permission to use copyrighted material: Miss Erica Oxenham, Worthing, England, for "Brothers in the Faith," "Who Answers Christ's Insistent Call Must Give Himself," and, "God Grant Us Wisdom in These Coming Days," all by her father, John Oxenham; Mrs. Thomas Curtis Clark for "While Mighty Earthquakes Rock the World's Foundations" by Thomas Curtis Clark; Lois Lundstrom Englund for "Some Folks Are Called to Mighty Acts," and Henry Holt and Company, Inc., for "Comrade Jesus" by Sarah N. Cleghorn.

EDWIN C. MUNSON

THE GOSPEL JESUS PREACHED

Luke 4:16-22

GREAT moments are not always recognized nor appreciated as such at the time of their occurrence. That was the case on that memorable Sabbath when Jesus participated in the service in His home synagogue at Nazareth and thus inaugurated a ministry that has been profoundly influencing the world ever since.

Although Jesus had lived in Nazareth practically all His life, He had been away for some time just prior to His participation in the synagogue service at Nazareth. He had been down to Judea where He had received baptism at the hands of John the Baptist, following which He had spent forty days in the wilderness in fasting and meditation. Before returning to Nazareth, He had visited Jerusalem where He had created something of a sensation by driving the money-changers from the court of the Temple. He had gathered a few disciples about himself, and these men had been with Him at a marriage feast in Cana, not far from Nazareth, where the first recorded miracle of Jesus was performed. In the light of these events, Jesus had returned to Nazareth with a certain aura of fame. He was the home town boy who had made good. Everybody was eager to hear Him, so it was arranged that He should participate in the synagogue service on a certain Sabbath. This was a privilege commonly accorded both members of the congregation and visitors.

1

What was the gospel that Jesus preached? What was the emphasis of His preaching? To know that should be valuable knowledge for all who strive to follow where He has shown the way.

1. *It Was a Gospel of Love.*

From the sixty-first chapter of Isaiah, Jesus read the words, "The Spirit of the Lord is upon me, because he has anointed me to preach the good news to the poor." In no country are the poor so near the rich in advantages as in lands where Christ's influence is strong. The Gospel of Christ, through its influence on laws, its development of a spirit of stewardship, and its fostering of concern for the underprivileged, has done much to reduce poverty. Especially at Christmas time, when the spirit of Christ is less bound than at other times, there is concern for the poor which is expressed in many ways.

Luke has not quoted the passage read by Jesus just as it appears in the book of Isaiah. In its original setting, it reads, "The Lord has anointed me to bring good tidings to the afflicted; he has sent me to bind up the brokenhearted." It is not a mutilation of the text to think of the afflicted and brokenhearted as poor. Money isn't everything. Economic limitations are not the only kind of poverty. Sickness and sorrow and despair can impoverish life as much as lack of money. To minister to this poverty, the Gospel of Christ has inspired medical missions, hospitals, the Red Cross, asylums for the infirm, a widespread ministry of sympathy for the afflicted and brokenhearted.

> "The healing of His seamless dress
>   Is by our beds of pain,
> We touch Him in life's throng and press
>   And we are whole again."

In the light of our Lord's subsequent teaching, we might expand the word "poor" to include the "poor in spirit," as Matthew seems to have done in recording the first beatitude. To those who are conscious of their spiritual poverty, the Gospel of Christ brings new enrichment. They come to realize that through Christ all things are theirs.

2. *It Was a Gospel of Light.*

In the book of Isaiah, reference is made to "the opening of the prison to those who are bound." In the Gospel of Luke, the text is changed to read, "recovering of sight to the blind." Was Jesus reading a spiritual application into the ancient manuscript, or did He have a version that has since been lost, or was Luke merely quoting freely? We do not know. In any case, the emphasis is upon light. Imagine a man lying in a dungeon prison having the doors opened and being told that he is free to go wherever he wishes. It would be the same sensation as a blind man having his sight restored.

There is all manner of darkness in the world—physical, mental, moral, spiritual. The Gospels record a number of miracles performed by Jesus through which sight was restored to those who had previously been blind. Yet, even in the performance of such miracles, He took occasion to point not merely to the seeing of objects, but to beholding the works of God made manifest. Until we see God at work in this world, we are blind.

That is why Christian education must never be allowed to suffer eclipse. It is not enough that men should learn to read; they must be encouraged to read the Bible. It is not enough that men should learn the age of rocks; they must be helped to know the Rock of Ages. One of the most unfortunate experiences a young person can have is to come under the influence of a teacher who has no faith or, what is worse, who scoffs at faith. Secularistic knowledge has not brought light into Russian minds. We can expect nothing better of it for American minds. One of the surest defenses against the darkness of Communism that seems to be creeping over this planet is Christian education.

To the morally and spiritually blind, Jesus is what the sun is to this earth—the source of health and the condition of life. I read somewhere that once a committee in charge of building an asylum for the blind decided that, since the patients could not see, no windows were needed. It did not take long before the patients felt restless and despondent. Some sickened. Some died. Windows were installed, and conditions righted themselves. The world has often thought that Christ is unnecessary, but without Him who is the light of the world, humanity becomes wretched and despondent. Mankind is ill with a mortal illness without Christ.

3. *It Was a Gospel of Liberty.*

The people in the Nazareth synagogue heard Jesus read, "He has sent me to proclaim release to the captives . . . to set at liberty those who are oppressed." Originally, those words had probably been spoken to captive Jews in Babylon. In time, they had been fulfilled in a literal sense, but physical freedom had not made life much richer and freer. Jesus looked beyond physical freedom to freedom of the spirit; for he knew that no man is free whose soul is bound by fear and sin and doubt. Later in His ministry, He stated this very clearly when He said, "The truth will make you free."

So often, when the world embarks upon a liberating program, it ends up in a new slavery. The French Revolution with its guillotine and worship of reason created new slaveries. Russia's foreign policy of liberating smaller nations is merely forcing them into a slavery of greater poverty and terror.

Christ's liberty is not one that can be won by force of arms. His freedom sets free by winning souls to a voluntary bondage. Just as that pilot who is slave to compass, stars, and chart is really free to sail the seas, so only that individual who has accepted Christ as absolute Lord and Savior is free to live an abundant life. George Matheson appreciated and expressed that truth:

> Make me a captive, Lord,
>   And then I shall be free;
> Force me to render up my sword,
>   And I shall conqueror be.
> I sink in life's alarms
>   When by myself I stand;
> Imprison me within Thine arms,
>   And strong shall be my hand.

The reference to proclaiming the acceptable year of the Lord probably had in mind the prescribed year of jubilee when all debts should be canceled, slaves set free, and lands restored to their original owners. A fresh start, a second chance, a new lease on life—is not this freedom?

Wherever the Gospel of Christ has been preached and accepted, it has brought release from paralyzing fears, from cramping doubts, from fettering legalism, from confining prejudices, from shackling superstitions, from imprisoning sins. Christianity has always been a liberating rather than enslaving force. No wonder Jesus could associate His Gospel with the Year of Jubilee. Gone will be the old sadness, heartache, and hopelessness when the Gospel of Christ has taken possession of heart, mind, and will.

It is a right understanding of Christ's Gospel that the Advent season radiates joy. In monarchies, it is customary that when a king is in residence the castle will fly the royal standard from its flagstaff. It is appropriate, likewise, to expect that a Christian should display the banner of joy as an indication that the King has come to take up His residence in that Christian's life.

WHEN COMETH THE KINGDOM?

Luke 17: 20-30

SOME of the greatest truths in life are expressed in paradoxes, in statements that seem to contradict themselves.
For example, if a man humbles himself, he is exalted, or if
a man would find his life, he must lose it. We could char-
acterize the Christian life by the paradoxical statement that
it is both contentment and discontent. If it doesn't have both
elements, it falls short of being Christian. We recognize, of
course, that many are discontented when they ought to be
contented, and contented when they ought to be discontented. That is not Christian.

Let us see how this matter of contentment and discontent
applies to God's kingdom.

One of the goals and hopes of mankind has been a society
where love and justice and righteousness prevail. Sometimes it has been a legendary Atlantis in the past. Sometimes it has been a fictional Shangri-la of the present. Sometimes it has been a future objective to be attained by ruthless revolutionary techniques. But religious minds have
always known that the perfect society can come only
through God's invasion of history. The great question has
been, "When?"

The contemplation of the coming of God's kingdom may
become a veritable obsession. Every happening in history,
every aberration in nature, every new invention may be
regarded as a possible indication of the ushering in of God's
kingdom. As dwellers in Latin America are said to overdo

7

the word, Mañana, which means "tomorrow," so there are those who, in discontent with things as they are, are always anticipating God's kingdom tomorrow. Their searching of Scripture is not with the purpose of finding God's will for today, but of discovering God's plan for tomorrow. As a weather prophet may scan the skies in order to predict tomorrow's weather, so these eager souls are always scrutinizing the horizon of events in order to detect signs of the approaching kingdom. The result is a perennial dissatisfaction, a chronic inability to find any reason for joy, contentment, or gratitude in the present.

Even before Jesus' time, there were those who were always saying, "Lo, here!" or "Lo, there!" Jesus had little respect for those whose exclusive interest was in that which was going to happen in the future. He said, "Do not follow them." He gave this counsel not because the purported revelations were altogther false, but because they were only partially true.

In answer to the question, "When is the kingdom coming?" a two-fold reply would have to be given. Jesus had much to say about the kingdom of God, and when we gather all of His teachings together we find we are holding on to one of those paradoxes which is often necessary to a complete understanding of truth; for the kingdom of God has come, and it is still to come.

1. *It Has Come.*

As the Gospels begin to unfold their story, you sense the air of expectancy. "Repent, for the kingdom of heaven is at hand," was the heart of the preaching of both John the Baptist and Jesus. "Will you at this time restore the kingdom?" was the great question among the disciples.

One of the charges that brought about Christ's crucifixion was that He called himself a king. He admitted before Pilate that the charge was true, but not in the sense that people understood it. "My kingdom is not of this world," said He.

On the basis of such passages, we can believe that Jesus did establish the kingdom of God while He lived and labored in Palestine. In His person He fulfilled the Messianic prophecies which had been a source of hope for the faithful throughout many centuries.

What characterizes the kingdom of God? It involves submission to the King and the desire to carry out His program. Christ is a King of Love and a Prince of Peace. His driving force is good will, not hate. Every rotten stone in the structure of Communism is a lie, and the cornerstone is the biggest lie of all, namely, that Communism seeks a classless society. There are more sharply divided classes under Communism than under any human system ever devised, each class living in fear and suspicion of every other class. The kingdom of God is the true classless society, for there all are brothers in Christ. Wherever you have a love of others that equals love of self, wherever you have respect for the infinite worth of each individual, wherever men regard each other as equals and do not erect false distinctions of color or wealth, wherever men call all brothers who have the same king, there is established the kingdom of God.

For almost two thousand years that kingdom has been on earth. It has no earthly boundaries, no standing armies, no glamorous palaces. Yet, it is firmly established, and all the gates of hell will not prevail against it.

The reason why the kingdom of God cannot be destroyed is because it does not rely on things that can be destroyed—

armies, fortresses, walls, ships, palaces. It relies on truth, on love, on faith. We might compare it to a powerful electric current which cannot be seen. It flows on and does its work or gives its light. If you smash light bulbs, you still do not destroy the current. It is a grave mistake to confuse the kingdom of God with earthly pomp and power, as the papacy has done. The kingdom of God has come as a vital force in hearts and minds. It is the rule which Christ personally exercises over the thoughts and actions of the faithful. Through the divine Word and the holy Sacraments, the current of God flows into human channels. Napoleon is reported to have said, "I have founded an empire by force, and it has melted away; Jesus Christ established His kingdom by love, and it stands to this day and will stand forever."

2. *It Is Coming.*

The fact that the kingdom of God has come and brought peace and joy into our lives is a wonderful source of contentment. Still, while we are contented, we should also be discontented. We should be discontented because the full glory of the kingdom of God is still in the future. It is far from realized. We must still continue to pray, "Thy kingdom come."

There are different opinions as to how the full glory of the kingdom will be realized. Some, remembering Christ's parables of the mustard seed and the leaven and the seed growing secretly, believe the kingdom will develop gradually. Others, thinking of the parable of the ten virgins, believe the kingdom will come as a sudden, divine invasion of earthly life. The common denominator in these parables is that the full coming of the kingdom of God is a future event.

On what will the fuller coming of the kingdom depend? For one thing, I am sure that the future consummation will gather up and make manifest what has always been, for Jesus Christ is the same yesterday, today, and for ever. There will be a continuing changing of men's lives brought about by the indwelling of Christ. This will express itself in ever-widening circles of human relationships. Take, for example, a business man who is ruthless in the competition he offers to others, hard in driving a bargain, unscrupulous in the practices he will resort to in order to gain power and wealth, suspicious or disdainful of other business men. Yet, that man may be a faithful and considerate husband to his wife, a kind and generous father to his children. For his family, he is ready to make any sacrifice. He trusts them implicitly, loves them sincerely. If only something of what he is in his home could be carried into business! Only when we regard others as we regard our parents, wedded partners or children can there be a beginning of that which will constitute the coming of God's kingdom in all its glory.

Our position, then, will be found neither among the worldlings like those of Noah's and Lot's days, who are content with things as they are, nor among those who find nothing encouraging in the present situation and always look for some divine intervention that will overthrow everything we know. Rather, we shall praise God that His kingdom has been established through Christ's redemptive work and is surely found in the midst of life's experiences, but we shall continue to believe that God has more wonderful things in store for this world and we shall not cease to pray, "Thy kingdom come."

Josiah Royce, an American philosopher, wrote something once that could almost be called a Christian creed as far as correct attitude toward this matter of the coming of God's kingdom is concerned. He said, "I believe in the beloved community and the spirit that makes it beloved, and in the communion of all who are in will and in deed its members. I see no such community as yet, but none the less my rule in life is: Act so as to hasten its coming."

A MAN AND HIS MESSAGE

Luke 3:1-14

THE FIRST century of the Christian era was a period of change, unrest, and disintegration. The political strength of the vast Roman Empire which had been developed by Julius Caesar and Caesar Augustus was beginning to wane. There was much graft in connection with the administration of colonial government. Tiberius, who succeeded Augustus in 14 A.D., began his reign with bright prospects, but no sooner had he obtained imperial power than he displayed his odious character. Talented and popular before his coronation, he now began to be cruel and tyrannical. He was brutal towards his wife and his mother; he poisoned his nephews; he brought about the death of many innocent persons by reason of his suspicious and cruel nature. At length, dreading the rage of his people, he entrusted the government to Sejanus in 27 A.D. and spent ten years in dissolute retirement on the Island of Capri.

Pontius Pilate, that unstable governor of Judea during the latter years of our Lord's ministry, attained an immortality of shame for condemning Jesus to the cross. Herod Antipas, tetrarch of Galilee, gained a doubtful distinction for his cunning, cruel, and sensual nature. He married Herodias, his niece and sister-in-law, and when John the Baptist denounced that immoral relationship, Herod caused John to be murdered.

13

With such unscrupulous leaders in the Empire as Tiberius, Pilate, and Herod, it was natural that there must have been economic and political unrest. It has been estimated that the slave population of the Roman Empire was almost equal to that of the free men. Poverty was widespread, particularly in the large centers of population. To keep the people's minds off of rebellion, food was doled out to them, and games were provided for their diversion.

This period was also one of religious decay. The people had come to realize that their pagan deities could not lift them from their hopeless situation. In their groping for something as a substitute, they were victimized by astrology and magic. A deification and worship of immoral, godless, and cruel emperors was springing up. Even among the Jews, the decline of religion was apparent when such despicable characters as Annas and Caiphas could attain to the priesthood.

The age was one of philosophic unsoundness. The two prevailing philosophies were the Stoic and the Epicurean. Both led to atheism and despair—the one by turning all high aspirations self-ward; the other by quenching ideals in the enjoyment of the moment. Everyone has a philosophy, whether he is conscious of the fact or not. A man is what his philosophy is. If his sense of values is distorted, if his objectives are selfish and earthly, if lofty thinking and the sense of personal responsibility find no place in his life, then that man can be said to have an unsound philosophy. Never, before or since, were the darkness of men's minds and the inadequacy of their philosophies more appalling than in the age of Tiberius.

Furthermore, moral degradation had reached epidemic proportions. Slavery and poverty bred vice, crime, and indolence. The theater, bath, and arena contributed to moral degeneration. Divorce was an open sore. The strictures and pictures of such writers as Suetonius and Juvenal represented the culmination of what was rapidly gaining ground during the first half century of our era. Starting in the capitals and larger cities, the tide of corruption flowed out through the whole Empire, reaching even Palestine.

1. The Man.

In the midst of this wilderness of spiritual chaos and social disintegration there was heard a voice, the voice of a prophet, yea, the voice of God speaking through a prophet. John the Baptist was the first inspired prophet to break the silence of the centuries which had elapsed since the days of Malachi. He was a great man. Jesus said that of those born of women there was none greater than John the Baptist. Wherein lay his greatness? What message did he bring to his generation?

As we see John the Baptist emerging from the pages of the Gospels, we see the perfect combination of a devout man who is exceedingly practical and a humble man who dared to thunder against the moral abuses of his day. In the austere discipline of his dress and diet we seem to see a monk, but a monk whose cloister was the desert, whose Father Superior was Jehovah, the God of righteousness and mercy.

Born of devout parents, he was consecrated to God before his birth. Although we know nothing of his early life, we are certain that he was instructed in the Scriptures, that he mastered the technique of prayer, that he did not sully his talents nor dissipate his strength in youthful follies. He did not waste his life in unessential things. His food was simple but substantial, his clothing scanty but sufficient. Into his life there flowed those forces that molded him after God's own pattern. He met the two requisites of a great prophet; for he saw with keenest penetration the life of his day and heard with acutest perception the still, small voice of God.

Like all great souls, he was humble. When the temper of the people was such that he could have proclaimed himself as the Messiah, he humbly and honestly confessed that he was not the Christ, that he was not worthy to unloose the latchet of the Messiah's shoes. He was satisfied to decrease, if only Christ and His kingdom would increase. He was content to be a voice, if that voice could prepare the hearts of men to receive the Messiah. I said that John the Baptist was practical. He saw through the shams and veneer of his contemporaries, but he did more. He exposed them. The advice he gave to eager questioners was adapted to each one's needs.

His courage is shown in his fearless denunciation of the shameless life of Herod and Herodias. It is exhibited also in his blunt criticism of the curiosity of the crowd. To multitudes who came out to be baptized by him he said, "You brood of vipers! Who warned you to flee from the wrath to come?" Because they sought the form of religion rather than its force, because they desired to escape from judgment rather than from sin, John felt compelled to shake them from their spiritual lethargy.

The picture that we get of this great man, John the Baptist, is that of a simple, humble, devout, rugged, practical, and fearless prophet. What was the great message with which this great man stirred his generation?

2. *The Message.*

John conceived his task to be that of preparing the way for Christ and His kingdom. Quoting from the Book of Isaiah, he said, "The voice of one crying in the wilderness: Prepare the way of the Lord, make his paths straight. Every valley shall be filled, and every mountain and hill shall be brought low, and the crooked shall be made straight, and the rough ways shall be made smooth; and all flesh shall see the salvation of God." As many commentators have pointed out, this preparation is pictured in terms of Oriental imagery. When ancient Oriental monarchs set out on journeys, careful preparations were usually made, even to filling valleys, lowering hills, making crooked places straight, and making rough stretches more smooth. Thus, before men would be ready to receive Christ, moral obstacles must be removed. Men must see themselves as sinners, truly repent, and turn from sin into the paths of righteous living. Christ will not come into a life where there are mountains of pride, valleys of degenerate living, crooked ways of dishonesty and deceitfulness, rough places of unkindness and hardheartedness.

The keynote of John's preaching was repentance. When he spoke of repentance, he was not thinking of a mystical experience or emotional spasm. He was seeking something far more fundamental and enduring. In its original setting, "repentance " means a change of mind. John wanted the people to have a new mental outlook upon life, a new set of convictions upon which to base their motives and actions. There can be no repentance, unless there is a sense of sin wrought by the Spirit, together with a desire to be delivered from the power of sin.

The Church of Christ has always had much to say concerning sin, but it has not always made sin in all its aspects sufficiently vivid. The emphasis upon personal religion, and it is a right emphasis, seems, however, to have blinded many to the social nature of sin and the need for social expression of righteousness.

Note the social emphasis in John's preaching. "He who has two coats, let him share with him who has none; and he who has food, let him do likewise." The principle of sharing wealth, the need of a more equitable distribution of the world's goods, so necessary even in our age, finds an exponent in John. Those words were not addressed to men of any particular class or vocation, but to the multitudes. At the same time, John had a timely message for each person. He struck at the besetting sins of each class. We hear him saying to publicans, "Collect no more than is appointed you," and to soldiers, "Rob no one by violence or by false accusation, and be content with your wages." Repentance, said John, meant to turn from the sin of selfishness, from the taking of unjust advantage over one's fellow men.

Sin separates from God, but since sin expresses itself largely in social ways, such as lawlessness, greed, and lust, then deliverance from sin must be reflected in a social way. Often, when the church lifts its voice against economic oppression and political corruption, it is accused of meddling in business or playing politics. Amaziah brought that complaint against Amos. It has been brought against prophetic pulpit voices time and again.

To divorce the personal phase of life from the social side is dangerous. It fosters the philosophy of Cain: "Am I my brother's keeper?"

A number of years ago we read of a certain well-known bishop who had been playing the stock market. In his personal life, he was no doubt a paragon of virtue, but in his social relationships, by his participation in mad speculation, he was contributing to man's greed for profits, and to the depression which resulted from that greed. He, and multitudes with him, did not realize that when we ride the crescendo of a delusive prosperity, we are sure to fall eventually into the diminuendo of a great depression. I know of another churchman, upright in character and a severe judge of the excesses of our age, investing his savings in a personal finance company that charged somewhere between thirty and forty per cent interest on its loans. If he had known how difficult it is for persons to become free from debt after having once become ensnared by loan sharks, he might have seen himself as a greater sinner than he ever did before. Do John's words, "collect no more than is appointed you," have no application on the stock market or in the placing of our investments?

It was not always religiously indifferent men who opposed the abolition of slavery. It has not always been unbelievers who have lent enthusiastic support to the institution of war. It has not always been godless Shylocks that have operated slum tenements. During the great depression in the thirties, it was revealed that a wealthy congregation in New York City owned some low-grade tenements and received part of its support in rents from them.

It is not heresy to point out the social side of sin. It is heresy to conceal the social implications of sin and the need for social expression of righteousness. If men had not carried their religion into business and politics, there would be no abolition of slavery, no pure food laws, no building codes, no penalties for short weight or misrepresentation. No sane person would advocate the repeal of those laws, yet seemingly sane people seem to think that there is no need of further legislative progress.

John consulted men's needs and not their tastes. The Holy Spirit had revealed to him that the kingdom of Christ will never be ushered in while pride and selfishness, injustice and violence are permitted to go uncurbed. He saw the impending judgment upon sin as clearly as the prophets who had gone before him. He knew that, even though the Messiah would come in the flesh, He could not come into the hearts of men until room was made for Him by sincere repentance, a repentance that brought a new mental outlook and that was ready to express itself in every department of personal and social life.

The reason why many reformers and preachers of righteousness are so unattractive is often because they see only the dark side; they have no message of hope. It was not so with John. He saw the crooked paths and the rough ways of life, and made them unmistakably plain; but he also saw the crooked made straight, and the rough ways made smooth. With Isaiah, he envisioned the time when all flesh would see the salvation of God. Under the dominant chord of judgment and repentance there was the strain of hope and redemption. He preached a religion of the broken heart in order that men might know the religion of the triumphant heart. He warned men of judgment because he was wooing them for Christ.

During the span of time that has elapsed since Tiberius and John, the natural human heart has not changed. We find about us the same sins, the same philosophies, the same need of a Savior that John found. Until man penitently and sincerely accepts Christ as Redeemer and Guide, the world will not change very much. But what creative energy is released in the soul that has found Christ!

Will you not open your eyes to the sin of this world and of your own life with which you are helplessly, but not hopelessly bound? I say "not hopelessly," for there is One who stands and knocks at the portals of your heart; and if you open to Him and permit Him to instruct you in the Way of Life, a new power and a bright hope will come into your soul.

WITNESSES TO CHRIST

John 5: 31-39

SOME things in life stand self-attested. They need no defense, for they are their own best witnesses. A glorious sunset, a majestic mountain, a beautiful flower, a noble and unselfish deed—such things are not made more significant or more beautiful by reason of any one's testimony. All that testimony can do is to direct someone's attention to what they ought not miss.

The same can be said of Christ. There He stands in the center of the ages. Time itself seems to revolve about Him. We date history B.C. and A.D. The quality of His spirit and the power of His personality shed a lustre over every century of the Christian era. Art, architecture, music, literature, legislation, home life, education, government have all felt the influence of His spotless life and His unselfish spirit. Nothing in the world can add anything to Christ. It is He who adds something to everything He touches.

Why, then, if He needs no defense and cannot be further exalted by testimony do I announce such a subject as "Witnesses to Christ?" For this reason: That witnesses may direct attention to Christ for those who might otherwise never behold Him.

1. *There Is the Witness of John the Baptist.*

Courts make a distinction between the testimony of questionable characters and the testimony of respected citizens. Let us see what kind of character John the Baptist was.

22

He was a man of simple tastes. Extravagance was foreign to him. He had no desire for luxuries. The poorest garment of camel's hair was sufficient for him. He was proof of the statement, "Clothes do not make the man." As for diet, he could be content with the honey and locusts he found in the wilderness. He ate to live. He did not live to eat. He fed on more important food than bread. He had discovered the principle to which Jesus gave voice—that man does not live by bread alone.

John was deeply religious. He believed the Scriptures. He hated sin, and was not afraid to denounce it in high places and in low places. He looked for the establishment of the kingdom of God. He knew that repentance must prepare the human heart for Messiah's coming.

He had moral courage. He told the publicans and the soldiers that they must change their ways. He did not talk against the rich and powerful behind their backs and fawn before them in their presence. He made Herod and Herodias feel the sting of his righteous rebuke. Because he dared to expose their immoral life, he suffered imprisonment and death.

He was humble. He sought no honors or glories for himself. He said he was unfit to unlatch the Messiah's sandals. He also said, "I must decrease. He must increase."

A man of such fine virtues and strong character should be an unimpeachable witness. And what was his witness to Christ? It was that Jesus was the Lamb of God who was to take away the sin of the world.

2. *There Is the Witness of Christ's Works.*

Jesus said, "The works which the Father has granted me to accomplish, these very works which I am doing, bear me witness that the Father has sent me." The obvious reference here is to the many miracles performed by Jesus which were such a powerful witness to the fact that Christ was more than an ordinary human being.

We should not think of Christ's miracles as devices to compel faith, but as signs to stimulate, strengthen, and develop the germ of faith already present, and to transform it into assured conviction.

The miracles of Jesus could probably be best described as unexplained phenomena of a higher law which a lower stratum of life finds difficult to grasp. I imagine that to the extent animals think, they must think of human beings as miracle workers. Likewise, Christ's miracles bear witness to His being on a higher level of life. If man could perform miracles, he would do so to make people marvel, or to bring them under his power. Jesus performed miracles to heal, comfort, and save. And what is the witness of Christ's works? Is it not this—that He drew upon divine resources to perform His redemptive mission?

3. *There Is the Witness of the Father.*

What did Jesus mean when He said that the Father had borne witness to Him? Could He have been thinking of the heavenly phenomena that attended His birth—the bright star in the heavens, the angelic choir heard by shepherds at Bethlehem, the divine messages to Joseph and Mary, to the Shepherds and the Magi? Was He thinking of the voice He had heard at His baptism and transfiguration: "This is my beloved Son, with whom I am well pleased"? Could He have in mind the divine attestation to the Saviorhood of Jesus which God plants within the heart of a sincere believer? However we are to interpret these words, Jesus means to say that there is something beyond the witness of our senses, and something beyond the witness of our reason, that proves the deity of Christ.

4. *There Is the Witness of the Word.*

If the Bible had never been written, I think we would still have some knowledge of Jesus; for such a life can never be forgotten. But we praise God that there is the written revelation of the hopes which preceded Christ's coming and of the love that was made manifest in His coming.

The Bible is many things, but primarily it is the interpretation of Christ, and we might add that Christ is the interpreter of the Bible. There are those who abuse the Bible by searching in it for everything but Christ. They look for science, history, predictions of future events, arguments to support preconceived prejudices; but they often miss the splendor of Christ's life and the sweep of His salvation.

Have you ever thought of how the whole Bible bears witness to Christ? In *Genesis,* He is the seed of the woman who will crush Satan. In *Exodus,* He is the deliverer and paschal lamb. In *Leviticus,* He is the atoning sacrifice, the object to which true ceremonialism points. In *Numbers,* He is the smitten rock and brazen serpent. In *Esther,* we see the propitiator and intercessor for His people. In *Ecclesiastes,* He is the goal of seeking souls. In *Isaiah,* He is the Prince of Peace, the rod of Jesse, the suffering servant. In *Luke,* He is the physician of souls. In *John,* He is the incarnate Word.

No wonder Jesus could say, "You search the scriptures, because you think that in them you have eternal life; and it is they that bear witness to me."

5.   *There Ought Also Be Our Witness.*

When Jesus was speaking of the things that bore witness
to Him, He did not mention His followers; but at His ascension, in the last words men ever heard spoken by Him, Jesus
said, "You shall be my witnesses in Jerusalem and in all
Judea and Samaria and to the end of the earth." For many,
this may be the only witness they will hear. Therefore, it
is not an unimportant witness.

Every human life bears witness to something—good or
evil, creative or destructive. Every word that we speak and
every act that we perform is some kind of witness. We
thought of the visitors in our Every Member Visitation as
witnesses for Christ. But did you think that you were
witnessing to something when you received the visitors?
You were witnessing to the interest or lack of interest you
have in the Church of Christ. You were witnessing to the
power of money over your life, or to the power of God's
grace in your life. You were witnessing to that which you
consider the most important values in life.

A Scottish writer has written a book in which there is a
story of a young minister who is to preach in his home
church just after completing his theological training. He
prepared a sermon that would reveal his acquaintance with
all the studies he had pursued in the seminary. He would
show the people how much he knew of theology, church
history, higher criticism, and many other areas of learning.
But the night before the great occasion, his mother, sensing
something of what might be coming, said to him: "I know
you'll be giving us a lot of theology and such things on the
morrow, but be sure to say a good word for Jesus Christ."
That plea caused him to discard his carefully planned sermon, and bring a simple testimony to Christ that was with-

in the understanding of those simple, untutored people. Are we saying our good word for Jesus Christ—in the kind of life we live, in the faithfulness with which we attend the public worship services, in the readiness to encourage others to become members of Christ's Church, in the unselfishness of our giving? Jesus admitted that He had witnesses to himself in John, the miracles, the Father, and Scripture. But He said at His ascension, "You shall be my witnesses." Have we taken that charge seriously?

THE SAVING NAME

Matthew 1:21

THERE are many instances of how an idea or a doctrine gathers momentum with the centuries, reaching ever wider circles of experience, invading one area of life after another, enriching or contaminating everything with which it comes in contact. Sometimes it can be a blessing; sometimes a curse. Communism is a good example of that which spreads evil and misery in its wake, and debases everything it touches. Christianity, on the other hand, never visits a home or a nation without leaving precious gifts; it never touches an individual life without making it better.

We cannot think of Christianity without thinking of certain days which have become inextricably associated with it—Easter, Good Friday, Pentecost, Christmas. Each of these days has its own associations, influences, and doctrines. Take Christmas, for example. It is like a great lake formed behind a tremendous dam. It has gathered waters from the heavens above and the springs below and from streams flowing into it from many regions in all directions. But it also sends its waters forth again to generate power, to spread light, to make arid areas productive. Children and adults, mystics and materialists, the learned and the illiterate, the rich and the poor, the ascetic and the pleasure lover all find something in Christmas that is appealing and satisfying.

But while Christmas has become a blend of doctrines, customs, symbols, legends, music, food, artistry, poetry, and pageantry, we must always bear in mind that its heart and center is a Person. There are many names associated with this Person, but the name by which He is usually designated is that by which His own family and friends knew Him, namely, Jesus.

On this most holy of all nights, I greet you in the name of Jesus. "There is no name so sweet on earth, no name so sweet in heaven." The great London preacher, Charles Haddon Spurgeon, once said that the name of Jesus is a jewel from the casket of heaven. Back in the Middle Ages, a monk by the name of Bernard testified that the name of Jesus was honey in the mouth, melody in the ear, and joy in the heart.

In this lovely and impressive Christmas service, we can use these hallowed moments to no better advantage than to consider anew the import of that blessed name which both Mary and Joseph were commanded by heralds from heaven to bestow upon the Child of Bethlehem. One verse of our text is sufficient to occupy our attention, namely, the words of the angel to Joseph: "You shall call his name Jesus, for he will save his people from their sins." For outline, we need search no further than the five letters of the name itself. Like the oft-imagined five points of a brilliant star they shine upon us tonight.

J

The letter J reminds us of the Jewish background of Jesus. From the days of Marcion in the second century to the manufactured religion of Nazism in our own century, there have been many attempts to dissociate Jesus from the Jews and to divorce the New Testament from the Old Testament. It cannot be done.

Christmas assures us that the Old Testament, as well as

the New Testament, is a revelation from God. Prophecies contained in the Old Testament were fulfilled by the events recorded in the New Testament. The Gospel of God's redemptive love is as real in the sacred Scriptures which preceded the first Christmas as in those holy writings which followed the first Christmas.

Hatred is sin, and it is never so great a sin as when it is directed toward whole nations and races. Whenever we are tempted to hate or despise whole nations and races, it is well to recall that Jesus sprang from a race which, above all other races, has been victimized by prejudice and hatred. In the Roman world of two thousand years ago, the Jews were a despised race, but God chose to bless the world through them, nevertheless. Let us remember that even today God can bring some blessing into the life of mankind from races we are tempted to disdain or dislike. Nations and races have a right to be judged by their best representative rather than by their worst. St. Francis was an Italian no less than Mussolini. Luther was a German no less than Bismarck. Mozart was an Austrian no less than Hitler. Kagawa is no less Japanese than the war-lords who perpetrated Pearl Harbor. Tolstoi and Tschaikowsky were Russians no less than Stalin and Khrushchev. When our judgments of whole nations and races threaten to become hasty and warped, let us remember that out of a race which has been hated and mistreated above all others came Jesus, a Jew.

E

E is for Emanuel which means "God with us." The Hebrew letter, "ayin," with which the word begins is usually translated as a short "i" in modern translations, but the older translations often render it as a short "e."

How tragically true it is that Christians often think of Jesus in the past tense—the Christ who was, or in the future tense—the Christ who will be, but forget Him in the present tense—God with us. In days of confusion, darkness and struggle, we need the assurance of a Companion for the way, a Guide for our difficult path, a Comforter in distress. This we have in Jesus, our Emanuel.

While it is true that Jesus was born of a Jewish mother, and lived his life against a Jewish background, it is imperative that we remember that Christ came *into* humanity, not *out* of it. The coming of Jesus into the world was a miracle. No greater miracle has ever taken place than that the divine Lord could tabernacle in human flesh. Without that fact as a starting point, there is neither hope nor joy in the Christmas message. Genuine Christianity demands that Jesus be regarded as more than mere man. "God was in Christ reconciling the world to himself." Upon our faith in that truth depend our higher joys, our deeper peace, our reconciliation to the changes and adversities of life, our freedom from doubt and despair, our confidence in the hope of immortality.

Robert Browning must have appreciated the significance of the name, Emanuel, as applied to Christ, or he could not have made this testimony in his poem, "Death in the Desert": "I say the acknowledgment of God in Christ accepted by the reason, solves for thee all questions in the world and out of it."

> "I know not how that Bethlehem's babe
>   Could in the Godhead be,
> I only know that the manger-child
>   Has brought God's life to me."

In the prologue to the Gospel of John, we are told that "The Word became flesh and dwelt among us." It is only another way of saying, "Emanuel, God with us." Not in some distant heaven, not on some faraway planet, but here among men we may find God, sharing our highest purposes, bearing our heaviest burdens, touched with the feeling of our infirmities, cleansing us of our sins, showing us the kind of life that has eternal value.

S

The letter S stands for Savior. "He shall save his people from their sins." That was the prophetic announcement before Christ's birth. Jesus was to save not from Roman power, not from galling poverty, but from sin. Sin destroys us, body and soul, for time and eternity. To be saved from sin is to be saved indeed. "To you is born this day . . . a Savior!" That was the angelic announcement at his birth. "We . . . testify that the Father has sent the Son as the Savior of the world." That statement of John has been the apostolic announcement ever since Christianity began to be preached.

There are those who might insist that man does not need a Savior, that sin is not very serious, that man is able by his own unaided strength to overcome sin. How blind can people get? How conceited can they become? Have not the crimes and terrors of our own era given conclusive evidence of the prevalence and the power of sin? Has any person who has rejected religion ever been a force for genuine good? Sin cannot be denied, for it is written indelibly over the face of all the earth. It holds not only individuals but whole nations in its thrall. There is only one solvent that can erase it from men's souls. "The blood of Jesus . . . cleanses us from all sin."

U

The letter U emphasizes the universal appeal of Christ, the universal scope of His redemptive work. "Behold, I bring you good tidings of great joy which shall be to all the people." Childhood and motherhood became exalted conditions of life after Bethlehem. The saving name of Jesus was first spoken to humble, working folk—to Joseph, a carpenter, and to lowly shepherds. But learned wise men, as well as working men, were led to the child of Bethlehem.

On one of the walls of our parish house hangs a picture entitled "The Hope of the World." It represents Jesus sitting in the midst of five children. One is black, one yellow, one red, one brown, one white. Jesus is for all races. No single race can monopolize him.

Our beautiful altar painting, "Come unto me," by Karl Heinrich Bloch, teaches the same truth in a slightly different fashion. Men, women, children, youth, and the old—all can come to him. "Him who comes to me I will not cast out."

Christmas can hardly be said to be a universal festival as yet; but the nations will yet kneel before the manger in love and hope. Christ has a universal appeal because He fills a universal need. It is for this reason that we sing at Christmas:

"Joy to the *world,* the Lord is come."

S

The final letter S stands for sacrifice. We cannot thrill to the gladness of the Christmas story, unless we understand what it cost Christ to come and be our Savior. He who shared the very glory of the heavenly Father emptied himself, taking upon himself the form of a servant, being obedient unto death, even death on a cross. It is that sacrifice of Christ which is referred to in the Christmas hymn,

> Thou didst leave Thy throne and Thy kingly crown
> When Thou camest to earth for me.

We have come to associate Handel's "Messiah" with the Christmas season, and we recall that a large portion of that musical masterpiece deals with the suffering and sacrifice of Christ on behalf of sinful humanity. The famous Christmas hymn by J. O. Wallin has a stanza which reads,

> He tears, like other men, will shed,
> Our sorrows share, and be our aid,
> Through His eternal power;
> The Lord's good will unto us show,
> And mingle in our cup of woe
> The drops of mercy's shower;
> Dying, Buying
> Through His Passion
> Our salvation and to mortals
> Opening the heavenly portals.

The weight of Christ's cross was not the wood, but the world's sin. You and I have added to His burden, because it was for you and me that He bore it.

The significance of the saving name of Jesus cannot be exhausted in one brief sermon. After all that we have said, we must add that it goes farther and deeper than that.

> "How sweet the Name of Jesus sounds
> In a believer's ear!
> It soothes his sorrows, heals his wounds,
> And drives away his fear."

It was the saving name of Jesus which an angel spoke at the annunciation. It was the saving name of Jesus which

Pilate caused to be written over the crucified Christ. In all ages, crusaders for Christ have asserted that there is no other name under heaven given among men whereby they can be saved than the saving name of Jesus. Let us enshrine that saving name in our hearts. Let us seal our prayers with it. Let us linger on it in this Christmas worship. And may it be that saving name which will be the last to fall from our failing lips.

GOD IN THE SHADOWS

Matthew 2:13-23

THERE are times when people find it hard to believe that God is in the maelstrom of those whirling events which we call history. There is so much suffering, cruelty, and tragedy in the world that people often ask why a good God allows such things to exist. Nevertheless, amid the sin and injustice of life, we can detect a restraining, guiding force.

James Russell Lowell was aware of both sin and grace in the world when he wrote those famous lines:

> Truth forever on the scaffold,
> Wrong forever on the throne,
> But that scaffold sways the future,
> And behind the dim unknown
> Standeth God within the shadows
> Keeping watch above his own.

There you have it—"God within the shadows." That truth is poignantly brought out in the sequel to the visit of the Wise Men. You will recall that these magi had gone to Herod on their arrival in Jerusalem, and inquired about the newborn king of the Jews whom they were seeking. Herod was surprised at first, then fearful, then crafty and cruel. He sought to kill Jesus, but when the Wise Men did not return, Herod had to devise a new and more diabolical plan. He ordered all male children in the vicinity of Bethlehem under two years of age to be killed. He felt that, by this plan, Jesus would be sure to be included among the victims. However, God overruled Herod's wicked plans. Through the medium of a dream, Joseph was warned of Herod's intentions, and ordered to take Mary and the child Jesus to Egypt, and to remain there until he was told to return to Palestine.

The story of the flight of the Holy Family into Egypt is one of the neglected portions of our Gospels, yet it is rich in lessons that comfort, cheer, and encourage us. The Bible does not say much about the childhood of Jesus. Some of the so-called apocryphal gospels give legendary accounts of our Lord's infancy and childhood, but they are too fanciful and unauthentic to have any value. The Gospel of Matthew, however, contains this brief record which reveals how the infant Jesus was the object of the Father's watchful care. It is this same divine Protector in whom we can place our reliance.

We should not pass over lightly the premature deaths of the innocent children and the anguish of the bereaved parents which were the consequence of Herod's bloodthirstiness; but had those children lived to maturity, they would certainly have experienced greater suffering and tribulation, for life was hard and harsh in those days, and misery was a familiar companion to the common people. The important thing for us to remember is that, within the shadows of martyred innocence, God was guaranteeing that His plan for redeeming the world would not miscarry. Within the shadows of persecution, suffering, and heartache, God was watching and working, defeating the evil purposes of Herod, and safeguarding His own redemptive plan.

What kind of God is it who is often concealed by the shadows of injustice and tragedy, but who is often most fully manifested in just such situations?

1. *He Is an Omniscient God.*

God knew the envy and wrath in Herod's heart, and saw the evil plot shaping itself in Herod's mind, so He warned the Wise Men in a dream not to return to Herod. There is a warning here to every evil-doer. God knows every thought and purpose. It is impossible to conceal the desires of our heart or the plans of our mind from Him.

When the Wise Men did not return to Herod, Herod was infuriated and conceived the outrageous scheme of murdering all male children under two in the vicinity of Bethlehem, sure that through such a procedure he would not miss the infant Jesus. But God would not allow His purposes to be thwarted, and warned Joseph in a dream to flee to Egypt. Later on, the all-knowing God revealed to Joseph in another dream that Herod was dead.

God is omniscient. There is nothing in all the world that can be concealed from Him. If we are receptive to His wise leading, there are ways such as intuitions, premonitions, insights, and inescapable commands by which He will guide us according to His purposes. By prayerful communion and constant searching of the Scriptures, we shall find many ways by which God's leading is recognized.

Not only does God know the course before us which many would give anything to know, and many more may be glad they do not know, but it follows that God must see and know each life, including our own. The psalmist stated it well: "Thou knowest when I sit down and when I rise up; thou discernest my thoughts from afar. Thou searchest out my path and my lying down, and art acquainted with all my ways." Knowing that we have a God who knows all things, even the deep intents of the heart, there ought to be profound moral implications for each of us. It is when men and women think that it is possible to keep attitudes and actions secret that evil flourishes. One of the most dynamic forces for noble living is faith in an omniscient God.

2. *He Is an Omnipotent God.*

The narrative of the flight into Egypt teaches us that God is able to frustrate the purposes of evil men. When Joseph was sold into captivity by his brothers, God overruled their evil, and made it the means by which those very brothers were to be saved. When persecution drove the Christians out of Palestine, God used the very dispersion as a means for spreading the Christian faith throughout the world. When white Christians are driven from Asia or Africa, God can make it possible for an indigenous Christian Church to rise out of the chaos and destruction. During World War II, a number of missionaries were sailing to Africa on a ship called the *Zamzam* when a German warship shelled the ship, took the passengers aboard the German raider, and then sank the *Zamzam*. The missionaries were taken to France and interned, Christians, throughout the world, felt that a terrible blow had been dealt to missions, but God's power saved all the missionaries and gave them a stronger faith in His omnipotence. The world had a glimpse of missionary faith and zeal which it would not otherwise have had.

"With God all things are possible." When we pray the Lord's Prayer, let us not be unmindful of the words, "Thine is the power." An almighty God is capable of miracles. Even as a wicked Herod was to die and make it possible for Joseph and Mary to bring the Christ child back to Palestine, so God may make the death of certain menacing figures of our world open up new opportunities for the true faith.

3. *He Is an Omnipresent God.*

In both the Old Testament and the New Testament, God promises faithful servants that He will be with them and uphold them. He not only promised His presence; He also proved it.

Have you not seen evidences of God's presence in your own lives? Some of you have been almost miraculously delivered from some danger, or from some tragic experience. Let us not confine God's protecting care to the spectacular, however. At a certain testimonial meeting in pioneer days, a man thanked God for His omnipresence; for as he had been riding across a treacherous spot, his horse had slipped, but God did not permit the horse to fall and plunge the man to serious accident or possible death. Another man testified that he had even more reason to be sure of God's presence, for his horse had not even slipped.

It is wonderful, if we can recognize God's presence in remarkable deliverances from danger; but it is no less wonderful to appreciate His sustaining and supporting presence in the ordinary, inconspicuous events of our normal life. God may be with us in dreams and visions, but He is with us even when there are no warning dreams or clear visions. In life's shadows, be they tedious vigils beside a loved one's sickbed, or dark uncertainties as we face some hazardous experience, or disappointing failures in spite of honest effort, we can believe that God will not desert His own, but will make it possible for His glory to be revealed in patient submission, in stronger faith, in untiring perseverance, or in sublime courage. After all, it is not necessarily success or joy or freedom from struggle that may fulfill God's will and plan for us, but trust and faithfulness and hope. Whether He spares us the long trek into Egypt or guides us

on the way, God's presence is there. Whether He removes
our burdens or gives us strength to bear them, God is in
the process.

> He leadeth me. O blessed thought!
> O words with heavenly comfort fraught!
> Whate'er I do, where'er I be,
> Still 'tis God's hand that leadeth me.
>
> Sometimes 'mid scenes of deepest gloom,
> Sometimes where Eden's bowers bloom,
> By waters calm, o'er troubled sea,
> Still 'tis His hand that leadeth me.

JOSEPH GILMORE.

ANOTHER YEAR OF GRACE

Luke 13: 6-9

NOTHING is surer than that our times are in God's hand, and no day emphasizes that truth more forcibly than New Year's Day, when we stand on the threshold of a new year and contemplate its possibilities for joy or sorrow, for good or evil.

The parable of the barren fig tree is an appropriate text for New Year's Day; for it speaks of many of the things that occupy our minds on this day—past failures, God's patience, human responsibility, divine grace.

The primary application of the parable was, of course, to Israel. Almost eight centuries before Jesus told this parable of the fig tree, the prophet Isaiah had voiced God's complaint against Israel in somewhat similar words: "My beloved had a vineyard on a very fertile hill. He digged it and cleared it of stones, and planted it with choice vines; he built a watchtower in the midst of it, and hewed out a wine vat in it; and he looked for it to yield grapes, but it yielded wild grapes. . . . And now I will tell you what I will do to my vineyard. I will remove its hedge, and it shall be devoured; I will break down its wall, and it shall be trampled down. I will make it a waste; it shall not be pruned or hoed, and briers and thorns shall grow up; I will also command the clouds that they rain no rain upon it. For the vineyard of the Lord of hosts is the house of Israel, and the men of Judah are his pleasant planting; and he looked for justice, but behold, bloodshed; for righteousness, but behold, a cry!"

Both passages assert that God has a claim upon man. He created man. He endowed him with certain capacities and surrounded him with various opportunities. This was especially true of Israel, the people God chose to carry the true faith to all peoples. Consider their privileges: the law, marvelous deliverances, great leaders. Behold their failures—apostasy, self-righteousness, wickedness. Israel's day of grace finally ended. The mission was taken away from her. Gentiles were entrusted with the extension of God's kingdom.

This suggests the larger application of the parable. The fig tree is every beneficiary of the grace of God. It may be you and I as individuals. It may be the Christian Church collectively. It can apply to any grouping of individuals. Nevertheless, no group can rise above the individuals composing it. Responsibilities are ultimately accepted or rejected by individuals. Righteousness or unrighteousness is, in the final analysis, the expression of individual character. Even when we speak of mass movements, we are thinking of similar ideas that have taken possession of many individual minds and of similar conduct expressed by many separate individuals.

While it is true that every person is responsible to God for the use to which he puts his life, it is especially true that you and I and every professing Christian are obligated to God. We became members of His kingdom of grace at our baptism. We have the lamp of God's Word to guide us. We have the assurance of peace and pardon and hope, the unfailing presence of Christ in our tasks and trials. All this should stimulate us to great fruitfulness.

What is fruitfulness? It cannot mean perfection, for there is no one who is perfect. Let us see what fruits in the lives of men pleased our Lord. There was the widow giving her contribution in the Temple—an example of unassuming liberality and sacrifice. There was the boy with five loaves and two fishes—an example of consecration of talents. There was the woman with an alabaster vase of precious ointment—an example of penitence, unselfishness, and courageous faith in Christ. Have these fruits grown in the vineyard of our life?

Today we look back over a year that cannot be relived, and we see failures and sins. In the parable of the fig tree, Jesus referred to three years of unproductiveness. Some Bible scholars claim that the figure three refers to the law, the prophets, and the ministry of Jesus. Some insist that it refers to the three years of our Lord's public ministry. It is not necessary to find some literal explanation for every expression of a parable. The parables of Jesus had one salient truth to teach, and all the details were only an implementing of the parable. To seek some allegory for every number may lead us far from the path on which Jesus is trying to lead us. Perhaps it is sufficient to regard the expression "three years" as indicating a sufficient period of time in which to produce fruit. God is not unreasonable. He is perfectly just. He does not expect us to do the impossible.

What Jesus is trying to say is that, with sufficient opportunities and ample time at our disposal, we have been unprofitable servants—as individuals, as a church, as a nation. Our world is in a muddle—like a worldling's feelings after a New Year's Eve carouse. Hopes of a brave, new world have turned to ashes. Dreams of new sources of power to run our machines have become nightmares in which hydrogen bombs are about to explode over us. Like the world of Noah's day, or the cities of Sodom and Gomorrah, we are failures in spite of our boasted inventions and discoveries.

However, we need not be pessimists. God's patience has not been exhausted. He gives us another year of grace. Many seem to have resigned themselves to coming destruction. The sense of inescapable crisis hangs over them like a morning fog. But with God all things are possible. That is why living is such a thrilling adventure. We are in the stream of history, and in history, unlike archeology and astronomy, the unpredictable is always happening. Who can guess what dynamic personality will emerge to steer the world in a right course, or what fresh dangers will arise to hasten the descent into the maelstrom of self-destruction?

As Christians, we should enter this new year with neither fear nor self-reliance, but rather with faith and hope, with repentance and renewed consecration. We are the fig tree, and God will cultivate and fertilize and prune through His means of grace—the Word and the sacraments. It should be our goal not to bring Christianity into harmony with our contemporary life, but to bring the objectives and institutions of this world into harmony with Christ. We shall have to start with the youngest children in our homes. We shall have to begin with the most insignificant assignments that fall to our lot. In all things, we must be loyal to Christ and His Church. We must rely on the gospel to leaven and transform. We must catch and translate into daily life the spirit of Jesus Christ.

Will it be a year of retrogression or a year of renaissance, a year when we shall feel the heavy hand of judgment, or when we shall bring forth the fruits of righteousness and truth which God seeks?

"One trial more! If then we bear no fruit,
  O God of justice! who shall longer stay
Thine arm? Behold, the axe is at the root.
  Oh, let repentance prune our faults away,
Thy grace, O Lord, in plenteous showers descend,
And bid the rescued boughs with clustering honors bend."

THE BAPTISM OF FIRE

Matthew 3:11, 12

ABOUT the time that our Lord was beginning His public ministry, there was one man whose personality and preaching were making a tremendous impact upon the life of Palestinian Jews. That man was John the Baptist. His sermons sat in judgment on the consciences of men. They awakened such a sense of sin in people's hearts that even grasping publicans and hardened soldiers came to him and asked, "What shall we do?"

However, it is one thing to awaken the fear of God in a soul; it is quite another thing to create a godly life in an individual. Vivid word pictures of the judgment may frighten sinners into repentance, but when the daily routine of living dims the luster of a spiritual awakening, and brings its strong and subtle temptations, there is need of something more dynamic than fear. Often, on the bed of sickness, men and women will turn to God for forgiveness and renewed hope, but when God's grace has restored them to health, they also often forget the spiritual longings and feelings which were theirs in the time of travail.

No one knew the failings and fickleness of human nature better than John the Baptist. He saw the limitations of his ministry. He realized that penitent sinners need power as well as purpose, a baptism of regeneration as well as a baptism of repentance. He knew that his ministry was incomplete and ineffective unless Another, greater than himself, crowned it with power and glory.

Emphasizing the preparatory nature of his ministry, John said, "I baptize you with water for repentance, but he who is coming after me is mightier than I, whose sandals I am not worthy to carry; he will baptize you with the Holy Spirit and with fire." John admitted that his baptism was only an outward cleansing. Christ's baptism would possess the power to cleanse the soul. Water touches only the surface. The Spirit reaches the heart.

What did John mean by his reference to fire? There is something about the very thought of fire that is at once terrifying and pleasing. The sound of a fire siren sends a shudder up our spine. News of people being burned to death is particularly horrifying. On the other hand, fire suggests light, coziness, and cleansing. It is this latter connotation that comes to a believer as he listens to the words of John.

Fire, the world over, represents divine energy. As a symbol, it suggests cleansing, light, warmth. Fire is, therefore, a fitting symbol of that reality to which John referred when he spoke of being baptized with the Holy Spirit. Let us see how the word "fire" serves to describe the nature of this baptism with the Holy Spirit.

Fire gives warmth. A true Christian is warmhearted. There is a glow of love which distinguishes him. He is not cold in his attitude toward his fellow men. Coldheartedness is a sin, but when one experiences the baptism of fire, his icy torpor is thawed and a new warmth of love and friendliness becomes evident. There is a fire of enthusiasm in the true believer for those things that belong to Christ's kingdom. In this connection, we should distinguish between fervor and fever. Fervor is an indication of health; fever is indicative of disease. Some seem to think that unless religion expresses itself in some kind of feverish excitement it is not genuine. Shouting, groaning, jumping, and extreme emotionalism are not the earmarks of a healthy religious life. They might rather suggest a fever. Religious fervor, on the other hand, is marked by earnestness, friendliness, sympathy, and love.

Fire does more than give warmth. It purifies. When water is not safe for drinking, boiling it over a fire will purify it. When instruments are to be sterilized against any possible infection, fire will accomplish it. When dross is to be separated from pure metal, that refining process calls for fire. After that, it can be molded to some purpose. When we have been baptized in fire, then we are ready to be molded to God's purposes.

There are many instances in Scripture where fire means cleansing, not destruction. In the third chapter of Malachi, the Lord is compared to a refiner's fire. "He will sit as a refiner and purifier of silver, and he will purify the sons of Levi and refine them like gold and silver, till they present right offerings to the Lord." In the prophecy of Zechariah, God speaks of the remnant that will remain after the destruction of the nation, "I will put this third into the fire, and refine them as one refines silver, and test them as gold is tested." In the great vision of Isaiah which led him into his prophetic work, we read: "Then flew one of the seraphim to me, having in his hand a burning coal which he had taken with tongs from the altar. And he touched my mouth, and said: 'Behold, this has touched your lips; your guilt is taken away, and your sin forgiven.'" Peter, in his First Epistle says, "In this you rejoice, though now for a little while you may have to suffer various trials, so that the genuineness of your faith, more precious than gold which though perishable is tested by fire, may redound to praise and glory and honor at the revelation of Jesus Christ."

Christian hymns refer often to the cleansing work of fire. In one of Thomas Cotterill's hymns, we pray,

> Come, Holy Spirit, from above,
> With Thy celestial fire;
> Come, and with flames of zeal and love
> Our hearts and tongues inspire.

Isaac Watts invokes the Holy Spirit to "light a flame of sacred love in these cold hearts of ours." Still another hymnist by the name of Relde has this prayer to the Holy Spirit: "Come as the fire and purge our hearts like sacrificial flame."

Fire not only warms and purifies. It gives light. We stumble and lose our way in darkness, but in light we walk safely and surely to our goal. God gives us that needed light.

Finally, fire suggests destruction. The same sun that conquers disease also produces sunstroke. The same electricity that heals and stimulates also electrocutes. The same pillar of fire which gladdened the ranks of Israel brought dismay to the hosts of Pharaoh. The same ark of the covenant whose presence hallowed Zion was a means of smiting the Philistines, and working havoc on their idols.

If men will not permit the Spirit's fire to melt their coldness and purge their dross and guide them to their heavenly home, then they must experience the fire as a destructive force. "God is love" but He is also "a consuming fire." He cannot abide and He will not tolerate an impenitent sinner.

We see and accept Jesus as a gracious Savior, but we see and accept Him also as Judge. If we do not let Him convict us of sin here and now, and thus remove the barrier which prevents union with Him, then we will be judged by Him hereafter. "His winnowing fork is in his hand, and he will clear his threshing floor and gather his wheat into the granary, but the chaff he will burn with unquenchable fire." Those are terrible words, and yet, even in their severity, they awaken hope; for who would not be rid of the chaff and the dross in his life?

God would have no soul perish. He does His utmost to purge the evil out of men's lives. Calvary is the climax of God's redemptive work. The benefits of that redemption are brought to us in Christian baptism, but they are not forced upon us. We must grow into an ever fuller appreciation and appropriation of those benefits; for it is tragic but true that many fall from the grace of baptism, drive the Spirit from their lives, and repudiate their heavenly inheritance. We must stand much beneath the cross of Jesus in order to realize with what a great price we have been redeemed.

The soul that has stood before the cross and seen Christ's blood shed for it and in penitent faith accepted the merits of that sacrifice is a new creature. A baptism of fire has judged him and purged out the chaff and dross of his life. Day by day, under the cleansing and vitalizing influence of the indwelling Spirit, the soul grows in the knowledge of the Son of God and glows with the spiritual warmth of sympathy, love, and zeal.

CARRYING RELIGION TO VICTORY

Matthew 12:15-21

EPIPHANY usually falls on a week day, and is therefore not generally observed in Protestant churches. This is unfortunate, for the festival of Epiphany has a great message that needs to shine forth. In fact, Epiphany comes from two Greek words which mean "shining forth." The emphasis of Epiphany is on the manifestation of Jesus Christ as the hope of the Gentiles, as miracle worker, as teacher, as healer, as Savior.

It may at first seem strange that, in view of the meaning of Epipany as "shining forth," we have a text which tells of Jesus' withdrawing and ordering people "not to make him known." Closer study of the text in its context will show that Jesus was withdrawing from controversy with the Pharisees. He was thus fulfilling the ancient prophecy from the Book of Isaiah, "He will not cry nor lift up his voice or make it heard in the streets." With regard to the commanded silence, it referred to the advertising of His miracles of healing. Jesus ministered to the physical needs of men, but His great ministry was to their spiritual needs. Until the redemptive act of Calvary, the disciples would not have a full gospel to proclaim. After that great event in time, they would be urged to go and preach the gospel to every creature.

In reading the various texts for Epiphany, one cannot help being impressed with the note of universality of the manifestation of Christ. "Nations shall come to your light."

"Wise men from *the East* came to Jerusalem," "Let light shine out of darkness." "I am the light of the world." "All the nations shall flow to it, and many *people* shall come, and say: 'Come, let us go up to the mountain of the Lord.'" "In his name will the Gentiles hope." It is interesting to note the recurrence of such words as "nations," "Gentiles," "world" in the Epiphany texts. Naturally, Christ will never be fully manifest nor shine forth in all His glory until He is known and adored by the Gentiles, i.e., by the world generally.

Various methods have been tried by professing Christians by which it was hoped that Christianity would prevail throughout the world. The Church of Rome, on one hand, has often employed techniques associated with earthly governments such as force, pressure, clever scheming. Some sects, on the other hand, have used flamboyant advertising and sensation-tickling methods which have virtually burlesqued religion. We would do much better, as Christ's followers, to emulate our Lord and Master. The Messianic prophecy from the Book of Isaiah which is quoted in Matthew's Gospel describes how the Messiah would act. Jesus truly fulfilled those prophecies.

Often, in Matthew's Gospel, the evangelist refers to passages of the Old Testament which found fulfillment in the life and ministry of Jesus. In this particular instance, the first four verses of the forty-second chapter of the Book of Isaiah are quoted. The expression, "till he brings justice to victory," is given a thought-provoking rendering by James Moffatt in his translation, "carrying religion to victory." The whole quoted passage indicates the means by which religion can be carried to victory.

1. *It Must Be Geared to Human Need.*

The Gospel of Matthew states that "many followed him, and he healed them all." Christ is always sufficient for man's need. He was and is able to satisfy men in their time of deepest need. He met their extremity with His boundless resources. Were they sick? He healed them. Were they hungry? He fed them. Were they ignorant? He instructed them. Were they oppressed by a sense of guilt? He forgave them.

A religion that will not meet the tensions and needs of human life will never be victorious. When Christianity has been true to Christ, it has followed Christ's example in being geared to human need. Hospitals for the sick, havens of refuge for the aged and the foundlings, adventure for courageous souls, profundity for the scholar, comfort for the sorrowing, a sense of vocation for those seeking to find their place in the scheme of things, a new start for those who have made a mess of life, inner peace and joy for those whose souls are torn by fears and frustrations—these are specific ways by which the religion of Christ has been geared to the basic needs of mankind.

Today, religion is being tested as never before. Ruthless ideologies, like Communism, are bidding for the loyalties of men and women. Promises of panaceas are not going to be enough. Whichever ideology can inspire a ministry to the universal needs of hunger, poverty, desire for racial equality, peace on earth and such legitimate hopes will win the field. Christianity has met our need for comfort, pardon, joy, and hope; and it can meet the world's need. But Christianity has neither hands nor feet except through those who are united with Christ through faith. Unless Christians go and give, the world's needs will go unalleviated.

2. *It Must Be Spirit Filled.*

The ancient prophet foresaw the Messiah as one filled by the Spirit of God. It was a person of whom he spoke, but those who come under the magnetism of His personality and power will be filled with the same Spirit.

When Jesus walked among men, they felt that there was a quality about Him that was unique. It set Jesus apart. It was the fullness of the Spirit that was always with Him.

The Spirit that dwelt with Jesus has come upon His Church. Through the church, the Spirit calls, gathers and enlightens souls, and places upon them the stamp of something not of this earth. The world feels that the true church is different from other institutions. With mingled animosity and admiration, the world sees how the true church, with meekness, love, unselfishness and prayer, goes on its way changing sinners into saints, weaklings into spiritual giants, broken lives into integrated personalities. It is true that sometimes a spirit of fear and selfishness and even cunning makes its way into the hearts and minds of professing Christians, but even the scoffers and unbelievers can see that that is not God's Spirit.

3. *It Must Be Mission Minded.*

I have already referred to the repeated reference to Gentiles in the Epiphany texts. The Wise Men were Gentiles. The Messiah was to establish justice and righteousness among the Gentiles.

The church is the body of Christ. Through the missionary

work of the church, Christ has been establishing justice and righteousness in the hearts of believers everywhere. Christianity is a world religion because it is adapted to men of every walk of life and of every color and clime.

No real Christian ever says that Christianity is good enough for us, but that we should let the Africans and Hindus keep their religions. If one were to give vent to some blasphemous oath against Christ, he would not be denying the Christian faith more completely than by urging heathen to be left alone with their unsatisfying husks.

We should be interested in mission work not only across the seas, but also across the tracks. Religion will never be carried to victory where there is self-complacency and lack of interest in winning all people everywhere for Christ.

4. *It Will Be Well Mannered.*

The quotation from the Book of Isaiah is freely rendered in Matthew: "He will not wrangle or cry aloud, nor will anyone hear his voice in the streets." Can you imagine Jesus shouting and pounding and carrying on with violent antics as some of his avowed followers do? Jesus was never rude. He did not force himself on anyone. He was never cheap or gaudy or blatant. He was always calm in His discourses. He was always dignified and well mannered.

Ours is a sensation-loving age, and religion sometimes stoops to cater to the popular demand. We may well wonder how much spiritual life there is in people who are not interested in Christianity unless there is something pugnacious or sensational about it.

5. *It Must Be Patient.*

"He will not break a bruised reed or quench a smoldering wick." We need never search far nor long before we find lives that have been beaten and buffeted until they are in utter despair. Patient comradeship and sympathy are needed to interpret the true Friend.

Sometimes, the patience and perseverance exhibited in non-religious work puts Christians to shame. Cyrus Field tried again and again before he was able to lay the first ocean cable. Every great scientist and inventor has failed often in attempts to produce a desired result, and it is only by patient perseverance that success is finally attained.

As the oak is not brought to its grandeur in a season, and as a cathedral does not reach its imposing beauty in a year or two, so Christian maturity is not produced by one sermon. After three years of patient teaching and inspiring example, Jesus had to say to one of His disciples, "Have I been with you so long, and yet you do not know me, Philip?" Even with time running out, Jesus dealt tenderly and patiently with those who had failed to catch all the implications of His teaching.

It is the mentally slow child that requires the most kindness and attention from a good teacher. It is those that have been alienated by life's hard experiences that need our loving patience, if their lives are to be brought within the orbit of Christ's radiant mercy. Let us never be weary in well-doing, for in due season we shall reap if we faint not.

KINSHIP WITH CHRIST

Matthew 12: 46-50

FAMILY pride distinguishes many people in this world, but when that pride is based on wealth, leadership in society, or worldly honors it can hardly be called laudable. Even when the family pride is based on a record of outstanding achievement and valuable service to humanity, it avails nothing if the individuals concerned have not themselves carried on the tradition.

Not all of us can glory in a long line of scholars, inventors, or otherwise distinguished ancestors; but it is not those things that are of supreme importance. It is a far more important matter whether we are in the family of Christ. That is something that matters both for time and for eternity.

Men talk a great deal about the fatherhood of God and the brotherhood of man; but it is only in the kingdom of God that we can speak properly of the fatherhood of God and the brotherhood of man. The reason we can do so is on the basis of Christ's redemption and regeneration, rather than on the basis of God's creation.

There is a broad and mystical relationship which binds men to God and to each other, and Jesus indicated the source and secret of it in the words of our text.

One day, while He was engaged in teaching and exhorting a large group of people, His mother and brothers came and stood on the edge of the crowd and sent a message to Jesus, saying they desired to speak with Him. We do not know what they intended to say. We do know that Jesus had aroused antagonism and anger, as every proclaimer of truth is apt to do, and it is possible that Christ's kin brought a warning of some plot against Him. Perhaps they thought Him overbold and indiscreet in stirring up such opposition, and hoped to persuade Him to be more diplomatic. Whatever they had to say does not matter as far as we are concerned. It is the reply of Jesus that matters.

The answer of Jesus to those who brought the message was in the form of a question: "Who is my mother and who are my brothers?" Then, stretching His hand toward His disciples, He continued: "Here are my mother and my brothers! For whoever does the will of my Father in heaven is my brother, and sister, and mother."

At first thought, the words of Jesus may seem harsh. We might feel that he was not giving Mary and the brothers the consideration that a dutiful son and loyal brother should give. But when we remember Christ's nature and mission, they become clear and eloquent.

1. *The Family of Christ Is Not Determined by Ties of Flesh and Blood.*

Mary and the brothers of Jesus were merely human. Jesus was divine. He was Mary's Savior as well as ours. Mary deserves honor, but she does not deserve worship. That can be accorded only to the Triune God, Father, Son, and Holy Spirit.

I do not think it is reading too much into the words of Jesus, if we find them suggesting the mystery of His supernatural conception. Notice that in His reply He does not introduce the term "father." He mentions earthly mother, but no earthly father. Listen to the words again, "Whoever does the will of my Father in heaven is my brother, and sister, and mother."

Jesus places spiritual ties above carnal ties. We can understand that better, if we look about us. Have we not known two people entirely unrelated to each other by blood who are closer to each other than those who may be blood relatives? Brothers and sisters can often be strangers to each other though they live under the same roof. Why? Because there is no spiritual affinity between them.

2. *The Family of Christ Is Determined by Fulfillment of Spiritual Conditions.*

Luke, in recording this episode, quotes Jesus as saying, "My mother and my brothers are those who hear the Word of God and do it." Matthew says nothing about hearing. He quotes Jesus as saying, "Whoever does the will of my Father." There is no contradiction, however. Doing the will of God implies having heard the word of God; and if we truly hear the Word of God, we take it to ourselves and translate it into action. Connecting the hearing and the doing is evidence of true faith. Many hear but do not have the faith which motivates to action. Jesus never gave the impression that it was enough to hear or read the Word. One must act in accordance with it. That can be done only when one truly believes it.

As a Christian's capacity and perception grow, so new phases of God's will are given to him. As we keep our minds open and our hearts sensitive, God reveals ever-widening areas for the doing of His will.

While Jesus hallowed and enriched all human relationships, He made possible a deeper kinship than that of blood, a kinship that transcends the barriers of class and race. All

can be members of Christ's family. Paul says, "There is
neither Jew nor Greek, there is neither slave nor free, there
is neither male nor female; for you are all one in Christ
Jesus." John Oxenham has stated the same truth in this
fashion:

> In Christ there is no East or West,
> In Him no South or North,
> But one great Fellowship of love
> Throughout the whole wide earth.

Though all have the privilege of becoming members of
Christ's family, each individual has the responsibility of
accepting or rejecting that privilege. Jesus said, "Unless
one is born of water and the Spirit, he cannot enter the
kingdom of God." By baptism and faith and the resulting
obedience to God's will, we become kinsmen of Christ,
"children of God . . . and fellow heirs with Christ," as the
New Testament says.

Privilege always brings responsibility. Noble ties are one
of the greatest restraining influences against evil. I once
read of how, during the French Revolution, the king's child
was in the custody of an evil person who endeavored to
corrupt the child, but the child said, "I am the son of a
king." We can say, "We are children of God and fellow
heirs with Jesus Christ." We would not want to bring dishonor on our kinsman. Being members of the family of
Christ is not primarily negative, keeping us from doing
those things that would dishonor Christ. It is a positive influence in our life. It spurs us on to do those things that
honor Christ and further His program. We do not prove
ourselves members of the family of Christ by vain professions, but by glad obedience. Jesus stated this fact on one
occasion when, to a woman's praise of His mother, He re-

plied, "Blessed rather are those who hear the word of God and keep it!" And let us not forget the promise given to those who do the will of God: "He who does the will of God abides forever."

It is easy to criticize Mary and the brothers of Jesus for their interference with the work and teaching of Jesus; but it would be far worthier of us to examine our own relationship to Him. Is there that in our lives which would hinder Him or hide Him? Do we pray sincerely, "Not my will, but thine, be done"? Are we deeply moved by the same feeling that moved Paul to exclaim, "When we cry, 'Abba! Father!' it is the Spirit himself bearing witness with our spirit that we are children of God, and if children, then heirs, heirs of God and fellow heirs with Christ, provided we suffer with him in order that we may also be glorified with him."

As you leave this service today, will you not carry with you the picture of Jesus stretching out His hand toward His disciples and saying, "Here are my mother and my brothers"? Imagine that, in the sweep of that gesture, He is including you and me. Ought it not give us a new outlook on life? Ought not the words, "Whoever does the will of my Father in heaven is my brother, and sister, and mother," challenge us to new efforts on behalf of the kingdom, and lift us to new levels of obedience to God's will?

HINDRANCES TO THE RELIGIOUS LIFE

Luke 19:1-10

THE VERY fact that people come to church indicates some kind of interest in the religious life. In the case of some, that interest may be shallow; in the case of others, it may be deeply rooted. In the case of a few, that interest may be very recent; in the case of others, it may be of very long standing. One thing, however, will be granted by all. That is that everyone of us finds hindrances to the religious life. They come both from within and from without.

There are many illustrations of such situations in Scripture. Take Zaccheus as an example. Zaccheus, a tax collector in Jericho, had some quickened interest in the religious life, or at least in a leading religious personality of that age, namely, Jesus of Nazareth. As a counterbalance to that interest, there were many hindrances.

Biography is always fascinating, partly because we see something of ourselves or what we might have been in the studies of other personalities. We are going to think about Zaccheus today, but in that thinking we may be able to see something of our own problems. I have said that he evidenced some interest in religion. He had heard of the sermons, miracles, and character of Jesus, and was determined to have a look at this greatest religious figure of that day. The desire may not have been of long standing, and it may not have sprung from the deepest motives. Nevertheless, there was a beginning, and every beginning is an opportunity. Just as people flock to hear some famous evangelist,

63

although they themselves may have no pronounced religious life, still, the very fact that they come indicates the presence of some spark of interest which may be fanned into flame. Many people in our day are reading books with a religious flavor—*The Robe, The Apostle, The Brother, The Song of Bernadette, The Keys of the Kingdom, Peace of Mind*—and in that very interest there is an opportunity to fan the religious spark into a pure and bright flame.

Unfortunately, however, there are many hindrances to the spiritual life. Look at Zaccheus!

1.   *There Was the Crowd.*

When Zaccheus set out to see Jesus, a large multitude already lined the road along which Jesus was to pass. The crowd stood between him and Jesus, so he got above the crowd by climbing into a sycamore tree. Most people will find themselves incapable of seeing over the crowd, not so much because of their physical stature as because of their small intellectual or spiritual stature. Few indeed are the individuals whose moral and intellectual stature is such as to enable them to see over the crowd. The last thing we want to be is "different." It is hard to buck the current of public opinion, whether it be in the realm of ideas, prejudices, fashions, or tastes. Let any practice make the first few hurdles and gain a following, and soon everybody will be doing it. It may be the latest song hit, the latest hairdo, or the latest prejudice.

People are prone to be stampeded by a seeming majority. Let the idea get loose that people are withdrawing money in large quantities from the banks of a city, and soon every bank will have a long waiting line. Let the rumor get started that there is a shortage of a certain commodity, and soon every store will be sold out of that article. Let some ugly gossip against a race or group find acceptance with a number of people, and it spreads like a prairie fire.

The crowd or herd mind has often been a hindrance to the religious life. Whenever some worldly, secular spirit becomes widespread, it soon becomes a temptation to nearly everyone. Sunday golf, the Sunday auto trip, or some similar fad have often stampeded people into falling in with the prevailing fashion. Sometimes, a few books like *The Modern Temper* or *The Twilight of Christianity* will start the idea that it is smart and sophisticated to believe that Christianity is becoming out of date, and soon there will be a wave of irreligion and immorality because the last thing people want to be is out of fashion. Sometimes a young person voices the desire to drop out of some activity in the church, influences a few others, and before long many are following the crowd away from some constructive and fortifying influence for human personality.

Of course, all this can work in reverse, as it does in the case of waves of spiritual revival, or even as it did in the case of Zaccheus. The fact that many Jericho citizens wanted to see Jesus awakened the desire in Zaccheus. The significant thing to remember, however, is that as long as he just followed the crowd he could not see Jesus. He had to get above the crowd. You may come to church because you have followed many others, but as long as the distinguishing characteristic is merely following the crowd, you will never really see Jesus. You must have that desire with such intensity that if the crowd turned against Jesus, you would be willing to stand alone against the crowd. Religion, if it is genuine, must be a personal experience. If the crowd has caused it, and if the crowd sustains it, it will crumble when the crowd is no longer a stampeding and supporting force. Not until we climb above the crowd and are willing to be laughed at or even persecuted by the crowd does our religion become vital.

If there are some here who are church attendants because they follow others, I say that isn't reason enough. You are letting the crowd stand between you and Christ. Ask yourself, "Would I stand for Christ if all these people stood for something else?" That is the test.

Zaccheus may have followed the crowd out of curiosity to begin with. That did not save him. What saved him was his readiness to rise above the crowd and to follow Jesus away from it.

I would urge upon all of you a suspiciousness of the herd mind, the crowd spirit. Learn to rise above it. Let Jesus single you out as He did Zaccheus. Then follow Him and stand with Him, let the fickle crowd do what it will.

2. *Another Hindrance to Religion May Be Our Work.*

Zaccheus was a publican or tax collector. In those days, one was not hired for that job. One bought it as a concession, and tried to make it pay as large dividends as possible. The very nature of the occupation, therefore, created many temptations to extortion, dishonesty, and materialism. There are many modern occupations, too, that are fraught with temptations and accompanied by low moral standards. Without much difficulty, we could compile quite a long list of occupations that no Christian would choose because of the temptations and low moral standards associated with them. Perhaps few, if any, of those occupations would be represented in a congregation of worshipers. It is more to the point to show that any occupation can be a hindrance to the spiritual life, if it becomes an end in itself.

Generally speaking, work ought to be a spiritual experience. It ought to make for fullness of life. It need not be a job that will make us rich, but it ought to enrich life. If it impoverishes the social, intellectual, and spiritual sides of our personality, it is a hindrance, not only to the religious life, but to our whole being.

In these times, as in all boom times, work has been a hindrance to the religious life of many people. It has robbed people of time to develop their souls. We think it a tragedy when polio withers an arm or a leg. It is a far greater tragedy when preoccupation with a job withers a person's soul. The desire to make money has made crass materialists out of many people. We get excited and concerned when we read that a few spies or saboteurs have gained entrance to our country. It is a far more serious matter when the spirit of materialism invades our society. We have often heard that slavery is evil because it stunts the spirit of man and prevents a well-balanced development. The person who allows his work to become a mere money-making mania is making himself a slave to that which stultifies his spirit and prevents a well-balanced development of the whole personality. Jesus knew whereof He spoke when He said, "What does it profit a man to gain the whole world and forfeit his life?"

Zaccheus refused to allow money-making to paralyze his soul. When he learned to know Jesus as his Savior, he determined henceforth to give half of his income to the poor, and to repay four hundred per cent any unjust acquisition of wealth of which he may have been guilty.

One reason why giving is always to be urged upon men

is not only because of the good it may do for others, but
also because of the deliverance from such soul-destroying
vices as niggardliness, materialism, and miserliness which
generous giving brings.

3. *Still Another Hindrance to Spirituality Is Often Found in Our Associations.*

Zaccheus was regarded as a traitor by his own people, the
Jews. A Jewish publican was very much like a Norwegian
Quisling or French Laval during World War II. He was a
collaborator with conquerors. Being a social outcast, he
was doomed by his position to associate with other outcasts.
Such association was hard on the spiritual life.

One does not have to associate with criminals and vicious
persons to discover that associations can endanger the religious life. Socially respectable people can often constitute
such a menace. A student's fraternity or sorority, for example, can be such a hindrance to the higher life. On a
certain campus, there was one fraternity which a few years
ago had the reputation of being a "booze" fraternity. Other
groups may be saturated with a sheer spirit of worldliness
and vanity. To become associated with such organizations
is to come face to face with a hindrance to the spiritual life.

Associates are important. They can help or hurt, bless
or blight. If associates are going to rob us of our faith, our
inclinations toward the spiritual life, our love for life's
highest values, we are associating with thieves of the worst
kind, no matter how many of the social graces they may
possess. I am sure that Zaccheus broke with his old associates after he found Christ, at least after having made an
effort to bring them to the spiritual experience he had
found. In order to maintain the spiritual glow, to retain

one's hold on Christ, it may be necessary for someone in this audience to sever certain associations which will in time destroy his religious life.

We could no doubt discover other hindrances to the spiritual life within the heart and mind of the individual, but these hindrances that come from without are serious enough to deserve consideration by themselves. The crowd, one's work, and one's associations may become saboteurs of the spiritual life. Let us be vigilant.

> "My soul, be on thy guard;
> Ten thousand foes arise,
> And hosts of sin are pressing hard
> To draw thee from the skies."

THE COMPASSIONATE CHRIST

Matthew 8:14-17

HOW DO you think of Christ? Do you think of Him as the fourth century theologians thought of Him —"God of God, Light of Light, very God of very God"? Do you think of Him as the medieval artists portrayed Him, a stern judge sitting upon the rainbow with a lily protruding from one ear signifying the redeemed and a sword symbolizing the doom of the damned protruding from the other ear? Do you think of Him as Sarah Cleghorn thought of Him when, in one of her poems, she represented Him as a Communist?

> Thanks to Saint Matthew, who had been
> At mass-meetings in Palestine,
> We know whose side was spoken for
> When Comrade Jesus had the floor.
>
> Ah, let no local him refuse!
> Comrade Jesus hath paid his dues.
> Whatever other be debarred,
> Comrade Jesus hath his red card.*

Do you think of Him as Bruce Barton described Him in *The Man Nobody Knows*—a shrewd salesman, a hale fellow well met, the most popular dinner guest in Jerusalem? Do you think of Him as He is often described—impractical dreamer, poet of Galilee, religious reformer?

There are many ways in which men think of Christ, for Christ is many things to many men—teacher, judge, friend,

---

* From *Portraits and Protests*, by Sarah N. Cleghorn. Copyright 1917, by Henry Holt and Company, Inc. By permission of the publishers.

example, redeemer. However, there is one attribute of Jesus that appeals to more people than any other, and that is His boundless capacity for compassion. From the beginning of His ministry to its close on Calvary, He was always thinking of others in a spirit of sympathy. Because of the inroads of sin upon human life, there is no generation, no nation, which does not need to feel the compassion of Christ.

We boast of our enlightened age with its productiveness, its labor-saving machinery, its conquest of disease, its progress along so many lines of endeavor. Yet, you cannot place your finger on a single spot of the earth's surface where there are people living where there is not need of compassion. There are refugees from Baltic countries and eastern Germany and Hungary stranded in free Europe without hope of ever resuming normal living again. There are the victims of Communism on half our earth who have been made slaves of a materialistic outlook on life. There are the colored races of Asia and Africa who have been objects of the white man's exploitation, or victims of their own pagan religions. There are those caught in the toils of some degrading vice. There are others who are desperately lonely, terribly frightened, or grievously disillusioned with life. Others are sick, unemployed, bereaved. One doesn't have to go beyond his own block, sometimes not even outside of his own family, to find a soul who stands in need of compassion.

It is this need for compassion that Christ meets today, as He always met it.

1. *See How He Met It When He Walked This Earth.*

We have before us a passage which describes Christ's compassion. Jesus was going to the home of Peter. As far as we know, Peter was the only one of the apostles who was married, and we can probably assume that Jesus was a frequent guest in Peter's home. On this occasion, Peter's mother-in-law was lying sick with fever. Fever can take many forms, but often it is marked by great discomfort, intense thirst, and delirium. Seeing the sick woman, Jesus was moved with compassion. We are told that He touched her hand, and the fever left her. Immediately, the word got around the city that Jesus had healed Peter's mother-in-law. It was not long before a strange crowd was gathered at the door of Peter's home—demoniacs, lepers, lame, deaf, blind, paralytics. In compassion, Jesus healed them all. Earlier that same day, in the same city, Jesus had healed the paralyzed servant of a centurion. According to Mark's account of the incident, and Luke's also, all this took place on the Sabbath. The evangelist, in recording the incident, could not but be reminded of what the Book of Isaiah said of the Messiah who was to come, "He took our infirmities and bore our diseases." To the evangelist, the expressions of Christ's compassion on this day were proof that Jesus was the long-looked-for Messiah.

That busy day was only the beginning of a long and active ministry of compassion. When great crowds of people listened all day to Jesus' preaching, and had a long journey home without food to strengthen them on the way, Jesus had compassion on them, and fed them. When He was entering the city of Nain one day, He met a funeral procession coming out of the city. A widow was burying her only son. Jesus had compassion on her and restored the boy to life again. One day, while worshiping in the Temple, there was brought to Him a man born blind. People wanted to argue about whose sin had caused the man's blindness, but Jesus felt there was something more important to do than argue. In compassion, He healed the man. On another occasion, as He was entering the city of Jericho, He was met by a blind beggar. Again, the compassion of Christ prompted Him to heal the man. How the heart of Jesus must have bled for the miserable people of His day, the lepers, who, because of the loathsome nature of their disease, were outcasts from society! Once He healed ten lepers by the power of His spoken word. On another occasion, when Jesus was preaching in the region of Decapolis on the eastern side of the Sea of Galilee, a deaf-mute was brought to Him. What a calamity it is for a person to be out of communication with his fellow men! We do not wonder that Jesus had compassion on him. This time, by the power of His touch, He healed that deaf-mute. And so it went. An endless stream of demon possessed, paralytics, lepers, blind, lame, and fevered felt the strength of Christ's compassion and received the wholeness of life He was able to give them.

Nor was the compassion of Christ limited to the bodies of men. When a woman taken in a grievous sin was brought to Him, He had compassion on her, forgave her, and told her, "Go and sin no more." On his last entrance into the city of Jerusalem, He paused at the brow of the hill overlooking the city and broke into tears. With pathos in His voice that we can never know, He said, "Would that even today you knew the things that make for peace!" He had compassion on the children which the adults tried to keep away from Him, saying, "Let the children come to me and forbid them not." When a thief, crucified beside Him on Calvary, asked to be remembered when He came into His kingdom, Jesus said, "Today, you will be with me in Paradise." Jesus' heart was torn by the ignorance, the unbelief, the sin which He found all about Him.

In His parables, too, Christ's compassion was evident. Best known to all of us are the parables of the good Samaritan and the prodigal son. Take compassion out of those parables, and there is no meaning left.

Asked to read the Gospels and to describe in the least number of words the content of those Gospels, it would be hard to find a better answer than "The Compassionate Christ."

2. *See How Christ Meets the Need for Compassion Today.*

It is because our Lord ministered in love to the souls and bodies of men, and because He opened men's minds and hearts to the duty and beauty of compassion, that whereever Christianity has gone there has arisen a ministry of mercy to the multitudinous needs of mankind—Bibles for the unsaved, hospitals for the sick, nurseries for unwanted children, havens of refuge for the aged, institutions of mercy for the afflicted in mind and body, fleets of ships bearing clothing, food, and medicine to the wretched millions of earth.

People who come into contact with Jesus usually catch something of His spirit of compassion. Long years after Peter had witnessed Christ's healing of his mother-in-law, as well as many other miracles of Christ's compassion, he urged upon the readers of one of his letters that they have "sympathy, love of the brethren, a tender heart."

Dr. Frank Laubach has recently written a book entitled *The World Is Learning Compassion*. Many would say that the title is too optimistic, but few would deny that we must change the world from an economy of scarcity to an economy of plenty, if the menace of Communism is to be removed; and that change can be effected not by politics or science or education, however much they may contribute, but by the awakening of a new spirit of unselfishness and compassion in the hearts of men and women everywhere. Science and education may give us the techniques by which an economy of plenty is possible for the peoples of the world, but only a right religion will be able to apply those techniques intelligently. The call of Christ is a call to sympathetic service. Where men are saved, they are interested in saving others, and because of this interest the Church of Christ will always be concerned with works of mercy.

The time will come when our earthly period of grace is ended, when we shall stand before the eternal throne of Christ as He gives the verdict upon men's lives. Not what men said they believed, not what honors the Church conferred upon them, not what display of piety they made in their lives will be the basis of that verdict, but faith working through love, compassion after the fashion of Christ's own compassion. God grant that on that day we may be among those who hear the blessed words: "Come, O blessed of my Father, inherit the kingdom prepared for you from the foundation of the world; for I was hungry and you gave me food, I was thirsty and you gave me drink, I was a stranger and you welcomed me, I was naked and you clothed me, I was sick and you visited me, I was in prison and you came to me."

THE STILLER OF STORMS

Matthew 14: 22-33.

ONE OF our great Christian hymns speaks of "life's tempestuous sea." We can readily appreciate the force of that figure of speech; for, whether we look at individual lives or at human existence in its collective experience, we can see how tempest tossed people often are.

Our expanding knowledge and rising standards of living of which we expect so much seem to have brewed new storms rather than to have eliminated them. We thought that the invention of printing would hasten the spread of the gospel, but it has also hastened the spread of false philosophies, deadly heresies, and demoralizing literature. We thought that a shorter work week would solve social problems, and lo, we are confronted with the problem of misused leisure. We thought that the eradication of child labor would take care of our youth, and then we run into the appalling problem of juvenile delinquency. We thought that airplanes would bring nations closer together in friendly understanding, but they have become potential weapons of mutual destruction. We thought that more deadly weapons would make war unthinkable, and we find ourselves standing aghast before the specter of possible global suicide. We thought that a higher standard of living would bring widespread contentment, but it has brought only a ferment of dissatisfaction.

Through the centuries, men like Metternich, Woodrow Wilson, Neville Chamberlin and Franklin Delano Roosevelt have conferred with other leaders to calm international storms, but their decisions have only brought on greater storms.

Is life doomed to this continual experience of getting out of one stormy situation only to find a stormier one? If mankind can arrive at no stable equilibrium, is it still possible that individuals, at least, find peace in the center of the stormy area?

One of the goals of life held before us by the Bible is the prospect of a society in which righteousness prevails and in which discordant forces may be harmonized. Scripture also reveals One who speaks a sure word of peace to the tempest-tossed soul. Whether it is Nicodemus, troubled with important questions, or a dying thief haunted by his past sins, or the Apostle Peter strangely torn by strength and weakness, or Martin Luther stormily beset by contradictory traditions and truths, Jesus stands near at hand to whisper, "Peace I leave with you."

You have just listened to a portion of the fourteenth chapter of the Gospel according to Matthew which speaks of different kinds of storms that were stilled by Jesus. These storms continue to rage in human hearts, but Jesus is still able to speak the word that calms and brings peace.

1. The Storm in the Souls of the Multitude. (Greed)

According to the gospel record, Jesus had just fed a large multitude in a miraculous manner. Because they had been so miraculously fed, the multitude wanted to make Jesus king, not that they might serve Him, but that He might serve them. How wonderful and easy it would be to have a king who took care of all their wants! With His strange powers, He could surely overthrow the power of Rome, and then He would be able to usher in an era of ease for them. Jesus, however, knew the futility of outward change when motives remained unchanged. Unregenerate Jewish hearts were no better than unregenerate Roman hearts.

I suppose that of all the temptations which lure us into sin, the most persistent is that of selfishness. The little child crying for another child's toys; the school boy cheating in an examination; the grown man seeking greater possessions or honors than those about him; the mother coveting special privileges for her children; one nation seeking dominance over other nations—such examples illustrate the pervading and perennial power of this subtle sin of selfishness.

The multitudes of Jesus' day who were seeking a king that would provide bread for them are not essentially different from the multitudes of today who want the government to provide them with all the necessities of life from the cradle to the grave. Under the specious argument that the mounting national debt is owed to themselves, they refuse to recognize the fact that they are saddling on unborn generations burdens which they are unwilling to assume. As long as they themselves have what they want when they want it, they care not what the future may hold for posterity. They are not as clearheaded regarding the future as that French king who, contemplating the spending orgy of his regime, said, "After us, the deluge."

Selfishness has many ways of expressing itself. All of us fall into its snares at one time or another, and all of us can testify, therefore, that it is a tempest in the soul. Greed, selfishness, and covetousness can so roil a soul that we stand aghast at the foul dregs that are stirred up. Whether it be an individual that has been stricken by its impact, or a whole generation that has bent before its terrible sweep, we can find no better description of the situation than that of a storm.

Is there any stilling of the storm? The history of Christianity preserves many splendid and stirring stories of how Jesus has stilled the storm of selfishness in human hearts, and sent forth men and women to serve others with little or no thought for their own comfort, strength, or life itself.

Just as Jesus did not change the multitude of his day, so he does not change nations today. He deals with individuals. One by one, we must permit His unselfish love to fill our hearts, and as we permit His gracious work to be done in us, so the storm of selfishness and greed subsides, and we know the meaning of a great peace.

2. *The Storm in the Heart of Peter. (Pride, Doubt)*

Peter is a puzzle. He had so many fine qualities, but alongside of them he revealed some very undesirable character traits. Have you been in a group where someone was always pushing himself forward? Peter may have been like that—aways ready to speak up before anyone else had a chance, always ready to play the hero, as when he drew the sword in Gethsemane, always ready to boast of his own powers to the derogation of others, as when he said, "Though all others may deny thee, yet will not I deny thee."

On this particular occasion of which we are thinking today, Jesus, after having fed the people, dismissed the crowd and persuaded His disciples to embark in a boat for the other side of the Sea of Galilee. He wanted to be left alone in order that He might find spiritual refreshment in prayer. How often do we, after a busy day that has taken heavy toll of our strength and patience, follow the example of

Jesus? How many times have we discovered the reality of
the experience for which Whittier prayed:

> Drop Thy still dews of quietness,
>   Till all our strivings cease;
> Take from our souls the strain and stress,
> And let our ordered lives confess
>   The beauty of Thy peace.

As He was praying and while the disciples were cross-
the sea, one of those sudden storms so usual to the Sea of
Galilee arose. The disciples were naturally overcome with
fear of what might happen. Then they saw Jesus walking
toward them over the water. At first, they thought they
were seeing a ghost, and were even more terrified. But
Jesus spoke to them, saying, "Take heart, it is I; have no
fear." Upon hearing Jesus' voice, Peter said, "Lord, if it
is you, bid me come to you on the water." When Jesus
said, "Come," Peter got out of the boat to go to Jesus. Perhaps he wanted to show the rest of the apostles that if Jesus could walk on the water he could also. But we are told,
"When he saw the wind, he was afraid." Then he began
to sink, and had to call on Jesus for help.

So often we start something, confident that we are going
to show up others. Then we lose our cocksureness. We begin to think of the difficulties. Soon we are overwhelmed
by the impossibilities. What was courage turns to cowardice. What seemed to have been faith becomes doubt. It is
a tempestuous experience to have one's pride humbled,
worse still, to have one's faith shaken.

The Apostle Paul said, "I can do all things in him who
strengthens me." He had discovered how the storm-torn
heart can be stilled. With Christ's help we can accomplish

the impossible. It was unthinkable that a little Jew like Paul could make an impact on the Greek and Roman world, but he did. It was impossible for a monk like Luther to break the tyrannical power of the Church of Rome, but he did. Christians will always be apostles of the impossible, "for with God all things are possible." When we are sure that we are committed to God's plans, then the storm of boastfulness, showmanship, impulsiveness and cowardice is overcome, and the peace of a high dedication of purpose prevails.

3. *The Storm in the Minds of the Disciples.* (*Fear*)

Jesus never promised His followers that they would be immune to storms and trials. Severe testings come to the righteous as well as to the wicked. When those disciples were tossed about by the winds in their little boat, they became frightened. When they saw a figure approaching over the water, they said, "It is a ghost." Fear of the elements gave way to fear of the supernatural. Then they heard the Master's voice, "It is I, do not be afraid."

It is hard to find a person who has not, at some time in life, experienced the storm of some superstition. It isn't only the pagans of Asia and Africa who are caught in the storms of superstition. Children often endure terrible anguish because of some superstition imparted to them by some older child or adult. Some of us remember the appearance of Halley's comet in 1910, and how reports of calamity resulting from some kind of contact with its tail filled the minds of many with dread and foreboding. Ordinary fears are bad enough, but when they are mingled with superstitious dread of the supernatural, they become sheer terror.

Into such tempest-tossed minds, the assurance of Jesus brings a great calm. We are asked to believe that at the center of the universe is not chaos or dissolving heat or whirling atoms, but Divine Love. Jesus says, "It is I, be not afraid."

The storms of life meet their Master in Christ. He can calm the storm of greed; He can cause the tempest of egotism or cowardice to subside; He can turn tumultuous fears into devotion and reverence. Out of such experiences resulting from Christ's manifestion in human lives in time of dire need, there develops the confident confession, "Of a truth, thou art the Son of God."

THE VITALITY OF GOD'S WORD

Mark 4:26-29

WITH THE most rigorous part of winter behind us, we hope and plan for spring with its warmth, vegetation, and refreshing showers. In the church, we begin to look forward to the Lenten Season, often called the springtime of the church, when a season of spiritual refreshment causes souls to radiate with spiritual warmth and to grow in grace.

When Jesus told the parable of the seed growing secretly, He called attention to a fact that we often forget, namely, that if we have been faithful in our sowing, God will see to the growth. Just as the farmer who has planted good wheat or oats leans upon the divine resources of rain, warmth, and sunshine to insure growth and guarantee harvest, so Jesus tells us that when we have planted the right seed, we should trust God to furnish the resources that insure growth and guarantee a rich harvest.

1. *We Should Make Sure That It Is God's Word That We Sow.*

It is possible to find churches where the preachers make no attempt to preach the Word of God. Current events, political issues, personal whims furnish the material for their pulpit discourses. There is no thundering from Sinai, no awe before the mystery of the Incarnation, no meditation before the cross on which died One who was wounded for our transgressions and bruised for our iniquities, no visit to an empty tomb from which rose our Lord to be King of kings and Lord of lords.

It is possible also to find churches where, though Scripture furnishes the basic materials of preaching, the messages are so bizarre in their interpretations, so lop-sided in their emphasis, and so intermingled with personal eccentricities, that one can hardly sift out the seed of God's Word from the chaff with which it is mixed.

A recent issue of *Life Magazine* contained an article about the shortcomings of Sunday schools. One teacher of fifteen-year olds is reported to have kept the interest of her girls by letting them use the class period to discuss dates, fashions, and dances. A man teaching boys devoted the class periods to discussing sports. Mickey Mantle, Paul Hornung, and Joe Louis took the place of Jesus and Peter and Paul.

2. *We Can Be Sure That the Seed of God's Word Is Good Seed.*

Moses said to Israel, "What great nation is there, that has statutes and ordinances so righteous as all this law which I set before you this day?" It is good seed because, as Paul said to Timothy, it is "profitable for teaching, for reproof, for correction, and for training in righteousness." Peter, in writing his first epistle, said to the exiles of the dispersion, "You have been born anew, not of perishable seed but of imperishable, through the living and abiding word of God."

The power of God's Word was early appreciated even by enemies of the early Church. In considering how to stamp Christianity out of the Roman Empire, one man said to the Emperor, "It is of no use to burn the Christians; for if you burn every Christian today and leave a single copy of the Scriptures, the Christian church will spring up again tomorrow." The Emperor, acting upon that advice, issued a decree to destroy all the Christian Scriptures. Though many copies were found and destroyed, enough remained, and wherever a copy was left, a church sprang into being.

Why did missionaries like Robert Morrison and Adoniram Judson spend so much of their time in translating the Bible rather than in preaching? It is because they realized that God's Word in the language of the people must be the basis of all preaching and study.

There is vitality in the Word of God. Instances could be multiplied of how people hearing or reading but a chapter or a verse have had their whole life changed. The important thing is to get it planted in the soil of the soul. It will prove that it is no ordinary seed. When Columbus discovered the Orinoco river, some of the sailors said he had found an island. Columbus replied, "No such river as that flows from an island. That mighty torrent must drain the waters of a continent." By similar reasoning, we say that the Bible is no insignificant book. It comes from the heights of divine wisdom, love, and grace, and is but a hint of the power and love that lies back of it.

We shall be hearing and thinking about Abraham Lincoln this week. It wasn't the public libraries or the public schools that could claim credit for his greatness. It was the good seed of God's Word planted in his soul. It had vitality. It did not remain dormant. Evidences of the Good Seed's growth could be seen in the style of his language, in the spirit of his speeches, in the gentleness and sympathy of his character.

3. *We Can Be Sure That God Watches Over the Growth of His Seed.*

It is mysterious how the seed of God's Word germinates and develops and matures. Jesus said, "The kingdom of God is as if a man should scatter seed upon the ground, and should sleep and rise night and day, and the seed should sprout and grow, he knows not how." How can a seed use air and light and water and soil, and incorporate these things into itself, and eventually multiply itself a thousand-fold? We know not how. It is a mystery.

Likewise, the seed of God's Word grows in a mysterious way. A boy in a Sunday school class was asked where heaven was and replied, "In our home since Father was converted and quit drinking."

The growth is not only mysterious. It is progressive. Jesus said, "First the blade, then the ear, then the full grain in the ear." All beautiful and worthwhile things are formed little by little. In the city of Florence stands the church of San Giovanni, at the entrance of which are two pairs of gates—the most beautiful in the world. They are modeled in bronze and are so lovely that Michaelangelo said that they were fit to be the gates of heaven. But it took a man, Ghiberti by name, forty-seven years to complete them.

Sometimes the Word can lie dormant in a person's mind and heart for many years, but it does not die. A Bible verse learned in Sunday school or confirmation class may be brought back to mind on a sick bed, in a time of temptation, in one of life's many crises, and it can alter the whole situation.

Man cannot say when the power of the Word will manifest itself. At a convention of the Salvation Army in England, everything was carefully scheduled with clock-like precision. At a certain hour of a certain day, the schedule read, "Descent of the Holy Spirit." That was impious presumption. Did not Jesus himself say, "The wind blows where it wills, and you hear the sound of it, but you do not know whence it comes or whither it goes; so it is with every one who is born of the Spirit." No one can predict when the Word will bring moral cleanness into a dissolute Augustine, or the light of truth into the mind of a groping Luther, or the call to a life of unselfish service to a young person standing on the threshold of life.

4. *We Can Be Sure That God Will Give the Harvest.*

There are times when a Sunday school teacher may wonder if it is worth while to work week after week with a small group of inattentive youngsters, trying to teach them the elementary truths of the Christian faith. There are times when a pastor sees worldly pleasures and earthly gain become main objectives in the lives of those to whom he has been breaking the Bread of Life, and wonders if he has failed. There are times when Christians contemplate the loss of whole areas to some new paganism, and ask if it was worth the investment of life and money. But Paul said, "The word of God is not bound," and Isaiah said, "The word of our God will stand for ever."

Let us read the Word of God. Let us ponder it. Let us believe it. Let us treasure it. Let us proclaim it. It is good seed. Its growth is watched over by God himself. It will produce a harvest in God's good time.

A PARABLE ABOUT WORK

Luke 17: 7-10

ON MOUNT PALOMAR in California, there is a 200-inch telescope which is capable of catching and reflecting more of the heavens than any other telescope has ever done. Nevertheless, however completely and perfectly the Palomar telescope reveals one aspect of the heavenly universe, there will always remain the opposite side of the universe which that telescope does not reflect.

So it is with the parables of Jesus. They catch, magnify, and reflect the character of God and His kingdom, but it is not easy to present the full picture in one parable. The mercy of God and the judgment of God, for example, can hardly be pictured in the same parable.

Man craves love and sympathy, and that is no doubt why the parables of the prodigal son and the good Samaritan are such favorites. On the other hand, it is natural to resent the implication that one is unfit or unworthy for the kingdom of God. That is why such parables as those of the wedding guest and bondservant are not among the popular parables of Jesus. Nevertheless, every parable of Jesus emphasized some needed truth, and we should shun no parable because its truth is hard or unwelcome.

The parable which we have before us today has a note of harshness in it. Because it tells of a slave working hard all day at plowing or tending sheep and then, on returning home at eventide, having to serve the evening meal to his master before he can rest or eat, it seems, on the surface,

88

to make God a slave driver. But that is to miss the point.

This parable of the bondservant brings out not the way in which God deals with those who serve Him, but rather the spirit in which we should serve God. God is love. He is merciful. Jesus once said, "Blessed are those servants whom the master finds awake when he comes; truly, I say to you, he will gird himself and have them sit at table, and he will come and serve them." That describes God's gracious character. This parable of the bondservant describes how the true Christian feels about himself and his service. He feels that he has received so much from God that he can never repay Him. After he has served to the utmost of his capacity, he still feels that he has done only a part of that which he ought to do for God. It is not God who calls the Christian an unprofitable servant. It is the Christian who calls himself that. This parable will take on added significance for us if we see in it not a rebuke but a challenge, not an indictment but an invitation.

1. *We Learn That There Is Always Service to Be Rendered to God.*

Jesus once said, "My Father is working still, and I am working." He sought continually to impress upon men that the challenge to work for God is always present. "Go, work today in my vineyard."

There is no room for the sluggard in the kingdom of God. There is always work to be done. Something of the intensity of purpose of Jesus must be found in every Christian. "We must work the works of him who sent me, while it is day." If there is anything that has to be worked at all the time, it is the business of cultivating the Lord's vineyard. When we have done our utmost, it is still not enough.

The forces of doubt and evil are like a leaky roof. You work diligently to stop the leak in one place, only to find that a new leak has developed elsewhere. Meet intellectual issues, and there arises an issue in personal morality. Meet that, and you may have to turn against some social problem like racial prejudice. Meet that, and you may find that evil forces have made inroads into some other area of life. An old Greek myth told of how a dragon's head, when it was cut off, was replaced by seven other heads. Jesus told of how a devil, when he was cast out, was replaced by seven other devils worse than the first.

Verily, we are slaves of heaven. There can be no letup in the service of God. We are never graduated or retired as long as life and strength remain. A Christian civilization involves unremitting struggle with the forces of evil and unbelief. There can never be consent to laziness or inertia. There can be no toleration of ignorance, no truce with selfishness, no capitulation to fear, no yielding to a mercenary spirit, no compromise with godlessness. Christian missionaries and pastors and Sunday school teachers and consecrated parents have been trying to spread the gospel for centuries, but where is their work complete? Is it complete in Jerusalem, in China, in Germany, in America, in our own homes, in our own lives?

Some tasks are so trivial that they can soon be performed. The great achievements of life are never complete. Madame Curie spent a busy lifetime in the discovery of radium, but many more lifetimes of service will be necessary to discover all the uses and applications of radium. David Livingstone spent a lifetime opening tropical Africa to missions, but it will take many lifetimes to follow up his pioneering work. In every field of knowledge, character development, and service, the importance is almost in direct ratio to the inability to close the circle, to write "Mission accomplished" after it. We can never exhaust the possibilities and opportunities for serving God and doing that which He would have us do.

2. *We Learn That We Should Use Our Full Powers for Service.*

The servant in the parable used his full day for serving his lord. God has a claim on your whole life, as He has on mine. We often speak of "full-time Christian service" as if it is only ministers, missionaries, and parish secretaries who are to give full-time Christian service. Christian service is the glorious possibility of every life. No one is either too young or too old to engage in it. A child can serve by being thoughtful of others and helpful to others. Many a child has been instrumental in leading parents to Christ. The aged person can serve by testimony out of a lifetime of Christian experience. Even in suffering we can serve God by manifesting patience and quiet faith.

In every life, there are resources that go untapped and opportunities that go unused. You may remember how this was demonstrated during the war. Waste paper, grease, tin, remnants of yarn or cloth, periods of time were all found to be unused resources that could be enlisted in the war effort. In like manner, we all possess talents, energies, periods of time that ordinarily go unused, but which, if dedicated to the Lord, might help the growth of His kingdom. We should never be satisfied with what we are already doing. We should search our hearts and our lives, and ask ourselves, "Am I giving all the strength, time, and talent I can to the service of God?"

> "To serve the present age,
> My calling to fulfill;
> O, may it all my powers engage
> To do my Master's will."

3. *We Learn the Spirit of Humility in Which Service Should Be Rendered.*

God does not despise or belittle any service we may render, but that fact should never foster the spirit of pride over our accomplishments. Remembering that all we are belongs to God should produce the feeling that, at best, we can only do our duty. None of us ever reaches that goal. Every one must pray that prayer of confession, "We have done those things we ought not to have done, and left undone those things which we ought to have done," for the plight of the whole world proves that Christ's followers have failed greatly in bringing their witness and in being the salt of the earth.

How often does it not happen that there is readiness to serve if the service is recognized, appreciated, and praised, but how often has not service ceased when there is not the stimulation of praise nor the comfort of appreciation! We all find it hard to serve unselfishly. How the cross of Christ condemns that spirit!

We need to be on guard against two temptations in the field of Christian service. One is the tendency to self-pity. The other is a conceited self-righteousness which thinks that it has won merit before God. In the case of self-pity, one doesn't feel that service is sufficiently noticed or properly rewarded. Peter expressed it at one stage of his life when he said, "Lo, we have left everything and followed you. What then shall we have?" Every type of Christian work suffers by the defections of workers who reach the point where they feel their efforts are not appreciated.

Very closely related to this type of thinking which pities itself when praise is not forthcoming is the type which thinks it can place God in debt. No service we render to God can ever be a claim on Him for special consideration and favor. God's boundless grace is so overwhelming that we can never understand its vastness. The better our insight into God's goodness and mercy, the greater our humility.

The more closely men and women approximate sainthood, the more the idea of merit before God fades from their mind. The more diligently and faithfully and sacrificially they work, the less they trust in their own work for salvation. Their only peace and joy and comfort lies in dependence upon the grace of God. Man never discovers the deepest satisfactions of Christian faith until dependence for salvation rests not upon good works but upon the unmerited grace of God through Jesus Christ.

ADVANCING THE KINGDOM

Matthew 10: 2-16

THERE is no program in the history of mankind that is so grand in all its proportions as the evangelistic endeavor of the Christian Church. Though at times the means used have been open to criticism, and though often the message proclaimed has lacked the richness and fullness of the Christian Gospel, there has always been at hand the corrective of Christ's own means and message as recorded in Scripture. It is always beneficial to go back to the simple statement of how Christ chose His men, set His goals, and stated His message.

1. *Consider the Men.*

Our Lord chose the twelve apostles not because of their proved ability or outstanding talents. He chose them because they had capacities and yearnings that could be useful in extending the kingdom of God. There wasn't a highly educated man in the group; for Jesus made a distinction that we often fail to make between intelligence and learning. There wasn't a rich man in the company; for Jesus knew how riches could be weights rather than wings to a person's spiritual life.

Christ did not wait until His followers had arrived at spiritual and educational maturity to send them out as builders of the kingdom of heaven. Shortly after calling the disciples He put them to work. Just as a candle begins to give light as soon as it is lighted, so a Christian should let his light shine as soon as his faith has been kindled.

Take a good look at those disciples. James and John earned the nickname, "sons of thunder," among their fellow disciples. Were they given to selfish ambitions? We do know that their mother came to Jesus and asked that when He established His kingdom one of her sons might sit on His right hand and the other on His left. Were they a couple of hotheaded young men, as might be suggested from the fact that when Samaritans of a certain village refused to receive Jesus they wanted to bid fire come down from heaven and consume them? Whatever the natural traits of James and John, Christ was able to transform them. No longer do we know them as "sons of thunder." We know James as the first martyr, and John as the disciple of love.

Andrew and Philip never wrote or said anything that was world shaking, but they had a natural interest in people. Andrew brought his brother Peter to Jesus, and Philip brought his friend Nathanael to the Master. During the week of Christ's suffering and death, Andrew and Philip came to Jesus to inform Him that certain Greeks desired to see Him. They were always on the alert for souls. We might well call them the patron saints of missions.

Thomas seems to have been an inquisitive soul. He had doubts at times, as all of us have, but there is nothing sinful about the relentless quest for truth. No true Christian would agree with the Sunday school child's definition of faith as "believing what ain't so." If tradition is true in claiming that Thomas went to Persia and India to proclaim the gospel, it seems perfectly natural that the intellectually inclined Thomas would go to just that portion of the world where the mind of man had made the greatest explorations and exploits which it is possible to make apart from divine revelation.

Nathanael, or Bartholomew as he is also called, was quick to form prejudices but equally quick to correct them. He wondered if anything good could come out of Nazareth, but he was the first to say, "Rabbi, you are the Son of God! You are the King of Israel!"

Why should we think it such a big step from politics to Christ? Matthew didn't. It would have been a beautiful sequel to learn that Matthew went back to politics from Christ. The world needs men today who will heed Christ's call to "follow," not out of politics but into politics. There are few fields that need greater Christian courage, integrity, and high-minded leadership.

Simon, the Cananean Zealot, is typical of the reformer type who wants action now, and is ready to resort to drastic means to obtain it. Does not Jesus demand sacrifice, enthusiasm, loyalty, obedience—the very qualities any zealot is always ready to give? Whatever motives led Simon to follow Christ, it is certain that he learned at last that man's wrath cannot work the will of God.

Christianity has always appealed to the humble and obscure. James, the son of Alpheus, and Thaddeus were unknown soldiers in the company of Jesus, but where would the Church of Christ be today without the unhonored and unsung?

Peter had as many strong points and weaknesses as could be crowded into one personality. Conceit and contrition, courage and cowardice—these are all a part of Peter. His ready tongue and impulsive action sometimes got him into trouble, but they also gained him recognition. Truly, Peter was a puzzle, but Christ took these puzzling fragments and made of them an ordered and beautiful masterpiece, the inspiration of all Christians down to our own day.

There was one disciple whom I would prefer not to mention. It was Judas Iscariot. Jesus chose Judas as He chose all the others, not because of what he was, but because of what he might become. How often great possibilities are thwarted by greed and dishonesty! The church has never been without its Judases who betray Christ into the hands of His enemies.

Such were the men that Jesus called. They have been called a "glorious company." There are incidents in the gospel narrative which would not justify the designation, "a glorious company," but as we follow them through the early chapters of the Book of Acts, as we see the impact of their labors on the rapidly expanding church of the first century, as we sense something of their influence in the traditions or legends that cluster about their names, we realize that the quality that played a more determining part than anything else was that of dedication. Are we dedicated to Christ? That is far more important than, "Are we educated? Are we charming in our manners? Are we masters of many techniques?"

One thing more should be noted about those men. Jesus did not insist that each one possess all the desirable qualifications, or that they all be cast in the same mold. He sent them out two by two in order that they might complement each other. When one became discouraged, the other could be a source of encouragement. When one could think of nothing to say, the other might have words on his lips. When one might be overcautious, the other would be unafraid. We need teamwork in the Christian Church. There is joy as well as strength in working together.

2. *Consider the Mission.*

The disciples did not begin their evangelistic endeavor by going to the Gentiles. They began by going to their fellow countrymen. It is possible so to stress the distant pastures that one overlooks the opportunities near at hand. Often, Christians can be more interested in the Negroes in Africa than in the Negroes of their own community. Sometimes, church members can be more enthusiastic about the missionary possibilities in some other community than in their own neighborhood.

In all evangelistic endeavor, we should not overlook the potential field near at hand—the unchurched in our own community, the indifferent and unassimilated members of our own congregations, the unused resources of talent and leadership in our own midst. Russell Conwell used to go up and down the land lecturing on "Acres of Diamonds," the point of the lecture being that we wander afar looking for diamonds only to learn that someone has discovered them in the ground that we had regarded as an unlikely source of diamonds.

On this mission on which Jesus sent His disciples, they were to heal the sick, cleanse the lepers, and raise the dead. In other words, they were not to be afraid of tackling the seemingly impossible. The record does not say how successful they were in all these undertakings. If they had actually raised the dead, I am sure there would have been some mention of it. The deeper meaning of Christ's charge to the disciples was certainly that they were to minister to people at the point of greatest need—sickness, disorganized personality, sorrow, despair. We must cultivate our sympathies. We must recognize how Christ's love, working through His followers, alleviates and conquers the ills of life.

Christian ministry is worthy of its hire, but it should not be soiled by a mercenary spirit. The questions of food, clothes, shelter, and such things are not the primary considerations. The important thing is: "What can we do? What ought we to do?" If we care for Christ's work, Christ will care for us. Dare we believe that?

Perhaps Christians have been prone to linger so long and concentrate so much on those words of Jesus which say in effect, "I give *to* you" that they have forgotten the challenging missions on which He sends us, saying, "I give *through* you." We should be more than chalices held up to receive blessings. We should be channels through which Christ blesses. "You received without pay, give without pay."

3. *Consider the Message.*

The gist of the message which Jesus told his followers to proclaim was, "The kingdom of heaven is at hand." That was two thousand years ago. With world wars and cold wars, was the cynic right who wrote:

> Two thousand years of mass
> And we've come as far as poison gas?

Was Jesus mistaken? What could He have meant by the words, "The kingdom of heaven is at hand?" Did He misunderstand His heavenly Father's timetable?

Are we not to suppose that these words were a reminder of the eternal and absolute sovereignty of God, and a promise of His eventual victory over evil and unbelief? Are we not to understand that in the coming of Christ, God's very nature had become incarnate in human life, and must be reflected in human lives? Are we not to believe that Christ alone can meet life in its crisis hours, and bring joy out of sorrow, victory out of defeat, life out of death?

Jesus was not mistaken when He asked the disciples to preach, "The kingdom of heaven is at hand." The kingdom of heaven is always at hand, as judgment upon the false and futile, and as promise of what shall ultimately be. Wherever men and women come to know Christ, catch His spirit, and imitate His life, there is planted the kingdom of heaven. Just think what an opportunity for evangelism every member of the church has to demonstrate the practical working of Christianity in his or her home life, in shop or office, in all the varied social contacts of life!

After World War II, we were talking of recovery. Now thoughtful people are talking about survival. Is it too much to say that there must be a radical change in the attitudes, outlook, and purposes of mankind, if civilization as we know it is to survive on this earth? The pastors and missionaries are too few to do more than touch the fringe of the problem. The laity of Christian churches must assume more responsibility for the evangelization of mankind. They must realize that the Christian message is not only "Come, and I will give you rest"; it is "Go, tell."

The perfect, ideal world may be ever so remote, but Christians know that a better world can come. Though millions may be outside of the kingdom, we can be citizens of it, and, as citizens of God's kingdom, we can work for its extension.

THE VALLEY OF VICTORY

Mark 10:32-45

WE ARE about to enter the Lenten season. It is like coming down from glorious, breath-taking heights into a valley of deep shadows filled with sin and suffering. The Passion of Christ is the most significant event in history, as is indicated by the fact that the Christian Church has set aside forty days for its consideration.

How simply the narrative begins! There is no flourish of trumpets heralding its approach. "They were on the road, going up to Jerusalem, and Jesus was walking ahead of them." To reach Jerusalem, Jesus and His disciples must first go down the Jordan valley to Jericho—down from the fertile and pleasant slopes of Galillee to the edge of the Dead Sea with its desolate and barren shores. It was while they were journeying through the Jordan valley that Jesus spoke of another valley into which He must descend before He could ascend. It was the valley of rejection, suffering, and death. How clearly everything in that bitter valley stood out! Listen to Him as he describes what he sees lying before Him: "The Son of man will be delivered to the chief priests and the scribes, and they will condemn him to death, and deliver him to the Gentiles; and they will mock him, and spit upon him, and scourge him, and kill him; and after three days he will rise." With what clairvoyance He saw not only the whole valley of shame and abuse and suffering, but the victory that lay at the other end! He was saying in words far more majestic and meaningful what the psalmist

101

had said in the words, "Though I walk through the valley of the shadow of death, I fear no evil."

As we journey through the valley of Lent, there will loom larger and larger above the horizon of our thought the figure of a crude and cruel cross. In its purple shadows many things will not seem as impressive or as glamorous as when viewed under the floodlights of man's stagecraft. What seemed to be precious jewels will turn out to be paste diamonds. What glittered as gold will be revealed as cheap tinsel. What bore the appearance of a healthy complexion will be exposed as anemic tissue disguised by the rouge of man's own making.

1. *Let Us See What It Is Which, in the Subdued Light of the Cross, Proves to Be False and Cheap and Tawdry.*

Man has always felt that it is necessary to use force in order to effect certain ends. The misdirected zeal which led the religionists of Jesus' day to persecute and crucify Him has had many a revival during the centuries that have intervened between then and now. Zeal is a good quality when it is directed toward good ends and by righteous means, but when it is enlisted in the obstruction or destruction of truth and righteousness, it becomes one of the most heinous sins that history records. Misdirected zeal is prone to use force; and force, as someone has aptly said, is the last argument of the wrong side.

It was this employment of force by misguided zealots that spread Islam over half of the Mediterranean world. It provoked the futile and foolish Crusades. It burned Huss and Jerome of Prague and Savonarola and Servetus. It plotted and perpetrated the St. Bartholomew massacre in which 20,000 French Protestants were slain. No thinking person can be proud of those gory chapters in the annals of history.

It is against all such error that believes force can ultimately settle anything that the Cross stands. The nails by which Jesus was fastened to the cross have long since rusted, and the wood of which the cross was constructed has long since rotted, but the Christ whom men thought they could destroy by force is loose in the world, judging humanity's little schemes, healing its hurts, offering to transform its institutions, drawing mankind to Him by a love that will not be denied.

It is in the valley of persecution and suffering that victory is born. That is why we believe that Russia and her satellities will yet know a Christian Church more pure and vital than they ever knew.

The scramble for worldly ambition and honor seems so pointless when compared with Christ's suffering and death. The request of James and John indicated that they had not yet understood the full significance of their Master's teaching. They were ambitious for honor and position, as is evident in their request, "Teacher, we want you to do for us whatever we ask of you. . . . Grant us to sit, one at your right hand and one at your left, in your glory."

The self-centered life shrinks to very small dimensions in the shadow of the Cross. Not the good of others, nor the success of right, but the enthronement of self is the goal of worldly ambition. And wherever self has been enthroned, injustice and oppression have obtained important cabinet positions. The world is slow to see the vanity of worldly ambition and honor, yet every generation has its own telling object lessons. Even a slight acquaintance with history enables us to recall the ambitious dreams of Alexander and Julius Caesar and Charles XII and Napoleon and Hitler, and how their vast empires crumbled with them. Those acquainted with the economic life of our century have vivid recollections of the ambitious outreach of Ivar Kreuger and Samuel Insull and Philip Musica, alias Donald Coster; and the debris of their fallen towers of self-glorification still clutters the economic landscape. We can make our argument more cogent and practical by looking at ourselves. What have we received of true peace and joy when we have yielded to the temptation to seek praise and worldly honor? Has not the reward been jangled nerves, unpopularity, more discontentment than ever, and a guilty conscience that reminds us that in the quest for praise and honor we have betrayed something true and beautiful?

The world wants thrones without the thorns, crowns without the cross. It expects a prize but is not willing to pay the price. The Passion story bids us not forget what Judas, Caiaphas, Pilate, and Herod got out of their ambitious scheming.

In this valley of Lent we shall learn the evils of envy and rivalry. As soon as the ten other disciples heard what James and John had requested, "they began to be indignant." Jealousy and envy are not strangers to those who profess to be followers of Christ. Churches have been built and broken by these evil traits. Friendships have been blasted as a result of these devils. Nations that could have lived side by side in amity have worn themselves out in ceaseless wars because they have yielded to the temptations of envy and rivalry. Bickering, spite, cutthroat competition, and similar expressions cannot begin to suggest the unhappiness brought into the world because of them. Think of the time and talent and wealth and energy that have been consumed by envy and rivalry! To what purpose? No enduring and honorable victory ever came as a result of envy and rivalry. Christ's rebuke upon His bickering disciples would still be heard, if we would but allow the strife of envy and rivalry to subside.

2. *If the Subdued Light of the Cross Reveals the Short-comings of Some Things, It Enables Us to See Other Things As True, Noble, and Worthwhile.*

Jesus said, "Whoever would be great among you must be your servant, and whoever would be first among you must be slave of all." No able-bodied Christian will ever be content to be a parasite, living off the industry of others, rendering no service in return. In hours of regular work, as well as in periods of leisure, the motive of service will always be present. Service need not be eminent to be real. If our lives are filled with the spirit of Christ, we will not always be conscious of good that is done. Have we forgotten the response that Jesus said would come from those on His right hand in the judgment? "Lord, when did we see thee hungry and feed thee? or thirsty and give thee drink? And when did we see thee a stranger and welcome thee, or naked and clothe thee? And when did we see thee sick or in prison and visit thee?" The answer they received was, "As you did to one of the least of these my brethren, you did it to me." Humble service is an avenue open to every life. Blind is he who cannot see that truth.

Service is a fine thing, but it is often nothing more than an enlightened selfishness. Service clubs and service slogans often emphasize how service can prove mutually beneficial as well as profitable to the ones rendering it. We are happy to know that there is a desire to render dollar for dollar value. But there is a higher plane of living than that of service. It is sacrifice. A city surgeon performing daily operations costing the patients hundreds of dollars is rendering valuable service, but a doctor going to some portion of the world to minister freely to poor and backward people is living on the higher plane of sacrifice. Educators having life tenure at comfortable salaries are rendering needed service, but teachers willing to serve on mission fields, where the work is difficult and discouraging and the financial return negligible, are in a position to know something of sacrifice. To give of our surplus for the support of Christian work may be rendering service, but to go without something important in our life that we may give more to Christian work is to taste something of sacrifice.

In the valley of Lent we shall be able to see the nature and glory of sacrifice. It was for us that Jesus suffered, bled, and died on the cross. He is the good shepherd, and "the good shepherd gives his life for the sheep." That is sacrifice. "The Son of man also came not to be served, but to serve, and to give his life a ransom for many." That was sacrifice. The writer of the Epistle to the Hebrews says, "He has appeared once for all at the end of the age to put away sin by the sacrifice of himself."

Were it not for the sacrifice that Jesus made, He could not have been our Savior. Were it not for His sacrifice, we would never know that the power of sin is broken. As we journey through this valley of Lent, may we appreciate more than ever before that it is a valley of victory. Without it, life would be only frustration and failure. With it, life may be for everyone something fruitful and wonderful; for Christ's victory is our victory, too, if we be found in Him.

THE ANSWER OF THE CROSS TO MAN'S BASIC SIN—PRIDE

Luke 10: 17-20

DURING the Lenten season, the Christian Church travels in spirit with her Lord as He goes that last, long road which culminates at Calvary. All of the church's preaching during this season should have some connection with the central message of the gospel which we call the Cross. The episodes that are considered may not have taken place during the last days of our Lord's life, but they should have some relationship to the message of the Cross. The testimony of Christians, as it has accumulated for almost twenty centuries, is that for most of man's problems and yearnings the cross of Christ has an answer. Therefore, sermons for this Lenten season will have the general theme, "The Answer of the Cross."

If, after having read the text for this day, you were asked to sum up as succinctly as possible its essential idea, you would probably answer without hesitation: Joy. Jesus had sent out seventy disciples to preach and heal and cast out demons. After a designated period which is not disclosed by the evangelist, the disciples returned to Jesus. They were elated. They were proud of their achievements. They had surprised themselves at what they were able to accomplish. "Lord, even the demons are subject to us in your name!" they exclaimed.

One would think that if ever pride were justified it would be when, in obedience to Christ's command, one has suc-

107

ceeded in carrying some high mission to a successful conclusion. Yet, even under such circumstances, Jesus does
not place His stamp of approval on pride.

Jesus did not compliment the disciples on their successes.
He knew that in war there might be victory one day and
defeat on another day. Battles won were of no avail if the
war was lost. It was because of this that Jesus said, "Do
not rejoice in this, that the spirits are subject to you; but
rejoice that your names are written in heaven." To say,
then, that joy is the central thought in this text is correct,
but it is not all there is in the text. Jesus was cautioning
His disciples against the wrong kind of joy. He was warning against the kind of joy that fostered pride.

Why should Jesus warn against pride? Look at that text
again. When the disciples had returned, and gloated over
the victories and successes, Jesus said, "I saw Satan fall
like lightning from heaven." Was He referring to Satan's
fall as the disciples cast out demons in Jesus' name? I think
not. I think His mind was going back to that event which
took place before any history was written. Lucifer had
been an angel of light. He had enjoyed the presence of the
heavenly Father. But pride had caused him to rise against
God, and consequently Lucifer lost the joys of heaven. Now
the disciples were gloating in pride over their successes.
They were drunk with power in a certain sense. Instead of
rejoicing in being instruments for good, instruments for
Christ, they rejoiced in possessing power. It made them
proud. Jesus knew what pride can do to character. Do we?

1. *Pride Takes Many Forms.*

Consider some of the forms in which pride may manifest
itself. There is pride of race. The Jews thought they were

better than the Samaritans. The Romans thought they were better than the Jews. The Greeks looked down upon all non-Greeks as barbarians. Whites often consider themselves superior to Orientals and Negroes. Some nationalities call other nationalities by such names as "wops," "bohunks," "kikes," and so on. It becomes a vicious circle, and soon passes beyond name calling to acts of violence, hatred, discrimination, and oppression. Pride of nationality and race has led to monstrous abuses and disastrous wars.

There is pride of family, but the pride is usually based on things concerning which there is no reason to be proud— the amount of money and extent of property that have been inherited, the power that has been gained over others, the wealth that has been accumulated and that can be displayed. It is not what people gain but what they give that should occasion pride, and when people are busy giving they have no time to show pride.

There is pride of neighborhood. It is true that some neighborhoods are better than others, but if we are fortunate enough to live in one of the better neighborhoods, it ought to make us humbly grateful to God, not disdainful toward those who live in the more undesirable sections of the city.

There is pride of accomplishment. One can hardly be blamed for rejoicing in achievement. Have you not seen the joy of a child which has taken its first steps? Have you not shared the joy of a child which has brought home a satisfactory report card? Have we not all thrilled in achieving some long-sought-for goal? The important thing is what the joy of accomplishment does to us. Does it make us feel that we have gained a means by which we may better serve our fellow men, or does it make us feel that we have gained a means by which we may get the better of our fellow men?

There is the pride of personal beauty. The classic illustration of how this form of pride can bring destruction is Absalom, David's son. Absalom was proud of his hair, but it proved his undoing. Many a woman who is vain over her beauty discovers that it is the cause of her downfall. It may become a barrier to the finer, higher, spiritual things of life.

How truly does the old proverb describe pride when it says, "Pride goes before destruction." Do we not begin to see why Jesus seemed almost to throw cold water on the high feelings of His disciples? The trouble with most of us is that we fail to see the evil of a thing until it is full fledged, and not always then. If only we could realize that it is the first step in the wrong direction that we must prevent, that it is the first tendency toward greed, lust, anger, and pride that we must thwart.

It is said that Lincoln's favorite hymn was by William Knox, and was called "Mortality." This is the verse that he liked particularly:

> Oh why should the spirit of mortal be proud?
> Like a swift-flitting meteor, a fast-flying cloud,
> A flash of the lightning, a break of the wave,
> Man passes from life to his rest in the grave.

Pride is condemned on many counts. It is exclusiveness, for it shuts out others. It is selfishness, for it withholds from others. It is ruthlessness, for it disregards the rights of others. It is laziness, for it will not do its share of work. Pride is rejoicing over the wrong things.

Somewhere in each life there is pride which contains within itself so much seed of evil—pride of race or nationality or family or position or accomplishment or beauty. It always exalts self at the expense of others. To this basic sin of pride, the Cross brings an answer.

2. *The Answer of the Cross.*

Against the exclusiveness of pride which seeks to shut out others, the Cross is inclusive, for it seeks to embrace all men. The extended arms of Jesus as He hung upon the cross is a true symbol of His desire to gather all men to himself. Just a few days before His crucifixion, Jesus had said, "And I, when I am lifted up from the earth, will draw all men to myself." Paul had seen how the preaching of the cross broke down barriers between men. In his Letter to the Ephesians, he says, "But now in Christ Jesus you who once were far off have been brought near in the blood of Christ. For he is our peace, who has made us both one, and has broken down the dividing wall of hostility, by abolishing in his flesh the law of commandments and ordinances, that he might create in himself one new man in place of the two, so making peace, and might reconcile us both to God in one body through the cross." In a real sense, the cross of Christ is the hub of the universe and, as in the case of a wheel, the farther the spokes extend from the hub the farther they are from each other, so, with people: the farther they are from Christ, the farther they are from each other. Rich and poor, learned and ignorant, black and white, can all find true fellowship in the shadow of the Cross. Any other fellowship will prove sham, shallow, and short.

Against the selfishness of pride which withholds blessings from others, the Cross is unselfish, for it gives freely to all men. Divine love is revealed at Calvary, and as some poet has said, "This is love's prerogative: to give, and give, and give." Why had Jesus sent out the seventy? Was it not to bestow blessings? Those disciples were to heal the sick, comfort the sorrowing, strengthen the weak, cast out demons. The history of colonialism has always had a twofold expression. There have been those who have gone out to find gold, raw products, rare gems, and merchandise to strengthen and lengthen the empire whose flag they set up in distant places. There have been others who have sought only to establish colonies of heaven. They have not sought earthly riches. They have desired only to bring spiritual enrichment, a more abundant life.

Against the ruthlessness of man's pride, which disregards and tramples the rights of others, the Cross is kind and gracious, for it is considerate of all men. As Jesus looked at the multitude on Calvary, He prayed, "Father, forgive them; for they know not what they do." As He listened to the humble plea of the penitent thief, He made the promise, "Today you will be with me in Paradise." As He beheld His grief-torn mother standing at the foot of the cross, He said to John, "Behold your mother!" The kindness, mercy, considerateness of Jesus on Calvary has overflowed into man's life. Something of the influence of the message of the Cross can be seen in the aftermath of war. Even before the war was over, the Christian elements of our nation were thinking in terms of helping the enemy nations rebuild on foundations that would insure a happier world. No one can say that Russia, with its anti-Christian philosophy, has been concerned about the welfare of the people it has brought into its orbit of influence. It has sought only to plunder and degrade and exploit for itself. Human rights are not considered where the pride of man is enthroned. They are recognized only where the Cross has shed its light.

Against the sterility and self-complacency of man's pride, the Cross comes with a tremendous power to transform the lives of people. Into the fetid air of the dying Roman Empire, the gospel of the cross came as a fresh and cleansing wind. Into the ignorance and corruption of paganism, the message of the cross brings regenerating power. Read the story of any missionary enterprise in Africa, Asia, or the islands of the seas, and you will thrill to the stories of transformations wrought. Jesus said on one occasion, "Unless a grain of wheat falls into the earth and dies, it remains alone; but if it dies, it bears much fruit." Then, to make His thought more clear, He added, "He who loves his life loses it, and he who hates his life in this world will keep it for eternal life." It is the life invested in the spirit of Christ's cross that has power.

Alexander Pope described the folly and futility of pride in these words;

> Thus unlamented pass the proud away,
> The gaze of fools and pageant of a day;
> So perish all, whose breast ne'er learned to glow
> For others' good, or melt at others' woe.

Sylvanus Phelps described the answer of the cross to man's basic sin, pride, when he penned those lines of one of our much-loved hymns:

> Some work of love begun,
> Some deed of kindness done,
> Some wanderer sought and won,
> Something for Thee.

THE CROSS IS THE ANSWER TO STRUGGLING FAITH

Mark 9:14-32

SOME people find it very easy to draw a line of demarcation through life, so that ideas, tastes, actions, and feelings are sharply divided between good and bad, between true and false, between right and wrong. To such a person, it would seem to be a contradiction to speak of "struggling faith." He would argue, "You either believe or you do not believe."

There is no question but that it is a wonderful ability to be able to discriminate so keenly between right and wrong and between truth and falsehood. Too many people never see in terms of black and white. They see only dull grays. They never develop a strong sense of justice because they never have felt a strong sense of injustice. They never come to have strong convictions on one side or another. They know neither radiant faith nor dull disbelief. They are like a lump of putty with no recognizable shape.

There are other people in this world who do not think in terms of black *or* white, nor do they think in terms of gray. They think in terms of black *and* white. One day they believe. The next they are floundering in a swamp of doubt.

The Passion story of our Lord presents all three classes of people. There were those who strongly believed and otehrs who strongly disbelieved. Like the faithful women, they were wholeheartedly with Christ, or like the high priests, they were uncompromisingly against Him. There were others, and I suspect that they were in the majority, who did not think much one way or the other. On Palm Sunday, they might be momentarily caught up in the enthusiasm of the disciples of Jesus, but on Good Friday they would be just as apt to be influenced by the rabble rousers before Pilate's palace. Then there were others who were really torn between faith and unbelief. They wanted to believe, but their lifelong prejudices seemed to be chains upon their minds and souls. Or perhaps they wanted to disbelieve, but there was that strange Prophet from Galilee who seemed always to haunt them. They could not escape Him. I find this class of people well described by the father of the afflicted boy who was waiting at the foot of the Mount of Transfiguration for Jesus to come down and heal his son. While Jesus, together with Peter, James, and John, was up on the mountain, the man had brought his afflicted son to the rest of the disciples asking that they might cure him. They were not able. When Jesus came down from the mountain after the transfiguration, the man laid his case before Jesus and added, "If you can do anything, have pity on us and help us." Jesus said, "If you can! All things are possible to him who believes." Immediately, the father of the child cried out and said, "I believe; help my unbelief!" Of course, Jesus healed the lad, but it is not of the healing power of Jesus that I wish to speak. I want to speak of Christ's power to strengthen faith. What He did for the struggling faith of that boy's father, He can do for many of you.

Perhaps there are some who are puzzled by the nature of faith. Is faith something that, by its very nature, is contrary to reason? Jesus did not so regard it. After He had told His disciples a number of parables about the kingdom, He asked, "Have you understood all this?" He did not say "Do you believe all this?" Often, Jesus would ask His hearers questions which put upon them the necessity of doing some hard, straight thinking. Jesus would never have approved the suggestion that we should leave our minds outside of the church as the Mohammedans and Hindus leave their shoes outside of their places of worship. However, He did realize that there are areas of knowledge and experience where faith can go, but where reason can never go.

True Christianity never despises reason, but neither does it permit reason to displace faith. An eastern college scheduled a panel discussion some years ago on the subject, "Faith on Trial. The Academic Mind a Challenge to Religion." It would have been more fitting to announce the topic, "Religion a Challenge to the Academic Mind."

The father of the afflicted lad who met Jesus when He came down from the Mount of Transfiguration is typical of a great number of people. They have problems and doubts, but, like Nicodemus, they have enough faith to bring those doubts to Jesus. It would be strange, indeed, if there were not quite a number here today for whom the expression, "struggling faith," is an appropriate description. There were a number who figured in the Passion story of our Lord who found in the cross of Christ an answer to their struggling faith.

1. *Consider the People Whose Faith Was Fortified at the Cross.*

There was the penitent thief. This man had been guilty of robbery, murder, and rebellion. He had been tried and found worthy of death. He did not question the justice of the verdict, for he told his fellow in crime, "We are receiving the due reward of our deeds; but this man has done nothing wrong." Then he went on to address Jesus, saying, "Jesus, remember me when you come in your kingly power." There can be no question as to the part which the Cross played in developing the penitent thief's faith. Both thieves had railed at Jesus, but one man's unbelief was conquered. Before he died, he was calling in faith upon Jesus as He hung upon His cross.

There was the centurion who had presided over the grim and ghastly rites of that day. It must have been a familiar experience for him. Nevertheless, there was something about the manner in which Jesus carried himself that day which shattered the centurion's hardness of heart and made him confess Jesus as the Son of God.

There were Nicodemus and Joseph of Arimathea. They were friends of Jesus and believers in Jesus. However, their faith had never been strong enough to risk the ridicule of friends or the persecution of the Jewish rulers. Nevertheless, when Jesus had breathed His last, these two members of the Sanhedrin came out openly as friends and disciples of Jesus by going to Pilate and asking for the body of Jesus that they might grant it proper burial. Something about the dying Jesus dissipated their doubts and brought their faith to clear conviction.

2. *What Was There About the Cross to Make it an Answer to Struggling Faith?*

Both Jesus and the two thieves were dying the slow, painful death resulting from crucifixion. Yet, what a difference! The thieves had been living as if all that mattered was what wealth and pleasure they got in this world. Evidently they believed that when death came, that was the end of everything. Jesus seemed certain that death was not the end but a beginning. Life could not be destroyed by a few nails. Life would go on with the heavenly Father. It was to save men for this larger life that Jesus was dying. Into the mind of one of the dying thieves this truth broke through. The Cross spoke of hope for a wasted life to that man. This is the answer of the Cross to everyone who wavers between believing that earthly existence is all of life and believing that there must be more to life than mere earthly existence. What comfort, in life's last hour, to be able to sing,

> "Hold Thou Thy Cross before my closing eyes,
> Shine through the gloom, and point me to the skies:
> Heaven's morning breaks, and earth's vain shadows flee;
> In life, in death, O Lord, abide with me."

The centurion had accepted the philosophy that might makes right. For him, meekness was weakness. He was sure that a stout sword could accomplish more than love and mercy. Nevertheless, something changed his set of values that day on Calvary. Love conquered him. The terrible meekness of Jesus overwhelmed him. He left Calvary exclaiming, "Certainly this man was innocent. Truly this was a son of God." Even today, the cross of Christ proves that love is stronger than hate, and that meekness is anything but weakness. Nuclear fission is only strong enough to kill. Divine love is strong enough to confer eternal life.

For Nicodemus and Joseph of Arimathea, the Cross showed them that faith is never true faith until it is marked by sacrificial love and courage to witness. This is something that many professing Christians of our own day need to learn. They feel that because they are not actively opposed to Christ, and because they have some relationship with the Church of Christ, that that is all that is required of them They have never in their life known what it means to make any kind of real sacrifice for Christ. They have never made the venture of speaking up for Christ, and making it known to others that they are wholeheartedly and adventurously with Christ. They are not sure that Christianity is worth a great sacrifice and a fearless witness.

There must have been times when Nicodemus and Joseph of Arimathea experienced terrific soul struggle. They wanted to be open disciples of Christ but they feared they might lose prestige, or be thought queer, or even be subjected to some kind of persecution. They were probably old men and did not live long enough after the Crucifixion and Resurrection to participate to any great extent in the phenomenal growth of the Church of Christ, but from that crucial day on Calvary they knew what peace and joy really meant.

There are no doubt some of you for whom Christian faith is a very perfunctory thing. The tryst with God on Sunday morning is never regarded as the event of the week. Every time there is presented an opportunity to serve or give, you feel that it is an imposition rather than a privilege. That is probably the way Nicodemus and Joseph of Arimathea felt before the Crucifixion. Faith is trusting Jesus all the way, in every way. If you haven't discovered that, you need to pray with the father of the afflicted son, "I believe; help my unbelief!" Take a good long look at your Savior on His cross, dying that life might be richer for you and for me. After that, does life's boundary extend only to the grave, do the powers that men wield seem so invincible, does giving sacrificially seem such an impossible and bur-

densome experience, does witnessing before others in order
to win them for Christ seem so difficult a thing to do?

"When I survey the wondrous Cross
   On which the Prince of Glory died,
My richest gain I count but loss
   And pour contempt on all my pride.

"Were the whole realm of nature mine,
   That were an offering far too small;
Love so amazing, so divine,
   Demands my soul, my life, my all."

THE ANSWER OF THE CROSS TO MAN'S QUEST FOR AUTHORITY

Luke 4: 31-37

MAN IS so constituted that he needs authority. If you doubt that, see what happens to those who try to dispense with it. There is no quicker way to make a mess out of life than to renounce authority.

There are different kinds of authority, however. Some kinds of authority can prove faulty and unreliable. History might be defined as a quest for authority. At times the witch doctor, or the soothsayer, or the state, has insisted on being the authority. At other times, the church, or some religious organization, has sought to exercise authority. There are those who believe that our only authority should be our conscience. All of these forms of authority have proved to be faulty or unreliable.

Mere claim to authority is not enough to constitute sufficient credentials. There must be evidence that it is wise and just. The only authority we should ever recognize is that of expert kowledge and ability. That is why, in the realm of spiritual values, Jesus furnishes the authority man needs.

We have before us a text which emphasizes the authority of Jesus most strikingly. In fact, the very word "authority" is used twice—once, when it is said that "his word was with authority," and again, when it is said that "with authority and power he commands the unclean spirits, and they come out."

Every aspect of Christ's life was an increasing revelation, reaching its fullest and finest revealing in the Crucifixion and Resurrection. Whether you are thinking of His sympathy, His prayer life, His courage, His faith in the larger life beyond death, or His power and authority, you find these qualities reaching their climatic revelation in the Cross and the empty tomb. That is why I do not hesitate to choose the topic, "The Answer of the Cross to Man's Quest for Authority," even though the event we are considering took place more than a year before Jesus walked the long and lonely road to Calvary.

In ascertaining the answer of the Cross to man's quest for authority, there are at least three areas in which Jesus establishes His authority.

1. *Jesus Is Authority for Us in the Goal of Our Living.*

What kind of life would be the best kind of life to find universally prevalent? Would it be some version of the law of the jungle where the strongest and shrewdest are the only ones who can survive? It would not be a very satisfying existence to live in constant fear and uncertainty, never knowing when a stronger and more clever person would get the best of us. Would it be the kind of life expressed in the philosophy of "eat, drink, and be merry, for tomorrow we die"? Those who have tried it have soon discovered the emptiness and futility of that kind of existence. Would it be a fatalistic acceptance that whatever is must be? There would be no growth or progress under such a system. We could go on asking questions concerning this way of life and that, but we would always find unhappiness or futility or stagnancy as the ultimate consequence. This cannot be said of the kind of life that would prevail, if the teachings of Jesus were universally accepted.

First of all, the goal of living for Jesus was an abundant life in which body, mind, and spirit were in harmony with each other. There have been religious systems, and among them have been perversions of Christianity, where the physical side of life was despised. Jesus taught that the body must be kept under control. He never meant that it should be tortured and despised. Christianity, at its finest, regards the body as the temple of the Holy Spirit. As to our thinking, the Bible says, "Have this mind among yourselves, which you have in Christ Jesus." We are to look at things from the standpoint of Jesus. Paul describes Christian thinking in this way: "Whatever is true, whatever is honorable, whatever is just, whatever is pure, whatever is lovely, whatever is gracious, if there is any excellence, if there is anything worthy of praise, think about these things." The Gospels speak of Jesus' casting out unclean spirits from men and women, but ideally the spirit of man should be a spirit of kinship with God. Paul says, "You have received the spirit of sonship. When we cry, 'Abba! Father!' it is the Spirit himself bearing witness with our spirit that we are children of God." The abundant life that Jesus brought to mankind embraces body, mind, and spirit.

Secondly, the goal of living for Jesus was marked by the practice of such moral qualities as sympathy, love, kindness, and good will. When we are in some unfortunate predicament and some one not only expresses sympathy but ministers in a spirit of unselfish love, do we not feel that that kind of conduct is right? When suspicion and envy increase tensions between persons, do we not see that a spirit of good will between those people would alter the whole situation? When we associate with conceited and proud and vain people, and then meet people who are humble and meek-mannered, do we not recognize which is the kind of life we would like to see prevail everywhere? When we come out of an atmosphere where all is anger and hatred and violence into an atmosphere where there is patience and gentleness and kindness, is it hard to know which is the true goal of living?

The healing of the man possessed of an unclean spirit seems to have taken place some time between Christ's launching of His ministry in His home synagogue at Nazareth and the preaching of the Sermon on the Mount. The people in Capernaum testified that "his word was with authority." What was the nature of that authority? Was it not in the sheer excellence and obvious transcendence of the ethical ideals He proclaimed? In His first public appearance, Jesus read from the Book of Isaiah what the ancient prophet had prophesied would mark the mission of the Messiah: "He has anointed me to preach good news to the poor. He has sent me to proclaim release to the captives and recovering of sight to the blind, to set at liberty those who are oppressed." In His first great sermon, Jesus set forth the qualities of character that would distinguish those who were to be the salt of the earth. They were poor in spirit, meek, merciful, pure in heart. They had learned the meaning of sorrow; they hungered and thirsted for righteousness; they were peacemakers rather than warmakers. Men hear or read these teachings concerning character and conduct, and if they are honest, they will have to bring the same testimony brought by the people of Capernaum, "his word was with authority."

2. *Jesus Is Authority for Us in the Way in Which the Perfect Goal Is Attained.*

On several occasions, Jesus revealed to His followers that if the kingdom of God was to be established "the Son of Man must suffer many things, and be rejected by the elders and the chief priests and the scribes, and be killed, and after three days rise again." In other words, the way of vicarious suffering would succeed where the way of selfishness must fail. Jesus expressed the authority of the cross in another way when He said, "I, when I am lifted up from the earth, will draw all men to myself." There is a sublime self-forgetfulness about the cross which condemns our self-centered philosophies of living. Yet, even in our selfishness, there is something within us that tells us that forgetfulness of self is a higher and more desirable trait. Even though we try to rationalize and justify our self-centeredness, there is always that strange Figure on the cross rebuking us, calling us with an authority that is not easy to resist or refuse.

It was not easy for Jesus to set forth God's will. He met with opposition. Nevertheless, the authority of His certainty that God's will was supreme was manifested in His unswerving loyalty to God even to His last breath when He prayed, "Into thy hands I commend my spirit." There is always something majestic and authoritative in that kind of unswerving fidelity to God. As men catch the spirit of Jesus in this respect, they gain a strange power which can be felt by others more than it can be understood. St. Francis had it. Luther had it. Schweitzer seems to have it. You and I can have it. When true followers of Christ gain that power, it is amazing what unclean spirits they can cast out of life.

3. *Jesus Is Authority for Us in His Revelation of the Resources Available for Attaining Life's Goal.*

Surely prayer must be mentioned. Jesus, though He was the Son of God, prayed much. Recall how intensely He prayed in Gethsemane. When He arose to meet those who had come to arrest Him, He was the most self-possessed person in the garden. As the poet said, "We kneel, how weak! we rise, how full of power!" The trouble with too much prayer is that it is conceived as some magic by which to bend God's purposes to ours. That was not the way Jesus thought of prayer. His oft-repeated petition was, "Not my will, but thine, be done." Light to see God's will and strength to do it—that is what prayer can give us.

Another resource of power is God's Word. It was the Word of God with which Jesus repelled the tempter after that long fast in the wilderness. It was the Word of God that He quoted against the scribes and Pharisees in His controversies with them. It was the Word of God that He recalled and recited while He was hanging on the cross, for the words, "My God, my God, why hast thou forsaken me?" are the opening words of the Twenty-second Psalm. It is possible that He was quoting the whole psalm in that hour of trial, but only the first verse was heard above the tumult and confusion around the cross. Fill your mind with as much of Scripture as you can. It will be like a bank deposit on which you can draw in some time of need. It will be like a compass which can guide you out of some wilderness experience. It will be like a miracle drug purging your life from some dread infection.

We cannot omit the forgiveness of sins as a resource available to the Christian. A sense of guilt can be a mighty weight on a man's soul; it can be a gnawing cancer in his memory. It can be a barrier ahead of him and an avenging nemesis behind him. Only as one finds in Christ the assurance of the Father's forgiveness for the Savior's sake can one find peace and joy and power. Jesus can do much for the bodies of men, but He can do far more for their souls. Once in healing a paralytic, Jesus said, "Your sins are forgiven," but when the scribes accused Him of blaspheming, He said, "That you may know that the Son of man has authority on earth to forgive sins," He then said to the paralytic, "Rise, take up your bed and go home." The healing of the body depended on the healing of the soul.

It was wonderful to hear all those words of Jesus that came with such authority. It was wonderful to witness His authority over the unclean demons that possessed men. But it is far more wonderful to see His authority exercised from the cross— an authority to forgive even those who are crucifying Him, an authority to command His disciple to care for that which is committed to him, an authority to open the gates of heaven to a penitent sinner. Verily, Jesus could say, "All authority in heaven and on earth has been given to me."

THE ANSWER OF THE CROSS TO THE EMPTINESS OF LIFE

John 6: 52-66

"UNLESS you eat the flesh of the Son of man and drink his blood, you have no life in you." Those words of Jesus were one of the central utterances in a discourse that had not the effect of drawing men to Him but of driving them away. We often hear it said that if preachers would only preach the pure gospel, the churches would be packed to overflowing. It didn't work that way with Jesus. The clearer He made it that He was the Son of God who was to give His life as a saving ransom for sinful mankind, the more people deserted Him. After the feeding of the five thousand, Jesus was so popular that they wanted to make Him king. Shortly after that, He made it clear that there was a greater emptiness than that of the stomach, which He had come to fill, and *that* they did not like to hear. With what pathos the evangelist describes the reaction of the people, "After this many of his disciples drew back and no longer went about with him."

What kind of emptiness is the church attempting to fill? We all realize that man has many wants. He desires fellowship. He wants a good time. He is hungry for thrilling experiences. He likes to have it as easy as possible. He is famished for praise and honor. He craves recognition. These are not necessarily lawless appetites any more than was the hunger of the crowd to which Jesus ministered in that most popular of His miracles. The important thing to remember is that there is a greater and deeper emptiness in man that needs to be filled, and when that fare is set before man he does not always seem to be as eager for it as he is for the bread that perishes.

You can see it revealed in many ways in modern church life. The colorful service with elaborate liturgy and brilliant music and splendid pageantry draws the crowds, but the prayer meeting repels the crowd. A potluck supper or a scavenger hunt will always bring out the members, but a Bible study hour does not have such magnetic power. It is not so difficult to find workers to plan social events, but it is a discouraging undertaking to enlist people in the work of evangelism. In satisfying some of the hungers of man for color and fellowship and pleasure, the basic hunger often goes unsatisfied.

We have heard about certain products of the field or forest which have the ability to still the pangs of hunger and make a person feel satisfied, but which, over a long time, will cause the person to die of malnutrition. There is a real danger that in many of the activities of a widely diversified church program people will feel that their emptiness is filled, yet they may die of spiritual malnutrition.

When Jesus spoke those words, "Unless you eat the flesh of the Son of man and drink his blood, you have no life in you," He meant that as long as men try to satisfy themselves with such earthly fare as fame and fortune, pleasure and power, they will always experience a gnawing emptiness. Something vital will be lacking, even though seemingly everything needed is theirs.

This sense of futility and emptiness is shown in many ways. Much of the dramatic, poetic, and literary output of our generation testifies to the gnawing emptiness of life.

Edna St. Vincent Millay has this line in one of her poems, "Life must go on. I forget just why." Noel Coward has a song in the last scene of his play, "Cavalcade," in which occur these lines, "In this strange illusion, chaos and confusion, people seem to lose their way. What is there to strive for, love or keep alive for,—say Hey, hey, call it a day. Blues, nothing to win or lose."

The movies with their great power for inspiration grant their highest award to Ingrid Bergman, whose immoral life caused only a ripple in that industry. Labor unions with their tremendous power to benefit not only the worker but the whole nation unveil one racketeer and embezzler after another. With our enviable standard of living, there is still a hunger and thirst in the soul of man that goes unappeased. If we could interpret the attitudes of many people, we would probably describe them as a fumbling and stumbling search for lost values.

There were those in Jesus' day who were also oppressed by a feeling of the emptiness of life. They had sought in wealth or sex or power that which might give satisfaction and contentment in life, but at the bottom of the cup they found only bitter dregs. There was the penitent thief. He had been a robber, but he never got enough money to satisfy himself, so he kept on robbing until he was caught. At Calvary he saw wealth of another kind. Mary Magdalene, according to tradition, had been possessed by the evil spirit of lust, but she only found herself in a blind alley until Christ led her out. The centurion at Calvary had put his faith in power, but at Calvary he learned that there is another kind of power than that which he knew. Here were three people hoping to satisfy their thirst at the brackish pools of life. The more they went on in their chosen course, the emptier life became for them. In the crucified Christ, however, they found an answer to the emptiness of their lives.

What is it that makes life empty? What is it that fills it with meaning? What is there about the Cross that can give us an answer to these pressing questions?

Shortly after the feeding of the five thousand, Jesus had said, "Unless you eat the flesh of the Son of man and drink his blood, you have no life in you." That was a vivid metaphor. Many took offense at it. He meant that He was ready to give himself that man might have abundant life, not emptiness of life. If we are to have the blessings that Christ would give us, we must feed on Him. This is another way of saying that we must appropriate Him to ourselves. We must catch His spirit, share His outlook, drink in His teaching, learn His ways. We must trust the Father's will, we must believe in the reality of heaven, we must believe in the ultimate failure and punishment of all evil. When we take Christ that completely to ourselves, we shall be able to say with Paul, "I can do all things in him who strengthens me."

The trouble with most people is that they think chiefly of themselves. They never know the meaning of that motto found on a college student's wall, "I am willing to be third." When asked what it meant, he replied, "I am willing to let God be first, and others second, and myself third." How hard it is for most people to be willing to be third! At Calvary, Jesus prayed for those who were crucifying Him. He did not cry over His bad fortune. He showed concern for His mother's future welfare and commended her to the care of John, but He showed no concern for His own future welfare. He spoke words of hope to a dying thief, but begged no words of comfort from those standing about the cross. To the end, He was pouring out His lifeblood for others, He was giving His very body for their salvation.

If we analyze the prevailing attitude of many people, by which they are overwhelmed by the emptiness of life, we would find not only that they are too wrapped up in themselves but that they need a new dimension for life. Like the man in Tolstoi's story who set out at dawn to mark off as much land as he would need, only to die at the end, so people will scramble and struggle, work and worry, to gather as many pleasurable sensations, flattering honors, and tawdry treasures as they can in the day of their life, only to find in the end that those things hem in life rather than enlarge it.

On the cross, Jesus promised Paradise to the penitent thief. That was giving a new dimension to life. At the end, He commended His soul to the Father. That was expressing faith that this existence was not all of life.

We shall soon be celebrating Easter, the day of victorious faith. It vindicates and verifies what Jesus revealed and asserted at Calvary—that life is delivered from emptiness only as it is poured out for God and for others, that life is no empty thing when it has added to it the dimension of eternity.

Turning again to the text for this day, listen to our Lord when He says, "This is the bread which came down from heaven, not such as your fathers ate and died; he who eats this bread will live for ever." When there is this complete appropriation of Christ, life has no boundaries. It goes on; it grows through all eternity.

There is one more thing that we must learn at the Cross, if the emptiness of life is to be filled. That is: we must have assurance that our life fits into God's plan and carries out His will. In Gethsemane, Jesus prayed over and over again, "Not my will, but thine, be done." When He had finished praying, there was no doubt in His mind but that He must go the way of the cross, if He were to carry out God's plan of redemption. Our nature stubbornly refuses to accept any way of life that is hard, or unpopular, or involves great sacrifice. Nevertheless, there seems to be something about the constitution of this universe that opposes ease and softness and selfishness. Whenever a civilization reaches the point where it becomes self-complacent and self-righteous, some other way of life that still knows what courage and sacrifice mean has a way of displacing softness and selfishness.

The Cross reminds us that life must never be allowed to look inward and live unto itself. The emptiness of life will never be replaced by the abundant life until man seeks and fulfills the will of God. That will involve courage and work and unselfishness. It may involve unpopularity and hardship and great sacrifice. But when it is truly God's will that we are doing, we are able to say with Paul, "I have learned, in whatever state I am, to be content," or we are able to say with Livingstone after his notable career in Africa, "I never made a sacrifice in my life." When God fills the emptiness of life, everything else is insignificant in comparison.

Let us think much about those strange and haunting words of Jesus, "Unless you eat the flesh of the Son of man and drink his blood, you have no life in you." Let it be more than meditation. Let it be mandate. Then we shall find life full. We shall discover that we have laid hold on something that creates no gnawing emptiness but which gives satisfaction and joy forever.

THE ANSWER OF THE CROSS TO MAN'S QUEST FOR FREEDOM

John 8:31-45

MAN seems to be endlessly engaged in a quest for freedom. Sometimes the emphasis is upon being freed from something. At other times, the emphasis is shifted to being free to pursue some given objective. There are not many words that cause the heart to beat more rapidly, the shoulders to be thrown back more squarely, or the eyes to shine more brightly, but one of those few words is certainly the word "freedom." Men have braved the cannon's mouth with that watchword on their lips. They have risked imprisonment, poverty, and death in order that freedom might be secured or preserved.

All too often, the coveted freedom, when obtained, has proved illusory. It has not brought the blessings anticipated. An old tyranny may have been overthrown, but the new freedom has proved to bring a new kind of tyranny, a new kind of slavery. Naturally, the question arises, "Can man ever be truly free?" To obtain an answer to that question necessitates, first of all, a clear conception of what is meant by freedom.

1. *From What Do Men Desire to Be Set Free?*

During World War II, men began to toss a phrase around rather freely. It was the expression, "The four freedoms." The four freedoms referred to were: freedom from want, freedom from fear, freedom of speech, and freedom of religion. Two of those freedoms indicated that there was something from which men desired to be free, namely want and fear. The other two freedoms referred to areas of life in which men desired to be free to express their thoughts and feelings.

Generally, men overemphasize the negative aspect of freedom. They think that if they are freed from something, then everything is settled, and they will live happily ever after. It doesn't work out that way. The Gospels tell of a man who was delivered from possession by a demon, but since nothing else took the demon's place, the demon returned with seven other demons more evil than himself, and the last state of that man was worse than the first. During the French Revolution, the French people thought that if they could be free from the king, all would be well, but Danton and Robespierre and the guillotine brought them a new kind of slavery. The Russian people thought that if they were free from the rule of the Czar, they would be free, but they did not find greater freedom under Lenin, Stalin, and the politbureau. Men become free from a certain want, only to find that they have developed new wants. They become free from the fear of certain diseases, only to find that they must face new fears. So it goes.

The old Roman writer and philosopher, Seneca, once flung out this challenge: "Show me anyone who is not a slave. One is a slave to lust; another to avarice; a third to ambition; all alike to fear." That sounds cynical, but there is an element of truth in it; for the moment we become free from one thing we become subject to something else. We become free from the slavery of preparing term papers and performing experiments and listening to lectures, only to become slaves of punching a clock and operating a machine.

From what do we want to be freed? From worry and anxiety? The Apostle Paul found freedom in Christ, but he still says that he had anxiety for all the churches. You cannot eliminate the element of uncertainty from life, but you can sublimate your anxieties. The person who never cares about anything lacks one of the finest endowments of the human spirit. Jesus was a free personality, yet He loved mankind so much that He was willing to be bound by fetters and nailed to a cross in order to bring the blessing of redemption to mankind. He rebuked Martha for being anxious for the morrow; but He was talking about the kind of anxieties that did not make any difference. He would have men be deeply concerned and profoundly anxious about matters that affected eternal destiny. Why fritter away life by being anxious about insignificant things when we ought to be concerned about big and vital matters? The "musts" of Jesus give us a clue as to what these larger concerns are. For example, He said as a mere lad, "I must be in my Father's house." That was something concerning which He could not be indifferent or careless.

Perhaps you want to be free from suffering. That is a legitimate desire, for one can hardly be expected to crave pain and sickness and sorrow. Nevertheless, it is doubtful whether anything truly worthy and noble comes into life without costing suffering to someone. Jesus could not effect the redemption of man without suffering on the cross. No great cause ever triumphed unless there were those who were willing to suffer for it. The Italian patriot, Garibaldi, who effected the unification of Italy, did not offer his followers wealth and pleasure, but long marches, hunger, suffering, and possible death. The great prime minister of England, Winston Churchill, did not offer his people ease and lower taxes and good times, but blood, sweat, and tears. Jesus did not offer His followers freedom from suffering and imprisonment. He challenged them to take up their cross daily, and follow Him.

Do people want freedom from work? Who really wants that kind of freedom? The most bored people in the world are those who have nothing to do. We need one day of rest out of seven and we need an occasional vacation; but to go month after month and year after year without having any work to do would make an able person go mad. We need to keep the Sabbath holy by using it for rest and worship, but we need to appreciate the sanctity and privilege of labor, too. Elbert Hubbard, famous writer and lecturer, once printed on the front cover page of his magazine, *The Philistine*, this wholesome suggestion: "Remember the Weekday and Keep It Holy." Never yield to the temptation of thinking that idleness is any kind of freedom. The poet was right:

> We are not here to play, to dream, to drift,
> We have hard work to do, and loads to lift.
> Shun not the struggle. Face it. 'Tis God's gift.

There are those whose conception of freedom is to be free from responsibility. That is the kind of thinking that creates dictatorship, whether it be in government, labor union, or any other institution. Freedom cannot be separated from responsibility. The moment we turn our responsibilities over to others, we relinquish our freedom. From the throne of His cross, Jesus conferred upon John the responsibility of caring for His mother. On the night when He was betrayed, He challenged His disciples to the responsibility of lowly service by washing their feet. The very idea of Christian stewardship is that of responsibility. We cannot evade it if we would. We would not evade it if we could.

2. *How Would Christ Set Us Free?*

Jesus had a great deal to say about freedom. More than that, He proclaimed himself as the Emancipator. "If the Son makes you free, you will be free indeed." He claimed that He had come to bear witness to the truth, and that He himself was the truth. In our text He makes the assertion, "The truth shall make you free."

All this is bold speech. Can Jesus support those claims? You do not have to go beyond the first converts to Christianity to find testimony that Jesus does all He claims to do. Paul, in writing to the Corinthians says, "Where the spirit of the Lord is, there is freedom. In his letter to the Galatians, Paul said, "For freedom has Christ set us free." In the letter to the Romans, Paul spoke of "the glorious liberty of the children of God."

What is this freedom which Christ gives? How is it related to the Cross? In a controversy with the Jews, they insisted that they were free, even though as they said it, they were in bondage to Rome, obeying her decrees and paying heavy taxes to her. It is an example of how deluded men can be—believing themselves to be free when they are anything but free. Jesus was free, but the Jews were not. How could that be? Were not both alike in that they were subject to the laws of Rome? Yes, but freedom is a moral and spiritual thing rather than a political thing. People can be politically free, and yet be in bondage. They can be in political bondage, and yet be truly free. Until we learn the moral and spiritual nature of freedom we shall never know the meaning of freedom.

On that fateful Friday when Jesus was crucified, Pilate offered to set free either Jesus or a criminal by the name of Barabbas. The people chose Barabbas as the man to be set free. But did the removal of his chains set Barabbas free? If he was a man of hate and lust and avarice, he was as much a slave when the shackles were removed as he was when he was in prison. It was Christ who was free, even though He stood before Pilate in fetters. The night before, in the Garden of Gethsemane, Peter, in a rash moment, had drawn a sword and charged into the crowd that had come to arrest Jesus. Before Jesus could stop him, he had cut off the ear of one named Malchus. Jesus healed the man's ear, freeing him from pain and deformity. But did that make Malchus free? Was Malchus, the servant of the high priest, prejudiced against Jesus like his master? We do not read that he ever showed any appreciation of the miracle nor that he ever became a Christian. If not, he was still a slave of prejudice and ingratitude and unbelief.

Pilate himself, who boasted that he could set a man free, was not free. The Jews threatened him, saying that he was not Caesar's friend if he set Jesus free. Trying one expedient after another to release Jesus, he finally capitulated to the clamor of the mob. "Their voices prevailed." Pilate was a slave to public opinion, a slave to fear. He did not dare to do what he felt to be right.

This brings us closer to an understanding of the nature of freedom. Real freedom is the freedom to think noble thoughts and to perform righteous deeds. How then can a man who clings to sin be free? The first requisite for true freedom is to be free from sin. Twice on Calvary did Jesus open the gates of freedom from sin to people—once for those who were crucifying Him when He prayed, "Father, forgive them; for they know not what they do," and again for the penitent thief when He said, "Truly, today shalt thou be with me in Paradise." There is freedom from sin through the forgiveness secured by Christ's sacrifice on man's behalf. Cold reason finds it hard to grasp that fact, as it does so many facts in the realm of the spirit. Yet, see how the assurance of forgiveness delivers from despair, bestows peace on the troubled conscience, empowers for holier living, inspires a forgiving attitude toward others, awakens sincere desire to serve God. Is not this freedom?

The Cross delivers men from the bondage of fear. Nicodemus and Joseph of Arimathea had been admirers of Jesus, but they had never had the courage to come out wholeheartedly for Jesus until that day on Calvary. The death of Jesus released them from the bondage of fear, and they went to Pilate asking for the body of Jesus that they might give it decent burial. Life does not end with the grave. Jesus testified to that when He spoke of being in Paradise, and of committing His spirit into the hands of the heavenly Father. When we believe in that great truth of eternal life, we have gained freedom from those who have power only to kill the body.

The Fourth Evangelist, as he begins the account of Christ's passion, says, "When Jesus knew that his hour had come to depart out of this world to the Father, having loved his own who were in the world, he loved them to the end." The Cross teaches us that the greatest freedom is the freedom to love our fellow men and to sacrifice for them. One of the most insidious dangers of the welfare state is at this point. Everyone is offered security from the cradle to the grave. No one has to feel the call to sacrificial service. No one has to assume the burden of another. The mission of mercy, which has been the glory of Christianity, may be gradually transferred to the state or be taken over by the state. Of course, the citizens pay for such things as truly when the state takes over as when the church assumes the burden, but people are not conscious of having a part, and therefore they lose the blessing that comes when one has the sense of being needed, and when one responds to the cry of need.

The Christian, realizing that freedom is a moral and spiritual experience, rather than a political experience, can find freedom anywhere.

> Stone walls do not a prison make,
>   Nor iron bars a cage;
> Minds innocent and quiet take
>   That for an hermitage.— LOVELACE.

Furthermore, the Christian, realizing that Christ has set him free, finds that freedom is not so much freedom from some evil as it is freedom to enter into His presence in order to experience His mercy, His peace, His joy, His power. It is the freedom of the mountain climber, for each time a summit is reached, there is a higher one beckoning the climber onward and upward. "If the Son makes you free, you will be free indeed."

PALM SUNDAY

THE ANSWER OF THE CROSS TO MAN'S HOPE AND EXPECTATION

Mark 11:1-11

WHEN PEOPLE do some straight and serious thinking, there are several things that they desire with all their heart; and when anyone comes who can supply or even shed light on these things, he is sure to find a royal reception. It was because people felt that Jesus had an answer to these great hopes and expectations that they were so eager to see Him when He came up to Jerusalem for the Passover Feast.

As you know, the Passover was the greatest holiday season in the Jewish calendar. It really marked the beginnings of the Jewish nation. For about four centuries, the Hebrew people had been slaves in Egypt. Then God raised up a deliverer in the person of Moses. On the night before the exodus from Egypt, the Hebrews had one last meal in Egypt consisting of lamb, herbs, and unleavened bread. Upon arriving in the promised land of Canaan, Joshua ordered that the Hebrew people observe God's gracious deliverance by an annual observance of that memorable meal. To this day, Jewish people regard it as one of the great seasons in their calendar.

In Jesus' day, Jews who lived in north Africa and Asia Minor and other places outside of Palestine endeavored to make occasional pilgrimages to the holy city of Jerusalem. I suppose it could be said that every Jew, no matter where

he lived, hoped that at least once in his life he could cele-
brate the Passover in Jerusalem. There were always many
thousands of pilgrims in Jerusalem for every Passover.
In this particular year of which our text speaks, there were
many who had heard stories of a remarkable preacher and
miracle worker, and they hoped that there might be an opportunity to see and hear him during their visit to Jerusalem. Therefore, when news seeped into Jerusalem that Jesus
of Nazareth was coming up to the Holy City to observe the
Passover as so many other Jews were doing, there was naturally a great deal of excitement.

Some time before, Jesus had added to His fame by raising
Lazarus from the grave. This great miracle, together with
His preaching about the kingdom of heaven being at hand,
led many of the people to go outside of the city to meet
Jesus and accompany Him into Jerusalem. They accorded
Him a welcome that must have rejoiced the heart of Jesus.
Waving palm branches, and casting their garments in His
path, and chanting some of the Messianic psalms of their
religion, they created a scene which has been remembered
through more than 1,900 years of Christian history as Palm
Sunday.

Recently, I read Pierre Van Paasen's book about his visit
to Palestine, and he has the feeling that the numbers participating in the ovation given Jesus on that occasion have
been greatly exaggerated. Evidently, he takes what he
wishes out of the Bible and discards the rest, for the records
which have been preserved through all these centuries
speak of crowds, not groups, and they say that the leaders
were so impressed that they said to one another, "You see
that you can do nothing; look, the world has gone after
him." To elicit such an extravagant statement, the first

Palm Sunday procession must have had greater proportions than Pierre Van Paasen wants to believe.

It is not the outward impressiveness of that entry into Jerusalem that concerns us, however. Whether the crowd numbered less than a hundred or many thousands is not important. Why did they receive Jesus in that fashion? What were the deep motivations in the souls of those people?

One thing is certain. It was not a cleverly planned and carefully executed reception, such as those we often read about in our day when some celebrity is coming to a certain community. Recently, we received a communication from a relative in Africa describing the elaborate preparations made for the visit of Princess Margaret to Arusha. Roads had been improved, flags unfurled to the breeze, and stands erected. Many years ago, a member of my former congregation was general chairman for the reception given to Col. Charles Lindbergh on his triumphant tour after his trans-Atlantic flight, and I recall how every detail was carefully planned in advance. There was nothing of all that in this Palm Sunday entry of Jesus into Jerusalem. It was spontaneous. It is true that He came riding on a donkey, the symbol of toil and peace, but if Jesus had been staging a coup of some kind, He would have chosen a prancing war horse. The very fact that He chose a donkey proclaimed Him as a man of peace.

What was it, then, about our Lord's coming to Jerusalem that elicited the enthusiasm of the welcoming throng?

1. *Jesus Had a Message of Redemption and Regeneration.*

There are always certain forces at work in this world which frustrate the health, happiness, and welfare of mankind. At times, these forces assume such proportions that mankind is threatened with utter despair. Some kind of intervention by God himself seems the only hope.

The Jewish people had long cherished the hope of a deliverer. At times, they had been ready to accept and follow some false Messiah, to their disillusionment and regret. In the claims and teachings of Jesus, many devout Jews saw a ray of hope in their darkness. Some hoped that He would proclaim himself as king, call for volunteers, and lead victorious armies against the power of Rome. Others began to catch the vision that a spiritual kingdom might be superimposed on the kingdoms of this world, effecting not their destruction but their regeneration.

Jesus had been saying that the kingdom of heaven was at hand. He had told men that His mission was to bring mankind abundant life. He had taught new standards of morality, not by abrogating the letter of the moral law, but by infusing a new spirit into moral conduct. Humility, kindness, forgiveness, and sacrificial love were given a greater emphasis than any teacher had ever given them. Purity of motive was set forth as equal in importance to purity of conduct. The spirit of penitence was urged rather than the spirit of self-righteousness. The man who was willing to minister to others was greater than the man who was being ministered to. Many of man's established practices and ideals were being turned upside down by this new teacher, but thinking and devout believers found a strange and irresistible appeal in them. They wanted to hear more. Therefore, they received Jesus with such enthusiasm when He came up to Jerusalem on that first Palm Sunday.

Little did they realize what the heart of that message of redemption was to be. They could not have guessed what the momentous week would bring forth. It is possible that as events began to shape up and a tide of opposition began to run against Jesus they thought their first impulses must have been wrong. They may even have joined the mob on Friday and clamored for the crucifixion of Jesus because Jesus' method of redemption did not harmonize with ideas of redemption which they had formed in their own minds.

One of the greatest mistakes people make is to want to spin their own ideas of God and of the way of salvation out of the gossamer tissue of their own minds. They will not listen to the revelation of himself and His will as God has given it through His Word. The Bible tells us that many walked no more with Jesus when the spiritual nature of the kingdom began to be made clear to them. They harmed no one but themselves. Likewise, today, those who turn from the message of the Cross and seek some other kind of redemption through legislation or education or increased production of material goods are bringing judgment on no one but themselves. We need to pick up the refrain of that first Palm Sunday, "Blessed be he who comes in the name of the Lord!" He is the way, the truth, and the life. There is no other.

2. *Jesus Had a Message of Life after Death.*

Some time before His coming to Jerusalem for the Passover, Jesus had raised his friend Lazarus from the grave. So great was the impact of the miracle that people were almost as eager to see Lazarus as they were to see Jesus. More than that, the leaders felt that if they were to prevent the growing popularity of Jesus, they must do away not only with Jesus but with Lazarus.

The idea of being imprisoned is one of the most frustrating feelings that can come to anyone. When we think of being imprisoned, we think first of all of being confined in a small cell or of being entombed in a mine cave-in. But think of what imprisonment implies. Does it not mean that we are not privileged to exercise our God-given powers to their fullest possibilities? Does it not mean that we are deprived of fellowship with many of our fellow men? In the light of such definitions of imprisonment, is not this world and this life a prison? Do we not feel that this earthly existence is not long enough to bring our finest capacities to fulfillment? Do we not feel that there ought to be a larger fellowship than with the few friends we know? Do we not feel that this world holds so many sorrows, so much disappointment, so much frustration that we need more opportunity to experience the full meaning of joy, and peace, and beauty, and fellowship?

In one sense, we are entering the saddest week of all the year. Yet, this week holds within itself the secret of eternal life. Jesus said, "And I, when I am lifted up from the earth, will draw all men to myself." As we see Him lifted up from the earth on His cross, we see Him lifted up above the meanness, the emptiness, the shoddiness of life. We see Him lifted into that realm where forgiveness is not an impossible virtue, where Paradise is no idle dream but a sure fact, where the hands of God are an encircling reality, where a cross of pain has become a ladder to heaven.

During this week, multitudes will flock to the churches of Christendom as at no other time of the year. Why? They come because they sense that in the Passion story of Christ they detect the very accents of God. They come because they feel that as they gather with Christ in an upper room, or kneel with Him in Gethsemane, or walk with Him the way of suffering, or stand beneath that old rugged cross, they are on holy ground. They come because they feel that here they find the gate that opens into life, that here they feel that vibrant power that can push out the imprisoning walls of earth, and reveal the untrammeled liberty of the life that is hid with Christ in God.

The Palm Sunday procession that started so long ago is an increasing and unending procession. All those who cherish high hopes and great expectations will soon or late be found in its ranks, for Scripture says that "at the name of Jesus every knee should bow, in heaven and on earth and under the earth, and every tongue confess that Jesus Christ is Lord, to the glory of God the Father." Come then, and lay not your garments but your lives at His feet; spread not leafy branches but your time and talents before Him; welcome Him not only into Jerusalem but into your hearts; follow Him not only to the garden of prayer and the hill of suffering and earth's last resting place, but follow Him through the tomb itself and into the glorious and eternal presence of the heavenly Father.

THE GLORY OF TOMBS

Text: Matth. 28:1-8

HAS IT ever occurred to you how much of the world's history is inscribed *in* tombs and influenced *by* tombs? We can learn much from tombs—how life was lived once, how far civilization had progressed, how ancient peoples regarded death, what standards men lived by. From the tombs by the Nile and from the burial mounds of American Indians, we have been able to reconstruct a great deal of the life and thought of dead civilizations. Tombs of martyrs have become shrines for annual pilgrimages. Tombs of influential men and women have kept alive certain values or philosophies of life. Surely, tombs have a glory all their own, but the glory is not all of the same pattern.

1. *The Glory of Some Tombs Is Because of What They Are in Themselves.*

We think of the pyramids built along the Nile long before the Israelites settled in Egypt. We might consider the Great Pyramid at Gizeh specifically. It is about 4,500 years old. To have survived the ravages of time and man for forty-five centuries is a glorious achievement. It is the largest structure ever built by man, being 756 feet square and 481 feet high. To have built something that massive, which humanity has not been able to duplicate in forty-five centuries, is no mean accomplishment. There is something to glory about in that. Herodotus claimed that 100,000 men worked for thirty years quarrying stone and building that huge structure. Considering the fact that there were no derricks, no blasting devices, no precision instruments in those days, we shall have to admit that it was a glorious engineering feat. The glory of that Great Pyramid lies in its vast dimensions and the manner in which it has weathered the buffetings of time; but the glory is dimmed when we think of the human slavery and cruel suffering involved in its erection.

We think also of the Taj Mahal at Agra, India. Shah Jehan built it for the last resting place of his favorite wife. Visitors have become rhapsodic in extolling the glory of that famous mausoleum. Never before or since have marble and alabaster and semi-precious stones been joined in such a perfect combination. It is said to be absolutely faultless, the most exquisite thing in existence. Twenty thousand laborers toiled for twenty-two years to erect that masterpiece. It cost about $50,000,000 to build, and could not be duplicated today for several times that sum. The glory of the Taj Mahal lies in its perfect symmetry, its harmonious setting, and the richness of its adornment; but its glory is dimmed when we think of the plundered poor who made its erection possible. Its glory has become a shame when we remember that the selfishness and vanity of the emperor caused him to blind the architect so that there would be no possibility of his ever duplicating or surpassing the jewel-like beauty of that magnificent structure.

2. *The Glory of Other Tombs Is Not Because of What They Are in Themselves but Because of the Bodies Which They Contain.*

There is Napoleon's Tomb in Paris where lies the little Corsican who rose from obscurity to rule over most of continental Europe. People will always marvel at the meteoric rise of Napoleon, at the genius he showed in military tactics, at the power he wielded over his followers; but Napoleon's glory is dimmed because of his reliance upon force, the baseness of his character, and his indifference to the value of human life.

There is Lenin's Tomb in Red Square, Moscow, before which millions of Communists have filed in tribute. The Communists see nothing but a glorious career represented in the figure lying so perfectly embalmed in his hermetically sealed glass casket. But Lenin's tomb possesses no glory for us. It stands for class hatred, anti-Christ, bloody revolution. No Christian will see glory in that tomb because of the ignoble and ruthless character that was Lenin.

There is Westminster Abbey in London in which we find the tombs of some of the most famous individuals that ever lived. Kings, poets, statesmen, queens, preachers are all represented. The body of Wilberforce, liberator of slaves, lies there. The body of David Livingstone, preacher of good tidings to those in Dark Africa, lies there also. But the glory of tombs which contain the bodies of noble men and women is only a faint reflection of the glory of Christ.

We could speak of Lincoln's Tomb in Springfield, Illinois, of the Tomb of the Unknown Soldier in Washington, D. C., and of many others; but, however great were the persons whose bodies lie in those tombs, we could only be reminded that the paths of glory lead but to the grave.

3. *While the Glory of Some Tombs Lies in Their Architecture and the Glory of Other Tombs Lies in the Bodies Contained, There Is One Tomb Whose Glory Lies Neither in Its Appearance nor in Its Contents, but in Its Emptiness.*

That tomb is the empty tomb of Christ outside the walls

of Jerusalem. Death is not there, for it was there that death yielded to life. Life has come forth from that tomb to rejuvenate the hopes of dying mortals in all ages. It would be revolting to speak of the contents of the world's tombs— the decay, the dust, the darkness. But Christ's tomb is glorious because of the thrilling message it proclaims and because of the glowing hope it brings.

Christ's tomb teaches that life's goal is not the grave. One of our hymns begins with this stanza:

> I near the grave, where'er I go,
>   Where'er my pathway tendeth;
> If rough or pleasant here below,
>   My way at death's gate endeth.
> I have no other choice;
> Between my griefs and joys,
>   My mortal life is ordered so:
>   I near the grave where'er I go.

But the hymn does not stop there. If it did, it would have no place in a Christian hymnal. It goes on as follows:

> I go to heaven, where'er I go,
>   If Jesus' steps I follow;
> The crown of life He will bestow,
>   When earth this frame shall swallow.
> If through this tearful vale
> I in that course prevail,
>   And walk with Jesus here below,
>   I go to heaven, where'er I go.

There is something beyond the grave. For the Christian, there is life and peace and joy. For the unbeliever, there is judgment and remorse and agony. Christ's empty tomb has lengthened our vista. Life on earth is not the blind alley it has often seemed to be. The world has received a re-sounding affirmative answer to the age-old query: "If a man die, shall he live again?"

Christ's empty tomb assures us that death could not hold Christ. Life's Redeemer is not there. The angel said, "He is not here; He is risen!" That was the stirring message on that first Easter morning. The post-Easter appearances of the resurrected Lord substantiated the evidence of the empty tomb. The disciples knew beyond all shadow of doubt that Christ was alive. He is loose in the world. We need not journey over sea and mountain to behold that empty tomb. There would be no special benefit in that. The Christ who rose from that tomb journeys to us wherever we may be to bring us the joy and peace and strength of His sustaining presence.

> The world cannot bury Christ.
>   The earth is not deep enough for His tomb;
> The clouds are not wide enough for His winding sheet.
>   He ascends into the heavens.
> But the heavens cannot contain Him.
>   He still lives—in the Church which burns
>   unconsumed with His love;
> In the truth that reflects His image;
>   In the hearts which burn as He talks with them by
>   the way.
>   —Edward Thompson

It is because Christ's tomb, of all tombs, is empty that it has a glory all its own. That is why Christians can exclaim defiantly at every open grave, "O death, where is thy victory? O death, where is thy sting? . . . But thanks be to God, who gives us the victory through our Lord Jesus Christ."

A PROBING QUESTION

Text: John 21:15-23

WE ARE living in a questioning age. No one's word is taken for granted. One often has to produce an affidavit to prove that he was born. When one seeks a position, he is given a long questionnaire to fill out. When one gets married, there are usually many questions on the license which must be answered and returned to the state. Even the radio has caught the questioning spirit, and it is reflected in "man on the street" programs and "quiz" programs of every description. The atmosphere in which we live, therefore, will not make it seem something out of this world if Jesus sees fit to ask some questions. One is frequently impressed with the trivial nature of many questions that are often asked of us, but the thrice-repeated question which our risen Redeemer put to Peter is tremendously vital. That probing question was and still is: "Do you love me?"

That seemingly sentimental question is far more practical than at first appears. We are sometimes tempted to think that the most important thing in our spiritual life is to belong to the church, or to have stipulated periods of prayer and Bible reading, or to have a zealous love for humanity. These things are not to be spurned or ignored, but undergirding them must be a genuine love for Christ. Church membership without love for Christ may even degenerate to the pattern of Judas who followed Christ without loving Him. Scriptural knowledge and devotional exer-

cises without love for Christ become pedantry and pageantry, like that of some of the scribes and Pharisees whom
Jesus rebuked so severely. Avowed love for humanity is
apt to be insincere and fickle, if there is no love for Christ,
the perfect representative of humanity.

Therefore, when Jesus asked Peter this probing question,
"Do you love me?" He was getting down to fundamentals.
It was not for the purpose of obtaining information for himself. It was for the purpose of organizing Peter's life around
such a solid principle that never again would he waver and
stumble in seeking the kingdom of God and His righteousness. We may detect a three-fold object in our Lord's purpose in asking this question.

1. *It Was to Encourage Self-inventory.*

Self-analysis is no easy undertaking. Many a person
knows a great deal about a great many things who does not
understand himself—his own likes and dislikes, his emotions, his prejudices, his temperament. What we often label
love may, on careful scrutiny and analysis, stand revealed
as sheer selfishness. It is a wholesome discipline for us to
subject ourselves to some examination from time to time.
The Church of Christ has always recommended that exercise as a worthy preparation for participation in the Lord's
Supper. "Let a man examine himself, and so eat of the
bread and drink of the cup."

We are often adept in analyzing others, in dissecting their
attitudes and motives, in discerning their faults and weaknesses. But we suffer from a strange astigmatism or blind-
spot when it comes to seeing ourselves. There is a story in
the Old Testament which emphasizes this tendency to see
clearly in others what we fail to see in ourselves. David had
committed murder and adultery in order to obtain Bath-

sheba as his wife. It caused him no qualms of conscience.
The prophet Nathan opened the eyes of David to his sin by
the indirect route of a parable in which was pictured a man
rich in fields and flocks stealing the only sheep of a poor
man. Immediately, David reacted to the sinfulness of such
an act. From that point, Nathan was able to help him see
the magnitude and heinousness of his own sin; for David
already had several wives, whereas Uriah had only one.

Jesus is aware of the struggle that is constantly going on
between the love of force and the force of love; and He
places His reliance on the latter. He would have us take
an inventory of ourselves in respect to the object of this
driving force of love. Do we ardently pursue earthly interests to the extent that we ignore Jesus? That is what
the rich fool in the parable was guilty of doing. Do we really concern ourselves with the spiritual aspects of life?
Wherever dead civilizations are discovered, there are
broken altars. Is there a connection? Isn't it possible that
spiritual indifference can lead to another dead civilization?

It is always good to settle down to some straight thinking. If life is to be nothing more than working long hours,
paying high taxes, and endeavoring to keep bodies decently
fed and clothed, perhaps it isn't so important what or whom
we love. But if we realize the reality of the spiritual values
of life for ourselves and for others, then it does become an
important matter. Our love determines our life. We ought
to become clear on this vital issue as to whether we really
love Christ or just think we do when in reality we may love
things which are altogether alien to His spirit.

2. *It was to Test the Real Motives Underlying Action.*

Educational and psychological studies have discovered
some strange reasons why we do certain things in life. The

reason is not always what we believe it to be. It is usually much deeper.

Why do we belong to church, go to church, contribute to church, work in the church? Is there a craving for popularity or praise? May it be that it ministers to our vanity? Is it because we anticipate some personal advantage? Or is it because we truly adore and revere Christ?

Paul said, "Love bears all things, endures all things." It cannot be love, then, that brought some people to the church when we see how a little lack of recognition, a failure to be re-elected to some office in the church, a thoughtless remark by someone, causes them to lose their interest in the work of the church, or even to quit. What would we do in the face of real persecution, when we are found wanting in the face of so many little things? Consider how love for Christ has inspired fidelity to Him in spite of persecution in Germany, Russia, and other countries. Would our motives stand such a test? Willingness to sacrifice and endure is a good test for the reality and depth of love. Will faith be stronger than fear? Will conviction rule over convenience?

3. *It Was to Deepen Love and Loyalty for Christ.*

Repeated avowals make denials more difficult. The whole idea of making promises or vows is fundamentally sound, provided that the thing promised is desirable. It is applied when people take out citizenship papers. It is used in army induction. It is employed in connection with reception of new members into the church. Paul reminded Timothy that he had made the good confession in the sight of many witnesses. We should not hesitate, therefore, to make our avowals of love for Christ and loyalty to Him. This does not mean that we sanction or recommend cheap, sentimental ways of asserting that love; for true love is majestic, never maudlin.

If love never grows from profession to proof, it is apt to wither and die. If we love Christ, we will also serve Him; for love always seeks to give expression to itself. Jesus asks not only Peter, but all His disciples to show their love by feeding His lambs and tending His sheep. On another occasion, Jesus had said, "As you did it to one of the least of these my brethren, you did it to me." A true love for Christ will be as wide as the world. It will count no sacrifice too great. Jesus knows that when our hearts are given to Him, there is nothing else that we will withhold. That is why this probing question gets down to fundamentals. Do you and I really love Christ? Are we sure in our own hearts that we love Him? The validity of all our actions will be tested by the love we have for Christ.

THE GOSPEL OF CHRIST

John 10:9

THE GOSPEL of Christ is profound enough to challenge the thinking of the world's wisest and most mature minds, but it is also simple enough to be understood by any one who wishes to understand it. One of the simplest statements on record regarding the Gospel of Christ is to be found in the ninth verse of the tenth chapter of John's Gospel. It reads as follows: "I am the door; if any one enters by me, he will be saved, and will go in and out and find pasture." It is so straightforward and compact a statement that it can be memorized in a minute or two. Yet, it will be found to contain most of the essential elements of the Gospel of Christ. Much of the chapter deals with Christ's relations to His followers, and there are many verses that deserve our reverent consideration; but, in order that our thinking may not become too diffuse and superficial, let us confine our attention to this ninth verse and see how adequately it describes the Gospel of Christ.

1. *The Simplicity of the Gospel.*

Jesus said, "I am the door." Nothing is more simple and more obvious than a door. Any one ought to be able to find a door.

There are religions in the world that are based on the principle that they possess mysteries or secrets that are reserved for a privileged few. In the ancient Greek civilization, such religions were called "mystery religions." If such religions could make any claim on Christ, they might conceivably change His words to read, "I am the secret panel." But Jesus never said anything like that. He said, "I am the door." In saying that, he meant, "Anyone who so desires can find me."

There are many edifices in the world that have doors before which visitors stand in admiration and awe; and, having seen the door, the visitors may pass on to other sights. There is no objection to having a door be beautiful, but we must always remember that a door is not something to look at or to look through. A door is something to pass through. It invites us to come to it in order that we may pass on into other areas. Likewise, Christ invites us to come to Him, the door, in order that we may pass on through Him to greater service and to eternal glory. First of all, therefore, the gospel is a simple invitation to come to Christ.

2. *The Exclusiveness of the Gospel.*

While the gospel is intended for every one, there is, nevertheless, an exclusiveness about it. Jesus said, "If any one enters by me, he will be saved." Christianity recognizes no other Savior than Jesus Christ. There have been attempts so to broaden religion, that Mohammed and Buddha and Zoroaster and other religious leaders are placed alongside of Jesus as doors for the spirit of man by which access may be had to God and His salvation. Scripture, however, recognizes no such broad road to life. "Enter by the narrow gate; for the gate is wide and the way is easy, that leads to destruction, and those who enter by it are many. For the gate is narrow and the way is hard, that leads to life, and those who find it are few."

No intelligent person would say, "It doesn't make any difference whether you eat toad-stools or mushrooms, just as long as you believe you are eating food." Yet, many supposedly intelligent people say, "It doesn't make any difference what you believe in religion, just as long as you believe something." There is hardly a sin or injustice that has not at some time been sanctioned by some kind of religion. The crucifixion of mankind through the centuries, as well as the crucifixion of Christ, are ample proof that it does make a difference as to what we believe.

Jesus made tremendous claims for himself which set Him completely apart from all others who might desire to share Messiahship with Him. The "I am's" of Jesus are claims to exclusiveness. "I am the resurrection and the life." "I am the bread of life." "I am the way, the truth, and the life." "I am the true vine." "I am the good shepherd." In the words of our text, "I am the door; if any one enters by me, he will be saved," Jesus again insisted on the exclusiveness of the gospel. He did so on other occasions as well, as when He said, "Apart from me you can do nothing," and "No one comes to the Father, but by me."

This exclusiveness of the gospel was taught by the early preachers of Christianity. Peter, speaking under the influence of the Holy Spirit, said in one of his sermons, "There is salvation in no one else, for there is no other name under heaven given among men by which we must be saved." Paul, writing to the Christians in Corinth, said, "No other foundation can anyone lay than that which is laid, which is Jesus Christ."

This exclusiveness of the gospel should deter us from giving a willing ear to those false gospels which seek to rob Christ of His unique position as the door to eternal life.

3. *The Inclusiveness of the Gospel.*

We are not to assume, however, that the exclusiveness of the gospel is a barrier to its inclusiveness. Jesus said, "If any one enters by me, he will be saved." Jesus placed no restrictions or limitations on those who could be saved. His invitation was always an inclusive one. "Preach the gospel to every creature." "Make disciples of all nations." "Him who comes to me I will not cast out." "Every one who acknowledges me before men, I also will acknowledge before my Father who is in heaven." "For God so loved the world that he gave his only Son, that whoever believes in him should not perish but have eternal life."

There is a universality about the Gospel of Christ which no other religion can match. It is for young and old, for rich and poor. It recognizes no racial barriers. The last, the least, and the lost are included in its evangelism program. The sons of sorrow and the pilgrims of pain are invited.

4. *The Demand of the Gospel.*

While the gospel is a proclamation of great blessings to all mankind, these blessings are not forced upon people. They must be desired, appreciated, and appropriated. The Gospel of Christ lays a responsibility upon each one who hears it. It demands a response, an acceptance.

The demand of the gospel is that we "enter in." By our own desire, by our own choice, by our own faith, we must "enter in." The blessings of the gospel are free, but they are conditional upon our acceptance. It is that idea that is voiced so poignantly in the fifty-fifth chapter of Isaiah, "Ho, every one who thirsts, come to the waters; and he who has no money, come, buy and eat! Come, buy wine and milk without money and without price." The benefits of the gospel have no price tag on them, but we must buy them with our desire and faith.

5. *The Sure Blessing of the Gospel.*

How clear and definite are the promises of God's blessings! "He will be saved." In other words, we can be as certain of our salvation as we can be sure of God.

Doubt and fear are terrible enemies of the soul. Many a person has missed the blessings of the gospel because of doubt and prejudice. We are urged to "be not faithless, but believing." We are told again and again, "Fear not," "Do not be afraid."

A quiet assurance is always a precious thing. It is especially so in the realm of the spiritual life. To know that our sins are forgiven, to know that we are not alone in our trials and sorrows, to know that our Redeemer lives and that because He lives we, too, shall live—these are values which we cannot afford to doubt. We can see how rich are the blessings of the gospel for this life. We can trust the promises which speak of blessings in the life to come. With Robert Browning, every Christian can confess, "The best is yet to be."

6. *The Liberty of the Gospel.*

There are people who think of Christianity as a set of fetters or shackles curtailing one's liberty. Nothing can be further from the truth. The saved man is a free man. There is a liberty in Christ that is not known in any other relationship. That is the meaning of the words, "will go in and out."

The Christian is free from terror, free from the dominion of sin, free from guilt, free to choose the right, free to serve God, free to speak the truth. "If the Son makes you free,

you will be free indeed." That liberation from bondage to
the lower interests of life is voiced in the hymn,

> Rise up, O men of God,
> Have done with lesser things.

7. *The Fullness of the Gospel.*

The Bible often uses the word "pasture" to suggest spiritual fullness. In the Twenty-third Psalm it is said of the
Lord, "He makes me lie down in green pastures." In the
thirty-fourth chapter of Ezekiel, the Lord promises concerning the enslaved people of Judah, "I will feed them
with good pasture, and upon the mountain heights of Israel
shall be their pasture; there they shall lie down in good
grazing land, and on fat pasture they shall feed on the
mountains of Israel." In our text, Jesus promises that those
who yield their lives to Him will "find pasture." The content of that expression would be plain to every one familiar
with the Old Testament, for the Hebrews were accustomed
to periods of drought when pasturage was scarce. Green
pastures suggested fullness and plenty. Jesus was bringing
home the idea more specifically when He summed up the
purpose of His mission in the words which are also a part of
this well-known chapter, "I came that they may have life,
and have it abundantly."

"I am the door." How simple Christ makes it! "By me."
What insistence upon His exclusiveness! How He refutes
the claims of other religious systems! "If any." How every
one should feel those words directed to him! "Enter in." Is
there any one who cannot do so simple a thing? "He shall
be saved." What a sure promise! What a hope-inspiring
vista is opened to the believer! "Go in and out." What
freedom it offers! "Find pasture." Who does not want to
realize the fulfillment of that abundant promise?

THE SECRET OF SECURITY

John 14:1-12

PEOPLE are interested in security, whether it be national security, social security for old age, or financial security in the disposition of their savings. Still, amid all the discussion about security, one senses that there is an element of insecurity about it. European nations had compulsory military training in the hope they could have national security. They had old age pensions and sick benefit insurance in advance of the United Sates. They had strong industries. But where are these things today in many of those European countries? Millions who thought they had social security are homeless refugees now. Business men who thought they had well-established businesses are bankrupt. It is not impossible that such conditions could take place here. History offers convincing proof that when nations get to the point where it seems that some measure of security has been attained, something goes wrong.

I do not desire to venture into the field of prophecy. Neither do I wish to underestimate the value of striving for national and social security. I am certain, however, that we stand in need of a more basic security than that which can be obtained by diplomacy or money. Powerful men and rich men are not the happiest or safest men in the world. They have to be surrounded by body guards and iron curtains and lawyers.

In the final analysis, security is a thing of the mind and spirit, and if you would discover the secret of security, you will find it not in politics or stocks and bonds or physical surroundings, but in religion.

Consider that last evening that Jesus spent with His disciples. The hopes which those disciples had entertained of a glorious kingdom were about to be dashed to pieces. The sustaining presence of their Master was to be denied them after that night. Their own physical safety was to be placed in jeopardy. In that situation of insecurity, Jesus said to them, "Let not your hearts be troubled."

When life is caving in, it doesn't help much to be told to keep one's chin up. When all the lights go out, it really doesn't help much to whistle in the dark. How, then, can such counsel as Jesus gives deliver men from the tyranny of trouble and give to them the secret of security? Let us look at the reasons He himself gives; for He reveals three sources of strength for troubled souls.

1. *There Is Belief in God.*

"Believe in God," said Jesus to His disciples. We know that many in our world do not have such a faith. Worse than that, many are out to undermine and destroy such faith. It may be understandable that one who has met nothing but opposition and failure and trouble might doubt that there is a God. But why anyone should consider it a worthwhile mission in life to destroy another's faith in God is beyond understanding.

Suppose, if you can, that there is no God. Then there would be no purpose to life. There would be no scale of values. There would be no sense to anything. Life would be just a crazy nightmare, and the sooner atom bombs destroyed all life, the better it would be. But there is a God. He has a plan, and we should find our place in it. There are true values and false values, and we had better learn to distinguish between them. There is logic to history. Truth is not always on the scaffold and wrong is not forever on the throne. The justice, righteousness, and power of God may be seen at work in the recorded history of mankind.

Still, it isn't quite as simple as that, for there are times that are sadly out of joint, when men's souls are sorely tried, when one wonders if God has forsaken the world. That is when we need faith in Him. And if we have faith in God, we have the most important thing in life.

Job lost his property, his sons, and his health, but he never lost his trust in God. The same tenacity of faith is expressed in the last verses of the prophecy of Habakkuk: "Though the fig tree do not blossom, nor fruit be on the vines, the produce of the olive fail and the fields yield no food, the flock be cut off from the fold and there be no herd in the stalls, yet I will rejoice in the Lord, I will joy in the God of my salvation." It would have been a good thing if that paean of praise had found its way into the historic liturgies of the Christian Church. The psalmist found God a very present help in time of trouble. Franz Werfel was right when he said that the world has forgotten in its preoccupation with Left and Right that there is an Above and Below. We need to come to a greater awareness of the Above. All through the ages, the noblest souls have found faith in God a secret of security.

2. *Another Source of Strength Is Faith in Christ.*

Jesus not only asked His disciples to believe in God; He added, "Believe also in me." This would have been arrogance of the first order, if Jesus had not been the Son of

God and the promised Messiah. God can sometimes seem terribly far away, but He is brought near to us in Christ. God can sometimes be the great unknowable, the *deus absconditus,* as Barth speaks of Him. He can be the unknown God to whom the Athenians had built an altar. Through Christ He becomes known. As Jesus said, "He who has seen me has seen the Father." Paul testified that Christians could behold the glory of God in the face of Jesus Christ.

It was Christ's mission to reveal God in all His saving power and redeeming love. "God was in Christ reconciling the world to himself."

Perhaps an illustration from science may shed light on a religious truth. Over a wire comes a mighty electric current. I cannot use it. It is too powerful for my motor. It would melt the thing, ruin it. But that current can be directed into a resistance box and transformed into voltage which is usable. My motor is no longer endangered, but empowered. Let us think of Jesus as thus transforming God. Through Christ, the almighty and awesome God becomes the accessible God. That is why Christ invites to himself those who are weighed down by trouble, burdened by sorrow, or possessed by sin. It is thus that God's grace and power are made available.

The great Scottish educator, Henry Drummond, was visiting in a Scotch home. The family told him they were not going to go with him to the station because their coachman was a brilliant scholar caught in the clutches of strong drink, and they wanted to give Dr. Drummond an opportunity to talk to him. Sitting on the seat with the driver, Drummond's gracious personality won the man's confidence so that he confessed his weakness and sin and failure. Then

Drummond said, "What if I who ride beside you were the finest horseman that ever drove a team of horses; what if I could control the wildest horses that ever pulled a carriage; what if these horses driven by you were such that you could not control them, you were helpless, and I said, 'Give me the reins and I will control them,' what would you do?" The man saw the point and exclaimed, "Is that what Jesus Christ will do for a defeated and helpless man?" "That is it," said Drummond, "let Christ have the reins; though your sins be as scarlet, He will make them white as snow."

What is true of sin is true of sorrow. We believe in God, but somehow it is through faith in Christ that God's love and sympathy and healing power become available. More than once, as I have preached a funeral sermon, I have seen some mourner's face fixed not on me but on the face of Christ in our chancel painting, and somehow a heavy heart has become lighter; for Christ's words have come with fortifying power, "Let not your hearts be troubled."

The shortest, surest way to the Father is through Christ. "No one comes to the Father but by me," said Jesus. No matter how dark may be the valley through which we must pass, He will be with us who said, in His last legacy of love, "Lo, I am with you always, to the close of the age."

3. *Still Another Source of Strength Is Belief in the Life Beyond.*

If this world were all of life, we would never know security, for as the hymnist says, "Change and decay in all around I see." We find something far more enduring in those words of Jesus, "In my Father's house are many rooms; if it were not so, would I have told you that I go to prepare a place for you? And when I go and prepare a place for you, I will come again and will take you to myself, that where I am you may be also." The Bible speaks of a city that has foundations, not here but hereafter. Foundations suggest solidity and security.

This world never brings perfect justice. God's righteousness is vindicated only by a day of judgment that punishes wickedness and blesses righteousness. Christ's mission was not merely to save from sin; it was to save to the uttermost; it was to bestow life everlasting. "God so loved the world that he gave his only Son, that whoever believes in him should not perish but have eternal life." Wherever men and women have laid hold on Christ, and through Him experienced this new dimension of life that is eternal life, there has been peace and security which nothing could destroy.

This lifetime is only the vestibule of eternity. What that life beyond will have in store depends on whether we have accepted or rejected Christ.

There are ways to coveted goals that are devious and difficult and dubious. Think of Columbus' search for the way to the East Indies, of the hunt by many for the Northwest Passage, of the fruitless search for El Dorado. It is not such devious, difficult, or dubious ways that lead to eternal life. It is the plain and simple way of Christ. It is the safe and sure way of Christian faith. If we are walking that way, it is in an aura of peace; for we have made the great discovery that God and Christ and the life beyond are all bound together. When we believe in God and Christ and in the eternal home, we have found the secret of security.

WHAT IS REAL FRIENDSHIP?

John 15:15

THERE ARE many names given to Christians—believers, disciples, servants, friends. There is a fitness to each one, for each one was given by Jesus himself. However, it was not until His last meeting with His disciples that Jesus called them friends, and then it was a name which was to supersede the word "servants." "No longer do I call you servants," said Jesus, "for the servant does not know what his master is doing; but I have called you friends, for all that I have heard from my Father I have made known to you." One group of believers has attached such value to the name "friends" that they have called themselves "The Society of Friends." We know them better as Quakers.

There have always been friendships of one kind or another, but Jesus seems to sift the ingredients of friendship, so that all chaff is removed and the pure virtue is set before us.

1. *The Nature of Friendship.*

Friendship is far more meaningful than acquaintanceship or companionship. An acquaintanceship can be casual and brief. On a railroad train, at a convention, at a party, we often meet, for a few interesting moments, people whom we can call acquaintances, but there is no real bond between us. As for companions, you can hire them. It is not uncommon to see an ad stating that a certain person desires another to occupy the same home with him or her as a companion. Friends, however, are not for sale.

171

Friendship does not rest merely upon being near someone. Enemies are often near each other, and friends are often separated by long distances and for a long time. Real friendship can stand the strain of separation, for as Emerson said in his essay on "Friendship," friendships "are not glass threads or frost-work."

The roots of friendship are spiritual. Friends build their personalities on the bedrock of life's basic interests—ideals, hopes, trust, mutuality, unselfishness. There may be a great difference in such superficial things as wealth, social position, and age, but there must be an affinity as far as the greater values of life are concerned.

I think the statement can be defended that great friendships are possible only to great souls. It is inconceivable that there can be real friendship between scoundrels, for scoundrels would want to use friendship. A real friend desires only to be used.

Jesus said, "Greater love has no man than this, that a man lay down his life for his friends." Friendship is pure love. Jesus not only set forth the principle in words, but carried it out in actual deed. He loved us so genuinely that He was willing to lay down His life for us. As a shepherd will put his life between the sheep and the wolf or thief, so Jesus proved himself the Good Shepherd by putting himself between us and our archenemy, Satan. "The good shepherd lays down his life for the sheep." The cross is the seal of Christ's friendship for us.

> What does it mean, this wood
> So stained with blood,
> This tree without a root
> That bears such fruit,
> This tree without a leaf
> So leaved with grief?

Though fool, I cannot miss
The meaning this,
My sins' stupendous price
His sacrifice
Where closest friendships end,
One Friend! My Friend!
                    AUTHOR UNKNOWN

Friendship seeks to carry out every wish of the friend.
"You are my friends if you do what I command you." This
may seem, on the surface, to contradict what I said about
scoundrels wanting to use friendship. Note, however, that
there is no selfishness in the commands of Jesus. His commands are intended for the good of others.

I saw a list somewhere of some organizations with the
word "Friends" in the name—"Friends of the Constitution," "Friends of Dumb Animals," "Friends of Hungary."
Without exception, one is able to detect some common ideal
that challenges or commands. When you are a friend of
someone or something, you are thereby pledged to a certain
loyalty. Otherwise, friendship is not real.

Friendship seeks to share. "All that I have heard from
my Father I have made known to you," said Jesus. Again
He said, "The servant does not know what his master is
doing; but I have called you friends." It is not the servant's
hard toil that is hard to bear. His hard lot is that he is
denied friendship. He knows nothing of the master's mind,
aim, goal, hope. Men are not degraded by hard work. Many
have toiled and risked much in a noble crusade. Men are
degraded when they are made to feel there can be no
equality of spirit, no sharing of purpose.

I said that friendship is sharing. I should have qualified
it by saying that friendship is a sharing of the best we have
to share. "Bar-flies" can never be real friends. Neither can

criminals. They share only the worst. Jesus said, "All that
I have heard from my Father I have made known to you."

2. *The Inspiration of Friendship.*

Whether you look at the friendships of others, or reflect
on your own friendships, you must see that friendship develops the finest potentialities of character. Friendship
brings out the best in people, not their worst. The Bible
records a number of friendships that are an inspiration to
study. There is the friendship between David and Jonathan.
Jonathan's father hated David. Jonathan had been reared
in a palace while David had grown up in a shepherd's hut.
Nevertheless, there were qualities within those young men
that transcended the conditions of social status. Concern
for each other, loyalty to each other, frankness between
each other—these were the elements of that friendship.
There is the friendship between Ruth and her mother-in-
law, Naomi. One was a Moabitess, and the other was a Hebrew; one was young, and the other old; but in God they
found a common basis for their friendship, and through
Him a great unselfishness which sought only the other's
welfare. There is the friendship between Paul and Timothy.
Paul was probably in his fifties, and Timothy hardly out
of his 'teens; yet in the spreading of the Gospel of Christ
they found a basis for their wonderful friendship. Their
difference in age was no barrier to a fine friendship.

Many a person's character has been ennobled through a
fine friendship. Qualities like honesty, courage, trust, unselfishness and the spirit of sacrifice are brought to full
development.

There is an inspiration about a beautiful friendship that
leaps over the boundaries of time. The friendship of Alfred

Tennyson and Arthur Hallam resulted in the great poetic masterpiece of Tennyson, "In Memoriam," which he dedicated to his departed friend. How the influence of that friendship has flowed over into other lives! Many of us recall the story which we heard in grade school of the friendship between Damon and Pythias. It revealed how friendship brings out the qualities of trust, courage, and willingness to sacrifice. Great friendships inspire mankind long after the friends have passed from this earthly life.

3. *The Basis of the Finest Friendship.*

What can be a higher goal in life than to be told by Jesus, "I have called you friends"? The person who is first of all a friend of Jesus is worthy of our friendship. He understands and possesses the ingredients that constitute genuine friendship. It is no wonder that we find the most perfect friendships among Christians.

"He first loved us." Having experienced that love, the Christian is able to reflect it. Surely, we live in a world hungry for friendship. Young people, neighbors, fellow workers, the downtrodden of the world—all need friends. Someone has defined a friend as "a person who comes in when every other person has gone out." That is what Jesus did for mankind. The philosophies, kings, and warriors had failed man. Christ saved, rejuvenated, and enriched life. That is why we can sing,

"I have a Friend so patient, kind, forbearing,
    Of all my friends this Friend doth love me best;
Though I am weak and sinful, yet, when sharing
    His love and mercy, I am ever blest."

THE PARABLE OF THE THREE FRIENDS

Luke 11:1-13

ONCE, while serving in a rural parish during my student days, a fire call went out over the rural phone, and soon the neighbors had grabbed buckets and were driving to the scene. I, too, went along, and soon found myself participating in a bucket brigade. One line went from the tank which provided the animals with water, another from the pump which was connected with the windmill. We would fill our buckets, rush to the burning building, hand up our buckets to the farmers on the roof, and dash back to the tank with our empty buckets, repeating the process until the fire was extinguished.

There is a parallel between that incident and the parable of the three friends which Jesus related in connection with some of His teaching concerning prayer.

A man is tired from a long journey. He has not had food for many hours. He is in need, just like that farmer whose house was on fire. A friend at whose house he was staying went in the night to see what could be done to help his friend. We might compare him to those who came to the assistance of the man whose building was burning. Then there was the man who possessed the means of helping those who were in need. In the case of that fire, it was God who gave the water with which to extinguish the blaze and the wind which turned the windmill. Without the wind and water, all our energies and good intentions would have accomplished nothing.

Let us take a close look at each of the friends of whom Jesus was speaking.

1. *The Friend in Need.*

We are not told much about the man, except that he was weary from a long journey and in need of food. It is enough to know that a person is in need. We do not have to have his biography. Jesus was trying to bring out the fact that a friend in need is our particular responsibility. The world has developed an "every man for himself" philosophy, and that is very largely what is wrong with the world. Jesus taught that we should love our neighbor as ourselves. Concern for others always had a prominent place both in His teaching and in His actions. Such concern calls for deep sympathy and sacrificial service.

We do not have to look long or far to find the modern counterpart of the weary and hungry friend in need. Which of you does not know some man or woman who is weary with a heavy burden of sorrow or shame, and hungry for understanding, sympathy, and love? Who does not know of some child, some sick person, someone living under a handicap who would rejoice at any consideration, help and guidance he could give? Who has not heard of the unfortunate masses of war-torn countries who are ill-fed, ill-clad, ill-housed, ill-informed, illguided?

These friends in need disturb our comfort and disrupt our schedule; but the fact that we cannot ignore is that they are in need. There are many who do not like to be reminded of the hungry, the unemployed, the dispossessed, the victims of injustice or oppression. It is so much more comfortable to beieve that "all's well with the world." Certainly, there is not much hope that anything constructive will ever be done about the maladjustments and miseries of life, unless people are informed about them. The friends in need make up a great company, and it is never "a convenient time" when we are brought face to face with their need.

2. The Friend in Deed.

Tolstoi wrote a story about a wealthy member of the nobility who attended a play one wintry night and wept copious tears at the misfortunes of one of the characters in the play. Outside, that individual's coachman, ill-fed and ill-clad, was freezing to death. It is not enough to have an abstract sympathy for some imaginary situation. It must be directed to concrete cases. A woman spoke to me once of her husband's neglect and harshness, but mentioned also that he could sit at the television set and weep over the fictional trials of actors in the plays being presented. It is a dangerous and sinful thing to keep our sympathies abstract and unreal, and never allow them expression in concrete and real situations.

A friend in deed will try to meet the needs and requirements of the unfortunate out of his own resources. In the parable of Jesus, the friend of the weary and hungry traveler was able to furnish a place of rest, but was not able to give the needed food. He did what he could but it was not enough. Everyone who honestly tries to be a friend in deed quickly discovers that the need is much greater than his ability to satisfy. Our help has to be supplemented with help from another source. We must say with the friend in the parable, "I have nothing to set before him."

Jesus told this parable of the three friends just after He had taught His disciples to pray. There may be needs beyond our capacity to satisfy—hungers of the heart and spirit. You no doubt remember the story of Peter and John at the Beautiful Gate of the temple in Jerusalem. As they were going up to pray, they met a beggar who was asking alms of the worshipers. Peter said to the beggar: "I have no silver and gold, but I give you what I have; in the name of Jesus Christ of Nazareth, walk." To bring our needy friends before God in intercessory prayer, to lead another to a living faith in Christ, to awaken a longing for righteousness and self-respect—these are gifts better than silver and gold. Let no one despise or minimize the spiritual gifts one may help another to receive.

The friend in deed did what he could to help a friend, but he had to go and ask another for that which he was not able to give. The Christians of the world will not withhold bread and clothing and medicine from the friends in need all over the world, but the gifts that will loom far more significant in the world scheme will be the gifts of faith, hope, and love. These are gifts which we must in turn receive from Him who is our Friend indeed. Jesus was emphasizing the need and importance of intercessory prayer when He told the parable of the three friends. It is easy for us to forget that praying for others is helping others. A true Christian will never permit intercessory prayer to become an excuse for failing to give the help that he is able to give. Intercessory prayer invokes that help which we find ourselves unable to give.

3. *The Friend Indeed.*

As I direct your attention back to that fire, I want to empasize that all our good intentions, and efforts, and buckets would have been unavailing if there had not been wind and water. It was what God supplied that enabled us to be of help. So, in the parable we are considering. What the friend was able to give to the weary and hungry traveler would not have helped much if he had not been able to go beyond himself and draw upon the resources of another.

All of us have experienced, both in prayers for ourselves and in intercessory prayers, what seem either rebuffs or unnecessary delays. We think that God seems indifferent to our plea. Perhaps we are annoying Him with our petitions. It was this feeling that we sometimes have that Jesus was illustrating when He represented the third friend as saying, "Do not bother me; the door is now shut, and my children are with me in bed; I cannot get up and give you anything." Jesus was not saying that God is reluctant about answering prayer. He was merely showing that to the petitioner, God's delay may appear to be reluctance or rebuff. But Jesus was building up to the lesson He wanted especially to teach, namely, the need of persistence in prayer. It is not the spasmodic, perfunctory prayer that reaches God, but the prayer marked by earnestness, persistence, and intensity to which He listens. "Ask, and it will be given you; seek, and you will find; knock, and it will be opened to you. For every one who asks, receives, and he who seeks finds, and to him who knocks it will be opened."

God is good, insists Jesus. Even His delays to our petitions are intended to deepen our dependence upon Him. It may seem, at times, that God is asleep, but Jesus teaches that we can go to Him at any time; and He emphasizes this by specifying a time which is usually the most unreasonable time of all, namely, midnight. Pressing His point about the goodness of God, Jesus said, "What father among you, if his son asks for a fish, will instead of a fish give him a serpent; or if he asks for an egg, will give him a scorpion? If you then, who are evil, know how to give good gifts to your children, how much more will the heavenly Father give the Holy Spirit to those who ask him?" To the materialist, it may seem to be an anticlimax that the Father should give the Holy Spirit. After the words, "how much more will the heavenly Father give," the materialist would expect the mention of all kinds of physical blessings. But Jesus desires to emphasize that the best things are spiritual blessings— comfort, strength, hope, guidance, divine companionship. The best in human life, purified, intensified, magnified, is what God in His love desires to grant us.

According to the parable, the friend of the traveler asked for three loaves. The Friend indeed gave him as many as he needed. Haven't we all discovered that that is the way God gives. He does not give gifts for us to hoard or waste. He gives according to genuine need. Sometimes, God's gifts surpass our expectations, for He is able to give and do exceeding abundantly above all that we ask or think.

Someone has summed up the parable of the three friends in these words: "A friend speaks to a friend for a friend." I would like to add to that summary three poignant sentences. Some time we will be the friend in need, for soon or late life's journey may leave us weary and hungry. Some time, yes, oftentimes, we can be the friend in deed, carrying out in some practical and unselfish manner the deed that will bring refreshment and restoration to some needy friend. Always, however, let us remember Him who is the Friend indeed to whom our petitions and intercessions are ever welcome, though at times, in our impatience and little faith, God tests us by deferring the answer.

THE SIGNIFICANCE OF THE ASCENSION

Luke 24:50-53

IT IS unfortunate that Ascension Day, observed on the fortieth day after Easter, always falls on a Thursday. This means that Protestant Christians, as a rule, give little thought to this important teaching of Scripure and confession of our faith, namely, that "He ascended into heaven and sitteth on the right hand of God the Father Almighty." With the exception of Christmas and Good Friday, Protestant Christians are not in the habit of going to church for worship except on Sunday. Consequently, many professing Christians, even though they are faithful in church attendance, have never heard a discussion of the ascension of Christ.

According to the Gospels, it was a public event. It was a well-attested fact, however we might explain or interpret it. The deity of Christ is the only explanation of the "How?" The Word of God gives us the only basis of explaining the "Why?"

1. *For Christ, It Meant the Completion of His Earthly Ministry and the Beginning of His Heavenly Ministry.*

In speaking to Cornelius, Peter had made a statement about Jesus that gives a cameo-like description of His earthly ministry, "God anointed Jesus of Nazareth with the Holy Spirit and with power;" and "he went about doing good and healing all that were oppressed by the devil, for God was with him." It was a beautiful life that Jesus lived upon earth. For all time, it demonstrated to mankind how our mortal bodies can become temples of the Holy Spirit, radiating faith, love, purity, humility. Nevertheless, our Lord's life was not without its bitter disappointments, its endless strife, its undeserved sufferings. When, on the cross, Jesus said, "It is finished," He meant that His mission was accomplished. He had revealed God to man. He had reconciled man to God. He had accomplished all that was necessary on His part for the redemption of man.

After various appearances following the resurrection, Jesus was seen by His disciples for the last time on a day forty days after the resurrection. In the simple words of Luke, "While he blessed them, he parted from them."

The ascension of Jesus did not mean that His ministry was at an end. Only His earthly ministry was finished. In his letter to the Ephesians, Paul, speaking under the inspiration of the Holy Spirit, says that God "raised him from the dead and made him sit at his right hand in the heavenly places, far above all rule and authority and power and dominion, and above every name that is named, not only in this age but also in that which is to come; and he has put all things under his feet and has made him the head over all things for the church." Again, in what seems to be an ancient credal statement that Paul is quoting to Timothy, he speaks of Christ being "taken up in glory." The writer of the Epistle to the Hebrews reveals that Christ "always lives to make intercession" for His own.

Because so much is said of the earthly ministry of Jesus and so little of His heavenly ministry, Christians are apt to emphasize the former at the expense of the latter. This is unfortunate, for if the earthly ministry of Jesus had not been confirmed and sealed by His resurrection and ascension, we could not now call upon the living Lord in our times of bewilderment and helplessness. But with Stephen of old, we ought to be able to testify, "Behold, I see the heavens opened, and the Son of man standing at the right hand of God."

2. *For the Disciples, It Meant the Completion of Their Training and the Beginning of Their Labors.*

For a period that may have been as long as three years, the disciples had spent most of their time with Jesus. They had conversed with Him, listened to sermons such as never before nor since fell from the lips of man, witnessed miracles which spoke undeniably of the power of God. More than that, they had learned attitudes of trust, sympathy, love, and mercy because these were the qualities of character which radiated from their Master constantly. As far as we know, Jesus had never taught His disciples how to preach, but He had taught them how to pray. He probably felt that if men are deeply aware and fully convinced of truth and if they are thoroughly persuaded that mankind needs the truth which they possess, preaching it will become a compelling necessity. In the age when Christianity developed, there was no lack of orators who, with beautiful rhetoric and studied gestures, spoke on all manner of topics except those which were most vital. What the world needed was a sincere witness born out of personal experience with Christ, not clever reasoning or oratorical display or passionate rabble-rousing.

It was at the Ascension that Jesus had given His followers their great commission to go and make disciples of all nations, baptizing them in the name of the Father and of the Son and of the Holy Spirit, and teaching them to observe all that He had commanded. In the words of Luke's Gospel, Jesus had referred to the Scriptures and said, "Thus it is written, that the Christ should suffer and on the third day rise from the dead, and that repentance and forgiveness of sins should be preached in his name to all nations, beginning from Jerusalem." Then He had added, "You are witnesses of these things." A witness is not one who knows great truths; he is one who testifies to that truth which he knows.

It was a glorious venture upon which the apostles embarked. They were no longer disciples, learning from a master teacher; they were apostles, emissaries sent forth to teach others that which pertained to life and destiny. It was a ministry to be crowned with both success and sacrifice.

3. *For All of Us, It Means a Spiritual Fellowship with Christ and a Finer Hope.*

A passage in the Epistle to the Hebrews led me to read that letter in the post-Easter season. I had been accustomed to thinking of the letter to the Hebrews as especially appropriate for Lenten reading since it sets the sacrifice of Christ over against the sacrifices with which the Jewish people were familiar. Although the Letter to the Hebrews will always be appropriate reading for Lent, its appropriateness for the post-Easter season must also be recognized. What a lift to faith is given in such a passage as this: "When he had made purification for sins, he sat down at the right hand of the Majesty on high, having become as much superior to angels as the name he has obtained is more excellent than theirs." Or consider the comfort of this sentence: "For Christ has entered, not into a sanctuary made with hands, a copy of the true one, but into heaven itself, now to appear

in the presence of God on our behalf." And consider the
challenge of these words: "Let us run with perseverance
the race that is set before us, looking to Jesus the pioneer
and perfecter of our faith, who for the joy that was set before him endured the cross, despising the shame, and is
seated at the right hand of the throne of God."

Jesus died, but He is alive for all eternity. He parted
from His disciples that He might be with all His followers
to the end of the world. He ascended that our lives might
henceforth be lived on a higher plane. No wonder that one
of Christendom's grandest hymns is an Ascension hymn,

> Let every kindred, every tribe,
> On this terrestrial ball
> To Him all majesty ascribe,
> And crown Him Lord of all.

THE SPIRIT OF THE WORLD VERSUS THE WORLD OF THE SPIRIT

John 15:18-25

MY TOPIC, "The Spirit of the World Versus the World of the Spirit," is more than a play on words. It is a description of a situation that is cosmic as well as personal. There are certain attitudes and desires that are so universally present among men that we can designate them by the general term, "the spirit of the world." However, arrayed against this worldly spirit is a world of spiritual values and ideals that can never be harmonized or identified with the spirit of the world.

1. *Let Us Try to Understand What the Spirit of the World Is.*

Jesus certainly spoke of the world as expressing a resistance and even hostility to His teachings. Paul in writing to the Corinthians says, "Now we have received not the spirit of the world, but the Spirit which is from God." The word that Paul uses most frequently to describe the spirit of the world is the word, "flesh." Jesus, too, used that word to describe man's disinclination or inability to do good when He said to His disciples in the Garden of Gethsemane, "The spirit indeed is willing, but the flesh is weak."

By "spirit of the world" we are to understand that natural alienation from and ignorance of God which is universally prevalent among men. It was this fundamental clash of which the ancient prophet was speaking when he said,

"My thoughts are not your thoughts, neither are your ways my ways, says the Lord." In his First Letter to the Corinthians, Paul seems to identify the wisdom of the world with this spirit of the world which is contrary to Christ and His kingdom. He says, for example, "The world did not know God through wisdom." The Greeks, even like our modern world, believed that the mind of man could unlock all truth, but Paul insisted that the wisdom of man's intellect could become a barrier to God. "If any one among you thinks that he is wise in this age, let him become a fool that he may become wise. For the wisdom of this world is folly with God." Paul's purpose and hope is that the faith of those to whom he ministers "might not rest in the wisdom of men but in the power of God." "No one comprehends the thoughts of God except the Spirit of God." Paul goes on to say, "Now we have received not the spirit of the world, but the spirit which is from God."

"The spirit of the world" is more than ignorance of God. It is complete absorption with the material things of the world. Jesus spoke, in His parable of the sower, of how "the cares of the world and the delight in riches choke the word." He illustrated the same thought in His parable of the rich fool who said, "Soul, you have ample goods laid up for many years; take your ease, eat, drink, be merry." Man thinks that by making money, increasing profits, owning real estate, possessing stocks and bonds he can find security. Marxism, with its philosophical principle of economic determinism, seeks to interpret all life on the basis of materialism. It leaves no room for trust in God or spiritual values. Jesus said to the tempter, "Man does not live by bread alone." Seeking to satisfy one's self with the material things of life will not dispel a deeper hunger which God has put within the soul of man. That is why Jesus could make the appeal, "Do not labor for the food which perishes, but for the food which endures to eternal life, which the Son of man will give to you."

"The spirit of the world" is a selfish spirit. It knows nothing of kindness, sympathy, consideration of others, vicarious suffering. Jesus condemned this selfish spirit in the parable of Dives and Lazarus and in the parable of the Good Samaritan. He condemned it by himself going the way of the cross. The world cannot understand the meaning of the cross. As Paul saw so well, "The word of the cross is folly to those who are perishing."

Perhaps the most evident expression of the spirit of the world is in its pride and vanity. Individuals, institutions, and kingdoms succumb to it. As long as pride possesses souls, there is no room for the world of the spirit. "For all that is in the world, the lust of the flesh and the lust of the eyes and the pride of life, is not of the Father but is of the world. And the world passes away, and the lust of it."

2. *Let Us Seek to Understand the World of the Spirit.*

When Jesus said, "My kingdom is not of this world," He was thinking of a world of the Spirit where spiritual values reign supreme. What are some of these values of the world of the Spirit?

Jesus assumes that His followers will not be imbued with the spirit of the world, for there is another Spirit which fills them. "If you were of the world," He said, "the world would love its own; but because you are not of the world, but I chose you out of the world, therefore the world hates you."

In His sermon on the mount, Jesus spoke of some of

those values which are recognized in the world of the spirit. Let us look at them. There is humility and meekness. There would certainly be far less friction and strife in the world, if men would forsake their pride and vanity and pomp, and exercise humility and meekness in attitude and act. There is mercy or the readiness to forgive and help. The world has always accepted the principle of an eye for an eye and a tooth for a tooth, but Jesus condemned the desire to seek revenge. He asks that we be willing to forgive without measure, to pray for those who persecute us. In the world of the Spirit, there is a hunger and thirst for holiness. Where the spirit of the world shows an indifference toward all that is righteous and holy, the children of God appreciate these qualities and seek to develop them in their own lives. In the world of the Spirit, there is readiness to suffer for the sake of goodness and truth and righteousness, but those who are infected by the spirit of the world desire only complacency and personal comfort. They recognize no responsibility for the furtherance or protection of spiritual values. The spirit of the world is an impure spirit, having a passion for literature and conversation and performances which reek with lust. The followers of Christ do all they can to promote peace. They heed the Biblical injunction to seek peace and pursue it. The spirit of the world, however, generates ill-will, prejudice, unfriendly rivalry, and hatred. Love is the fulfilling of the law in the world of the Spirit.

As followers of Christ, we are committed to do battle against the spirit of the world. Jesus said, "If the world hates you, know that it has hated me before it hated you . . . If they persecuted me, they will persecute you." It was this great struggle of which Paul was speaking in his letter to the Ephesians, "We are not contending against flesh and blood, but against the principalities, against the powers, against the world rulers of this present darkness, against the spiritual hosts of wickedness in the heavenly places."

3. *On Which Side of the Struggle Are We?*

When Jesus explained to His disciples that there is an irreconcilable difference between the spirit of the world and the world of the spirit, He was forewarning and thus forearming them. There can never be peace between right and wrong, between virtue and vice, between truth and error. Christians cannot be satisfied with a mere truce. Complete victory must be their goal. Therefore, as long as unbelief poisons souls, as long as injustice breeds misery, as long as greed and lust wreck human lives, so long must Christians persevere in the task of bringing the spirit of man into obedience to the spirit of Christ. That it is a glorious responsibility, none can deny. That it is beset with many dangers and disappointments, only adds to the challenge. That progress has been so slow and slight should only be a spur to greater loyalty. "A servant is not greater than his master." Take a stand with Jesus against exploitation and injustice, and the opposition of the world spirit will soon become apparent, as Jesus prophesied.

There are many who agree with the principles of Jesus, who know that man does not live by bread alone, who long for the realization of the kingdom of heaven, but who have not the courage to stand up and be counted on the side of Jesus. In a probing sermon, Dr. Carl Lund-Quist, executive secretary of the Lutheran World Federation, asked, "Why was there only one Bishop Ordass?" Against the insidious advance of Communism in Hungary as well as in other countries, there have been many Christians who have paid dearly for their opposition to the spirit of anti-Christ represented in Communism, but those who have furnished conspicuous opposition have been relatively few. Take a stand with Jesus for the loving of all men against all injustice and corruption, and see what happens.

It is in the fifteenth and sixteenth chapters of the Gospel of John that Jesus reveals the sources of power for the Christian in his stand against the spirit of the world. They promise a blessed union with the Father and the Son, and the gift of the Holy Spirit with His comfort and power.

It would be a marvelous thing if our worship today will have aroused in us a deeper desire to be in harmony with the world of the Spirit; if it will have made us willing to be hated by the world because we do not share its spirit; and if it will have led us to rely more implicitly on God for comfort and power, as we stand with the world of the Spirit against the spirit of the world.

PENTECOSTAL BLESSINGS

John 14:15-21

THE CHRISTIAN CHURCH ought always to make much of Pentecost, for it was on Pentecost that she came into being. Centuries before the coming of Christ, the prophet Joel had envisioned the rapturous experience which would one day come to the body of true believers. Jesus himself promised the coming of the Holy Spirit to His disciples, and foretold the blessings which would be made available to mankind through His work.

During these past weeks, Christians have dwelt on the joy and hope which came into life because of the resurrection of Christ, but the early Christians needed more than joy and hope if they were to dislodge the entrenched power of pagan religion. That something happened on Pentecost which gave new purpose and enthusiasm and power to the band of Christian disciples is beyond question.

It would be a fitting observance of this day to reflect upon the blessings which Pentecost emphasizes. Time and again the Christian Church settles down into a dull routine, and seems to lack the zeal and the power which the Early Church had following the Pentecost experience. It was the outpouring of the Holy Spirit that was the essential element in that Pentecost experience. That was what the disciples were waiting for. Jesus had promised that the Spirit would be given to them. Pentecost marked the fulfillment of Christ's promise. What were the blessings which Christ had promised and which Pentecost fulfilled?

193

1. *One of the Chief Blessings of Pentecost Is a Love Which Inspires and Empowers Obedience to Christ.*

There are many who believe in God, but who do not obey His will. Jesus said, "If you love me, you will keep my commandments." Obedience, then, is more closely related to love than to belief. Love is a strange force. It inspires and empowers. It is true all through life that we serve that which we love.

When the Holy Spirit is active in a person's life, that person is given such an insight into Christ's nature that he cannot help but love Christ. When we remember the healing ministry of our Lord to the bodies, minds, and souls of men; when we recall His sympathetic understanding of heavy-hearted humanity; when we reflect upon the shame He endured and the sufferings He bore in order to accomplish man's redemption, we wonder how people can do anything but love such a Savior. Still, we need only look about us to observe how men and women fail to appreciate what Christ has done for them. They may be acquainted with the record of Christ's life, but there is no upsurge of appreciation and gratitude in their hearts for what Christ has done for them. Because they do not appreciate, they do not love. Because they do not love, they do not obey.

Listen to the words of Jesus in which He emphasizes the relationship between love and obedience! "He who has my commandments and keeps them, he it is who loves me; and he who loves me will be loved by my Father, and I will love him and manifest myself to him." "If a man loves me, he will keep my word, and my Father will love him, and we will come to him and make our home with him. He who does not love me does not keep my words."

When we permit the Holy Spirit to work in our hearts,

one of the first blessings we receive is such an appreciation of Christ's work on our behalf that we cannot but love and, loving Christ, we cannot but obey.

2. *A Second Blessing of Pentecost Is the Ability to Grasp Spiritual Truth.*

It requires something more than intellect to grasp the highest values of life. A number of years ago, the famous mathematician and philosopher, Bertrand Russell, gained much notoriety because of his opinions regarding certain moral standards. There could be little doubt as to his mental powers in the fields of mathematics and philosophy, but his sanctioning of looseness in morals by espousing free love revealed the truth of what Jesus said about the world not being able to receive the Spirit of truth. How true the words of Paul, "The world did not know God through wisdom"! Paul put it still more strongly when he said, "Has not God made foolish the wisdom of the world?" The world has abounded in intellectual giants who have missed the goal of life and who, with all their insight and foresight, have been unable to apprehend spiritual truth and eternal values.

Even when Jesus was here on earth, the world did not see the greatness of His life and spirit. The eyes of faith in the humblest believer saw more than the brilliant minds of the age. To grasp spiritual truth, we must keep ourselves open to the illumination of the Holy Spirit. There is one danger, however, that may arise; for it is possible so to rely on direct inspiration that we confuse subjective aberrations with divine inspiration. Men may regard certain feelings as Spirit-inspired which are only the agitated reaction of mingled fears, hopes, and hazy religious knowledge. The very word "Pentecostal" has fallen into reproach because there are certain religious groups whose lop-sided interest in the Bible and whose emotional excesses present Christianity in a false light.

J. S. Whale in *The Right to Believe* says, "The Holy Spirit which is the sole agent of God's grace, operates in this three-fold way, so that the appeal to history (the Bible), the appeal to living tradition (the Church), and the appeal to conscience (the inner light) are one and the same appeal to every Christian." Those words state very clearly the balanced position which the true Christian will seek to hold. There can be little doubt that when the Holy Spirit is permitted to operate in these ways, through the Bible, the church, and the conscience, He does endow us with ability to gain and grasp spiritual truth. The profound insights to which the Christian Church and individual Christians have been led confirm this.

If science is that which is verifiable, this statement is truly scientific, for it can be verified. Let two people read the Bible. Let one read with a critical mind, looking for everything that may seem to be out of line with modern thought, for everything that may seem to contradict some other part of the Bible, and the result will be nil as far as any contribution to the spiritual welfare of that person is concerned. Let the other read with an eager heart, asking the Holy Spirit to guide him into an understanding of the truth of Scripture, and the result will be peace, light, and power.

3. *A Third Blessing of Pentecost Is the Comfort of a Sustaining Presence.*

When Jesus was with His disciples in that upper room on the night before His crucifixion, He told His disciples that they would know the Holy Spirit as an abiding presence. "I will pray the Father, and he will give you another Counselor, to be with you for ever, . . . He dwells with you, and will be in you."

In promising the Holy Spirit, Jesus used a word which should be properly translated "Paraclete," but it is so unfamiliar that its significance would be lost. The R.S.V. uses the word "Counselor," and the King James version uses the word "Comforter." The word, in its original setting, means helper, defender, advocate, intercessor, one who comes to rally us, one who supports. All this the Holy Spirit proved to be to the first disciples, and all this He is still today to every believer in Christ. He braces us for the hard road ahead. He gives us fresh vigor and high courage.

Sometimes we are apt to long for a new Pentecost and a new coming of the Spirit from heaven, forgetting that the Spirit once given at Pentecost is always with us in the means of grace. Through the Word and sacraments, the Holy Spirit convicts us concerning righteousness, and sin, and judgment. Every prompting to turn from sin is the work of the Holy Spirit. Every impulse to lay hold on divine grace and to walk in the way of light and life is also of the Holy Spirit.

We are not left alone in a friendless universe. We have a Comforter, a Counselor, a divine Helper who is always with us.

4. *Still Another Blessing of Pentecost Is Mystical Union with the Triune God.*

There are experiences in the lives of people which they cannot describe to others who have not had the same experiences. For example, a person deeply in love cannot convey to one who scoffs at love, and who has never been in love, the nature of his feelings. Jesus said, "In that day you will know that I am in my Father, and you in me, and I in you." He was speaking of a genuine experience which Christians through the ages have designated as mystical union. This is, without question, one of the sublimest mysteries revealed to men. To feel that we are a part of God and that God is a part of us is what has brought dignity, joy, and power into men's lives.

"You in me." Jesus means that we shall be lifted above the frets and fears of life to be with Him in the realm of spiritual things. "I in you." He means that we shall be possessed and ruled by Christ in our hearts, minds, and faculties.

Pentecost enshrines the person and work of the Holy Spirit. For most people, that means that the mystery of the Holy Spirit occupies their thoughts. It ought to mean that the mastery of the Holy Spirit fills our lives.

WHY THE CHURCH OBSERVES TRINITY SUNDAY

Matthew 28:18-20

WITH THE OBSERVANCE of Trinity Sunday, the Christian Church begins the second half of the liturgical year. There is a large segment of the Christian Church that pays no heed to the Church Year. Even in the denominations which observe the liturgical year, there are no doubt very many who would find it far from easy to give a satisfactory explanation of it to anyone entirely unacquainted with it.

The Church Year came about by gradual development rather than by decree. At first, there were only a few festivals, such as Easter and Pentecost. Later on, the Christmas and Epiphany festivals and seasons of Advent and Lent were added. Finally, the whole year was divided into fixed cycles with appropriate themes for each Sunday and festival.

There are two main parts of the Church Year: the festival season with Christmas, Epiphany, Easter, Ascension and Pentecost in it, and the Trinity season. During the first half of the Church Year, from December to June, the texts deal with some phase of Christ's life. During the second half of the Church Year, which is the Trinity season, the texts pertain to the Christian's life. The line is not finely drawn and cannot be, but in principle this would be the difference.

I like the way in which Phillips Brooks describes the

Church Year in his famous *Lectures on Preaching.* "The great procession of the year, sacred to our best human instincts with the accumulated reverence of ages,—Advent, Christmas, Epiphany, Good Friday, Easter, Ascension, Whitsunday,—leads those who walk in it, at least once every year, past all the great Christian facts, and, however careless and selfish be the preacher, will not leave it in his power to keep them from his people. The Church Year, too, preserves the personality of our religion. It is concrete and picturesque. The historical Jesus is forever there. It lays each life continually down beside the perfect life, that it may see at once its imperfection and its hope."

As the first half of the Christian Year takes us from Christ's birth through His crucifixion, resurrection, and ascension, so the second half of the Church Year takes us through the life of the Christian from baptism to the judgment. The Trinity season sets forth the Christian's life in all its trials and triumphs, its duty and beauty. The texts for Trinity Sunday should somehow be a fitting introduction to that grand theme.

The text which is set before us today gives three reasons for observing this day which starts the Church of Christ thinking about the privileges and responsibilities of the Christian life. The Church observes Trinity Sunday

1. To Reaffirm Its Knowledge of the True God.

The Bible reveals one God who is Lord of stars and earth, of hills and seas, of Jews and of all other races. For more than twenty-five centuries, Jewish services of worship have begun with those stately words from the Book of Deuteronomy: "Hear, O Israel, the Lord, our God, is one Lord." But Scripture speaks often of the Spirit of God or the Holy

Spirit, and also of the Son of God, Christ the Lord. It is not three gods of whom the Bible is speaking, but one God manifested in three activities, as Creator, Redeemer and Sanctifier. A man may be a stern policeman to some people, a loving father to his children, and a congenial and helpful neighbor to those about him. There is only one man, but he is known in three aspects of his personality.

Likewise, God is one, but in the godhead there is an eternal Trinity—Father, Son, and Holy Spirit. Trinity Sunday emphasizes this triune nature of the one true God. In the Great Commission which occurs in one of the Trinity Sunday texts, we have the words: "Baptizing them in the name of the Father and of the Son and of the Holy Spirit." Trinity Sunday emphasizes the beginning of our experience of God.

The Triune God or Trinity might be compared to a spring of water, welling up in a pool and flowing away into a stream. The spring, the pool, and the stream each has its separate function, and yet they form a unity by being the same water. God is not simply Creator, not merely God who has revealed himself as our loving Redeemer, but God who is the indwelling Spirit within our lives. The full Christian life needs this full experience of God. In fact, there might be less difficulty in understanding the Trinity if we thought of the Triune God in terms of experience rather than belief. Therefore, it is a fit introduction to the Trinity season and its presentation of the Christian life to be reminded that God touches the Christian life in the three-fold function of Creator, Redeemer, and Sanctifier. Not to recognize God in this three-fold experience is to have but a partial knowledge of Him.

The Christian Church observes Trinity Sunday

2. *To Rededicate Itself to Missionary Endeavor.*

Life is always an ongoing thing. It can never become static. If it does, it dies. We are Christians because others were Christians before us. We speak, for example, of the doctrine of the Trinity, and doctrine, to many people, is simply some belief that they hold in their minds. The very word "doctrine" comes from the word "doceo" which means teach. Teaching implies sharing on the part of one person with another. Doctrine never stands in splendid isolation from life. It is a part of life, a sharing of truth with others. If there is to be Christian doctrine, there must be missionary endeavor. Jesus realized that, and made missionary work an integral part of the Christian experience. God never intended that the true knowledge of Him should be the monopoly of any single people. The Jews were not the chosen people in the sense that they alone knew the one true God. They were the chosen people in the sense that they were chosen to be the medium through which this knowledge of God was to be brought to every race. This is the great truth and teaching of the Book of Jonah, for example; for the Bible teaches that God "desires all men to be saved and to come to the knowledge of the truth."

Someone has said, "The whole business of the whole church is to preach the whole gospel to the whole world." That is the commission which Trinity Sunday enshrines. People are not only to be baptized into the name of the Triune God; they are to be taught all things that Christ has commanded—truths, duties, hopes, blessings.

The finest picture painted on the canvas of history is that of those confessors of Christ going forth into age after age to rebuke, redeem, change, and glorify individuals, communities, and nations which, without that gospel of salvation, would be lost and condemned. The greatest odyssey ever written is not the mythical adventures of some wandering warrior, but the world-changing adventures of soldiers of the Cross.

Sometimes we become so engrossed in the power of the gospel in the hearts of Africans and Orientals that we forget the power of the gospel near at home. What about the parents who fulfill their God-given responsibility in seeing that their children are made recipients of God's grace as early as possible? What about the husband or wife who can never gain peace of soul until the mate is sharing the joy of salvation? What about the little child who becomes a missionary to parents who are estranged from God? What about the friend who speaks to a friend about the riches, both of the wisdom and knowledge of God? Until missionary endeavor becomes the business of every professing Christian, the Church of Christ will only plod and stumble along. If every Christian would earnestly set for himself the goal of winning one more Christian for God's kingdom, the whole course of history could be changed from one fraught with much foreboding to one radiant with hope and promise.

The Christian Church observes Trinity Sunday

3. *To Reassure Itself of Christ's Abiding Presence.*

Over against the morbid expectations of those who stress the return of Christ in some spectacular manner in the future, we need to set forth the heartening words of our Lord wherein He promised His continued and unending presence with His disciples. You may have known sick people who in the delirium of fever have called for a relative who was even then beside them. Christ's last words to His friends were: "I am with you always, to the close of the age."

In time of weakness, Christ is near to give strength. In time of temptation, He is near to give victory. In time of sorrow, He is with us to give comfort. In time of uncertainty and confusion, He gives direction. In time of trouble, He gives deliverance. In time of idleness, He gives us a task. In our task, He gives us the sense of usefulness. In our despair, He gives us hope.

How may we feel this presence of Christ? There are means by which He comes and abides—through the Word and the sacraments. In worship, Christian fellowship, Christian service, Christ fulfills His promise to be with us.

THE FOURTH CROSS

Matthew 16:24-27

SOMEWHERE in the experience of everyone there is a cross.

It may be a cross like that of the impenitent thief at Calvary which illustrates the truth of those stabbing words, "The wages of sin is death." Many have known that cross. It is proof of the inexorable law that if we sow unto the flesh, we shall of the flesh reap corruption and death. God will not be mocked. If a person chooses the way of unbelief and vice and crime, he will have to take what goes with it—an accusing conscience, a dishonored name, an unhappy end, and a condemned soul.

It may be a cross like that of the repentant thief at Calvary which proves Christ's power to snatch a brand from the very flames of hell. As in the case of the first thief, there has been a mistaken sense of values, a misplaced allegiance, a mismanaged life. There has been the price of suffering and shame which goes with sin; but, before the sands of time have run out, there has come a loathing of the ways of sin, and a wistful longing for pardon and peace. The cry of repentance and faith has worked a miracle of grace. The cross of deserved punishment becomes a ladder that reaches to heaven, and one does not have to climb it alone; for there is the hand of the Lord reaching down to help and reclaim. Too late, the commitment of strength and service to Christ, but not too late the demonstration of divine love and mercy!

It may be that, like Mary, one has lived one's life in the shadow of the third cross, the cross of Christ. In joy and sorrow, in strength and weakness, the love of Jesus has been nearer than hands and feet. It has kept before us the assurance that the grace of God is new every morning. It has shed an aura of peace and joy over life. It has been a perpetual comfort, as the extended arms of Jesus have reminded us that we are never far from His ready love and welcome presence. It has been a magnetic force drawing us toward those things which are good and true and kind and worth while; for did not Jesus say, "I, when I am lifted up from the earth, will draw all men to myself"?

We cannot, however, live beneath the cross of Jesus without discovering a fourth cross.

"Jesus told his disciples, 'If any man would come after me, let him deny himself and take up his cross and follow me.'" What is this fourth cross?

1. *It Is a Voluntary Cross.*

Words are strange instruments. A word which had one meaning three hundred years ago may have quite a different meaning today. That is one reason why we must make new translations of the Bible from time to time. Again, the same word may have entirely different content to different people. We have discovered how true and tragic this is in international relations. Communists interpret words like "democracy," "liberation," "free elections," "integrity" in an entirely different manner from what we Americans do. Russians and Americans can use the same words and still mean entirely different things by them.

So it is with the word "cross." To some people, the word "cross" can mean any misfortune that has happened to a person. For example, a man has driven a car in an intoxicated condition, and had an accident which left him permanently crippled. That is not a cross in the Christian sense of the word. Or, a person has invested life savings in a business which failed. The poverty resulting from that gamble is not a cross. Again, an individual may possess a hot temper or a sensitive spirit or an impatient disposition, and call it a cross. Jesus would never use the word "cross" to cover up some nasty trait of character.

Jesus spoke of a cross as some burden, privation, or suffering which could be avoided, but which is voluntarily assumed and borne out of love for Christ and love for mankind.

This fourth cross involves a voluntary denial of self. "Let him deny himself," said Jesus. This means far more than curtailing some luxury, making some generous contribution, or assuming some worthwhile responsibility.

To deny self means to suppress our ego, to push the personal pronouns "I," "me," and "mine" into the background, and to place ourselves entirely at the service of Christ. In the light of our Lord's meaning, many seemingly conspicuous Christians stand condemned. In practically every congregation and in the work of the church at large, one is amazed to find how much of the ego seeks expression. People want honors, praise, and recognition. They want the rest of the people to know how important they are and how much they do. They play politics, and even resort to underhanded methods in order to push through their pet ideas. It is bad enough to discover these practices in the political, social, and business arenas, but when one finds them within the church and bearing the name of religion, they are especially repugnant and reprehensible. The per-

son whose self is always in evidence knows nothing of the
fourth cross, which Jesus said one must take up if one is
to be a true disciple.

There are many who are doing some worthwhile task in
Christ's kingdom, but it cannot be called a cross, for there
is too much of self, too much of personal ambition, left in it.
The pride, the praise, the honor, the financial return, the
security have all worked together to prevent the experience of the voluntary assumption of a cross.

2. *It Is a Bearable Cross.*

One would think that taking up such a cross as Christ is
talking about would be such a complete act of renunciation
that people would break under the burden, but those who
have taken up the cross have discovered the truth of
Christ's words when He said, "My yoke is easy and my
burden is light." Christ's cross is not as heavy as the world's
cross. It is the worshiper of mammon, power, and pleasure
that finds the price too high. Livingstone, after many years
of hardships in Africa, said, "I never made a sacrifice in my
life." When the fourth cross is a reality in one's life, one
discovers what Paul meant when he said, "I can do all things
in [Christ] who strengthens me."

The worldling, looking at one who is bearing this fourth
cross, may say "It's a dog's life," but there are lap dogs and
there are St. Bernard dogs, and there is a vast difference
between them. To brave the storms of life in order to bring
faith, love, and hope into the souls of those who are numbed
and lost and helpless is high adventure.

Recently, a request came to the Lutheran World Federation from Siberia for 1,000 confirmation certificates. Evidently, somewhere behind the iron curtain, there are those

who have taken up the fourth cross. Persecution and exile has been their lot, but they carry on. They find the fourth cross bearable. The saga of those who, in our generation, have taken the cross and followed Jesus will some day be written in letters of living light, even as now it is written in blood and tears. The very contemplation of that story makes our comfortable, complacent Christianity seem insipid, unromantic, and uninspiring.

3. *It Is a Rewarding Cross.*

People do not renounce life when they accept the fourth cross. They find it. Jesus said, "Whoever loses his life for my sake will find it." It is always a thrilling experience to find something. We think of the great discoveries of Columbus, Madame Curie, Thomas Edison, and a host of others who, in the fields of science, archeology, and exploration, have made great discoveries. However, these discoveries in the material realm cannot be compared to the discoveries of spiritual truth and spiritual values. Think of Moses' experience at the burning bush, when he found that God had a task for him to do. Think of Isaiah's experience in the Temple, when he saw the Lord in a vision, and felt called to do His work. Think of Andrew's joy, when he could report to Peter, "We have found the Messiah." Think of the thrill which those had who found the evidence of victory over death in the empty tomb and the risen Christ.

Great discoveries are always costly, but they are worth the cost. The immigrant who discovers this country by coming over the Atlantic in a few days can never know the joy which the Pilgrims knew after one hundred days of uncertainty and privation on the stormy Atlantic. Those who might land on Mount Everest in a helicopter will never

know the thrill which those had who, after long climbs
through storms and snow and bitter cold, finally stood on
the top of the world. To bear the fourth cross and then to
discover that, in proportion to the life of the sensualist, the
criminal, or the miser, the yoke is easy and the burden is
light is one of the richest satisfactions in life. To find one's
life in fellowship with God, in the working out of His purposes, in the bringing of other souls from darkness to light—
this is life indeed. There is no greater reward than to find
life solid with truth, vibrant with divine love, rich with
self-forgetfulness, and radiant with eternal hope.

> "Must Jesus bear the cross alone,
>   And all the world go free?
> No, there's a cross for ev'ry one,
>   And there's a cross for me."

DIFFERENCES OF DISCIPLESHIP

Luke 9: 51-62

THERE ARE SIGNS that there is an awakening of religious interest in our country. Church attendance is better than usual in most areas. Evangelism meetings attract large audiences. As one travels about the nation, one cannot but be impressed by the many and beautiful church edifices that are being erected. Stewardship in all denominations has reached high levels. It would seem that Christ has more disciples than He has ever had.

Then we read the front pages of our newspapers. They seldom have any news about religion, but have much news about crime and juvenile delinquency and divorce. We read the statistics about the growing menace of alcoholism and the increased use of narcotics and drugs. We are shocked by the disclosures of dishonesty and greed in high places in government and labor unions. We cannot help wondering what depth there is to much of the so-called awakened interest in religion. Certainly, the tares are growing amongst the wheat. Even among the professed disciples of Christ, we find marked differences.

1. *There Is a Great Deal of Deluded Discipleship.*

The gospel record informs us that when Jesus entered a village of the Samaritans and they would not receive Him, the disciples suggested that it might be a deserved punishment for those Samaritans to call down fire from heaven and consume them. Jesus, however, would not sanction

211

such punishment. Instead of rebuking the Samaritans, He rebuked His disciples for thinking that He would consider such action. Christian discipleship should be made of better stuff than a spirit of vengeance and persecution.

Nevertheless, as we read church history, it is surprising how often the pages are marred by some kind of deluded discipleship. People profess to be followers of Christ, but they have not caught His spirit of patience and kindness and mercy. As a result, we have often had persecution of those who do not accept the full creed of the majority. Protestants have been persecuted by Roman Catholics. Baptists have been persecuted by Puritans. Liberals have been condemned by fundamentalists.

Long before Jesus came into the world, the prophet Micah had enunciated the spirit of all true religion when he spoke those plain demands of discipleship, "He has showed you, O man, what is good; and what does the Lord require of you but to do justice, and to love kindness, and to walk humbly with your God?" In the light of the preparation for Christ by the prophets and in the light of our Lord's teaching and example, how can professed disciples ever believe that persecution and even execution of those who do not see eye to eye with them in religious matters is compatible with Christianity? There has been too much deluded discipleship in the history of Christianity. Jesus made it clear that love to God and love to man were to be the essence of the religious life.

2. *There Is Too Much Defective Discipleship.*

We are told that one man came to Jesus and said, "I will follow you wherever you go." Instead of accepting that promise, Jesus seems to have discouraged him, for He said to the man, "Foxes have holes, and birds of the air have nests; but the Son of man has nowhere to lay his head." Beneath the fine profession, Jesus detected the lack of self-denying devotion. It is not what we say and profess but what we do in the way of denying self that wins the approval of Jesus. All of us must bow our heads in shame at this point, for our avowals of discipleship have not always been followed by that quality of loyalty and love that subordinates our own comfort and pleasure to the welfare of Christ's kingdom. Christ's test for discipleship is clear: "If any man would come after me, let him deny himself and take up his cross and follow me." Until we have accepted and experienced that fourth cross, our discipleship is defective.

3. *There Is Too Much Delayed Discipleship.*

One man to whom Jesus issued the invitation, "Follow me," replied, "Lord, let me first go and bury my father." It is inconceivable that Jesus would have denied to anyone the duty of performing the last rites of burial of a loved one. Evidently, our Lord understood the man to mean, "Wait until my father is no longer living. Then I will follow you." That might have resulted in many years of delayed discipleship, and delayed discipleship is not only lost service for Christ, but it is apt to result in lost souls as well.

The Roman governor, Felix, postponed hearing the defense of Paul, and that delay probably cost him his soul. He said, "When I have an opportunity, I will summon you." That opportunity never came.

There are many who say, "When I am through with my education, I will become an active disciple of Jesus." Others say, "When we are married and settled, we will become

active church members." Still others assert, "When our
children are old enough to go to Sunday school, we will begin fulfilling the responsibilities of church membership."
Always some excuse for delay!

People need to be reminded repeatedly, as Paul reminded
the Corinthians, "Behold, now is the acceptable time; behold, now is the day of salvation." They need to hear the
clear challenge of Jesus, "Leave the dead to bury their own
dead; but as for you, go and proclaim the kingdom of God."

There are words in the prophecy of Jeremiah which describe with awful accuracy the price of delayed discipleship, "The harvest is past, the summer is ended, and we
are not saved." May those words find no echo among those
who are present here today.

4. *There Is Too Much Divided Discipleship.*

One man to whom Jesus gave the invitation, "Follow
me," replied, "I will follow you Lord; but let me first say
farewell to those at my home." This was not only delayed
discipleship; it was divided discipleship. The ties of group
loyalty were stronger than those of loyalty to Christ. The
comforts of the old life were more appealing than the dangers of discipleship. Once back in the old ways, the call of
Christ would be forgotten. The words of Jesus in the parable of the sower would find fulfillment, "the cares of the
world and the delight in riches choke the word, and it
proves unfruitful."

There are many who have no time for the Lord because
they want to give time to lesser things. One man says he
has only Sundays on which to hunt, or fish, or play golf. A
woman says that her clubs and household duties and social
interests leave her no time for activity in the church. A
young person allows friends and worldly pleasures and

mere laziness to usurp time that rightfully belongs to the Lord. What right have they to complain if, as they stand before the judgment throne, Christ has no time for them?

One of the greatest tragedies of life is the warped sense of values that people have. They do not know how to separate the wheat from the chaff. The illusion of the near obscures the vision of the far. They give a first-rate enthusiasm to a second or third-rate interest.

Most of people's so-called allegiance to Christ is a leftover loyalty. People think and act more as members of a certain nationality, economic class, or political party, than as disciples of Christ. Secular bonds often seem stronger than the bonds by which Christ binds men together. The New Testament gives many tragic examples of divided discipleship. Judas professed to love Christ, but he loved gold more. Ananias and Sapphira claimed to have accepted the principles which guided the Jerusalem church, but they loved economic security more.

During the war, we heard a great deal about an all out effort to win the war. If Christ is to win our generation, it will require an all out discipleship. We will have to be Christians every day of the week, not just on Sundays. We will have to be Christians in the way we vote, in the way we make, use, and invest our money. We will have to be Christians in the class room, at the factory bench, in the business deal, on the highways. We will have to be Christians in the use of our leisure as well as in the practice of our vocation. We will have to be Christians in our associations with Negroes and Orientals, as well as with those of our own race. Any other kind of discipleship is a divided discipleship, and a divided discipleship is not really Christian discipleship.

5. *There Is, Fortunately, Much Determined Discipleship.*

Jesus said, "No one who puts his hand to the plow and looks back is fit for the kingdom of God." There are some who start but never stick, who commence but never complete. Jesus asks for perseverance, stick-to-it-iveness. It is not enough to make vows of loyalty and allegiance when we are confirmed, or when we are accepted into the church. We must abide by them. We must not fall away. "Seek first his kingdom and his righteousness." That is the only standard by which we must order our lives.

Have you ever tried to plow? If so, you know that if you concerned yourself exclusively with the way the soil was being turned, you could not plow a straight furrow. Discipleship must have the forward look. It cannot look backward or downward. Victory by God's grace and eternal glory are always before the faithful disciple. The writer of the Epistle to the Hebrews says, "Let us run with perseverance the race that is set before us, looking to Jesus the pioneer and perfecter of our faith, who for the joy that was set before him endured the cross, despising the shame, and is seated at the right hand of the throne of God." The older translations used the word "patience," but the new rendering "perseverance" injects a more positive and resolute quality, a discipleship that is not easily discouraged.

> Who answers Christ's insistent call
> Must give himself, his life, his all,
> Without one backward look.
> Who sets his hand unto the plow,
> And glances back with anxious brow,
> His calling hath mistook.
> Christ claims him wholly for His own;
> He must be Christ's, and Christ's alone.
>
> JOHN OXENHAM

CALLED TO A HIGHER LOYALTY

Matthew 9:9-13

IT SHOULD not be a big step from politics to open Christian discipleship, but it is a big step from active participation in a corrupt political organization to sincere Christian discipleship. It was this latter step that Matthew took when he gave up his loyalty to the Roman Empire for the higher loyalty to the kingdom of God.

Matthew, or Levi as he was also called, was Jewish both by birth and religious heritage. He had been trained from youth in the moral law of his people. The Messianic longing of his countrymen had been instilled in him from childhood. Nothwithstanding all this, he had broken the law, stifled the Messianic longing, and placed himself in the employ of the nation that was ruling his people. It was the old but ever modern story of a young man or a young woman despising spiritual blessings and deserting them for the glitter of gold or the pride of position.

We first see Matthew sitting in a tax collector's booth. From time immemorial, people have detested taxes, and their dislike has also embraced the agents through whom taxes are collected. This was especially true of the Jewish attitude toward those who acted as taxgatherers for Rome. Disowned by his fellow Jews, and being nothing but a tool in the Roman political organization, Matthew was virtually a man without a country.

Taxes

Taxes are neither good nor bad in themselves. They have nursed extravagance, invited graft, financed wholesale murder, perpetuated oppression, and alienated the good will of citizens. They have also built good roads, preserved law and order, encouraged education, strengthened national defense, and contributed to the common good of social groups. Generally, there has been an admixture of good and evil in taxes, but in imperial Rome, the bad was more in evidence. The selling of the right to collect taxes was in itself a prolific cause of injustice and oppression. Then, too, since most of the money collected went out of the country to enrich foreigners, the Jews were especially antagonistic to all who had any part in the system. That is why the word "publicans" became joined to the word "sinners" in an expression often used by the Jews in Palestine in Jesus' day.

Matthew's Call

One day as Jesus was passing down a main street of Capernaum, He passed by the tax collector's booth. He had often gone that way. He may have stopped on occasion to chat with the man who sat there. The man's name was Matthew. On this particular day, Jesus addressed a brief command to Matthew. He said, "Follow me." We do not know how much Matthew knew about Jesus, but if he had never received that personal invitation, he almost certainly would never have become a follower of Jesus.

In our offices and shops, in our neighborhoods and social groups, there are those who are not ignorant of the life of Jesus, men and women who know the location of any number of Christian churches, but who will never follow Christ, nor associate themselves with other followers of Christ, until they have been given a personal invitation. Few and far between are the disciples who have volunteered. The importance of the personal invitation to those outside of the Church of Christ cannot be overemphasized. Let each and every one of us be lavish with our invitations, in season and out of season. It is better to be rebuffed by man than to be rebuked by Christ.

One reason why we are apt to neglect inviting certain persons to follow Christ is because they seem so unlikely to accept. They may not be of a certain nationality. They may not have come from the same denominational background as ourselves. They may be so preoccupied with their business, so taken up with social activity, so interested in worldly pursuits, so tied up with sinful living, that we feel that it would only be wasting breath to invite them. But where was there more unlikely material for Christian discipleship than in the souls of Matthew, Zaccheus, Mary Magdalene, or Saul of Tarus? The whole history of Christian endeavor is replete with instances where unpromising individuals, bitter enemies, sodden sinners have become distinguished disciples because someone took enough interest in them to invite them. It is always in order to call someone from a lower loyalty to a higher loyalty.

The Decision

It is almost inconceivable that Matthew would have paid much attention to the invitation of Jesus, if he had never heard of Him. It is surprising enough that, knowing something of Jesus, he would, upon hearing the invitation, rise from his tax collector's seat and follow Jesus into an entirely new domain.

This decisive action on the part of Matthew furnishes us with a striking example of the value of promptness in accepting or grasping opportunities. "He who hesitates is lost" is more than a mere adage. It is a concise statement of eternal truth. The rich young ruler, Pilate, Felix, Agrippa, and a host of individuals since their time have been lost because they did not accept Christ when He was standing and knocking at the portals of their hearts. "Today, when you hear his voice, do not harden your hearts."

The name Matthew may have been assumed after becoming a disciple of Jesus, for we know that Matthew is spoken of as Levi by Mark and Luke. As Simon became Peter, and as Saul became Paul, so it is possible that Levi became Matthew after dedicating his life to Christ. A new name fitted a new loyalty.

For Matthew, the call to follow Christ led him from one occupation into another. It need not always do that. As far as we can learn, Zaccheus did not cease to be a tax collector. He merely brought to his work the principles and spirit of Jesus. Many Christians feel that politics can do nothing but contaminate them. It would be better for all of us if Christians, instead of studiously avoiding politics, would be more ready to go into politics and take with them the principles and spirit of Jesus. The important issue in every situation is to be sure who is our master. Where is our loyalty? The only one who has a valid claim to our lives and our loyalties is Christ, for He purchased us unto God with His blood. When men recognize that claim of Christ, they will gladly yield allegiance and obedience to Him in every sphere of their life. Where does the Lord want us? We must find that place; for no real success can come in any other place.

Feast for the Publicans

Of the feast which Matthew gave for his fellow publicans, and to which Jesus was invited, Matthew, very modestly, says little. The purpose of the feast was, no doubt, to introduce Jesus to other publicans and outcasts. A banquet is a strange setting for evangelization, but those associates of Matthew probably would never have accepted an invitation to come to the synagogue or Temple.

Nothing can displace reverent worship in the sanctuary as a means of communing with God, but there are times when a social atmosphere may be more conducive to making an impression on souls than formal worship. Because of this fact, the church provides for social features in its program in order that through them it might introduce the appeal of Christ to men and women. There is nothing wrong with banqueting and social life, if Christ can be invited and be able to smile with the rest. Sin enters only when Christ goes out, or when we timorously apologize for anything that savors of the spiritual.

Matthew believed that, as far as his former associates were concerned, friendliness would be more apt to bring results than formality. One reason why many churches repel rather than attract is because they lack a spirit of friendliness. Nearly every congregation would be a stronger congregation, if members were more friendly toward strangers and toward each other.

Criticized for Doing Good

Good intentions are nearly always impugned by someone. Even our Lord was not exempt from criticism. The Pharisees who criticized Jesus' presence at Matthew's feast had a "dog in the manger" attitude. They would never interest themselves in the spiritual welfare of a publican or outcast, and they found fault with anyone else who did. The Pharisees regarded others as spiritually sick, but they could not see the seriousness of their own spiritual affliction. They suffered from a "holier than thou" attitude. It prevented them from seeing the spiritual potentialities of their fellow men. It distorted their vision, so that even the compassion of Christ seemed to them to be compromise. That attitude never wins men from a lower loyalty to a higher loyalty.

Where a Physician Is Needed

In His reply to the faultfinding Pharisees, Jesus said, "Those who are well have no need of a physician, but those who are sick." In the spiritual sense, there are no whole people. In every soul, there is the taint of sin. "All have sinned and come short of the glory of God." Every man, woman, and child stands in need of the great physician of souls, Jesus Christ. None is so bad that Christ will not receive him; none is so good that he does not need to receive Christ.

Quoting the prophet Hosea, Jesus said, "I desire steadfast love and not sacrifice." The Pharisees were conscientious about offering all the sacrifices which the law commanded, but they knew little about practicing mercy and forgiveness. In making people outcasts, they did not convert them to a higher loyalty, but rather confirmed them in their slavery to evil. Jesus was exposing and condemning the hollowness of the religious formalism of the Pharisees. It is so easy for men to perform the externals of a religious system, but so hard to practice the essential elements of religion. It is so easy to see sin in others, so hard to see it in ourselves. We can be loyal to standards that condemn extortion, adultery, and unbelief, and still be disloyal to those higher standards that condemn pride, hatred, and lack of sympathy.

It is God's mercy in Christ that saves men. It is men's mercy toward each other that lifts life to higher levels. Jesus calls men from the lower loyalties that are based on pride, rivalry, and selfishness to the higher loyalty based on sympathy, mercy, and love. Never look down on your fellow men. Love them. Lift them. Show them what the spirit of Christ dwelling in a soul is like. It is by such conduct on the part of professing Christians that discipleship becomes meaningful. It is only by such higher loyalty that men can be won from lower loyalties.

IS CALAMITY GOD'S PUNISHMENT?

Luke 13:1-5

THE PROBLEM of suffering and disaster is one of the oldest problems with which the human mind has occupied itself. Why do afflictions come? Why does calamity overwhelm men and women who seem no more deserving of it than others, and often seem entirely innocent? Are these recurring troubles purely accidental and coincidental —entirely out of gear with the customary working of cause and effect? Are they a divine visitation brought upon certain individuals because they have broken some fixed law of the universe? Or are there other ways of regarding affliction?

1. *Much Affliction Is the Result of Sin.*

You may recall that in the Book of Job, after Job has experienced one calamity after another, some friends call on him. In the course of their conversation, they suggest that Job suffers greatly because he has sinned greatly. Those who were talking to Jesus on the occasion mentioned in our text seemed to have the same opinion, for Jesus asked this challenging question, "Do you think that these Galileans were worse sinners than all the other Galileans, because they suffered thus?" Then He went on to refer to another incident that had taken place, challenging them with another question, "Or those eighteen upon whom the tower in Siloam fell and killed them, do you think that they were worse offenders than all the others who dwelt in Jerusalem?" Jesus did not deny that much affliction is the result of sin. He merely denied that the answer to life's troubles could be explained as easily as that.

We must admit, of course, that this is a world of moral consequences, and that sin does bring trouble. Men speed, and if, because of that excessive speed, they fail to negotiate a turn and go off the road into a ditch, incurring severe injuries, we can understand how sin has caused misfortune. A man forms the habit of drinking. Eventually, it takes such a hold upon him that poverty and illness become his constant companions. Here again, we can understand how much trouble is the result of sin. A parent may spoil a child by never disciplining that child for disobedience, and by permitting the child to have everything desired without having to work for it. It is a simple working of the law of cause and effect, if that child turns out bad, and brings disgrace and sorrow to the parents. A child may refuse to study school lessons. If that child never makes a success of life, we can understand how the sin of idleness brought on the consequence of failure.

In the political realm, we find that selfish tariffs, armament races, contemptuous treatment of other races, eventually bring on a day of judgment. There can be no doubt that sin brings on a judgment of one kind or another.

2. *However, the Affliction Does Not Always Come to the Sinner.*

Jesus indicated that the victims of Pilate's wrath and those who were killed by the falling tower at Siloam were not more sinful than others who escaped those misfortunes. Calamity and sin are connected, but sometimes others suffer vicariously for the guilty. It is possible that the men who built that tower in Siloam had used poor materials, or had not been sure to make it plumb. It was their sin, but some innocent people happened to be beneath it when it toppled to the ground. A few men in the village of Lidice had killed one of Hitler's henchmen who was named Heydrick. For this deed, Hitler ordered the whole population of the village wiped out. The great majority of them were innocent of any crime, yet they had to die. The ones who precipitated World War II—those who financed Hitler's rise to power, those who taught Nietzsche's and Machiavelli's ideas, those who took the teeth out of the League of Nations Covenant, those who exploited weaker nations—all these suffered far less than millions who were caught in the throes of World War II.

Long before Jesus came into the world, an Old Testament prophet was given a vision of the Suffering Servant whom God would send to save mankind from sin. Of the Messiah this prophet said, "Surely he has borne our griefs and carried our sorrows; yet we esteemed him stricken, smitten by God, and afflicted. But he was wounded for our transgressions, he was bruised for our iniquities; upon him was the chastisement that made us whole, and with his stripes we are healed." There is a redemptive power in vicarious suffering. No wonder the Cross has become the chief symbol of Christian faith. The suffering of Christ not only draws men from the power of sin, but inspires in them the power to reflect in their own lives something of the spirit of vicarious suffering. The defenders of the faith, and those who have brought the gospel into pagan lands, have often died for their efforts, but they have been willing to make the sacrifice because they knew that they were thus enriching other lives.

3. *We Should Look Upon Calamity As An Opportunity.*

In writing to the Christians in Rome, the Apostle Paul said, "We know that in everything God works for good with those who love him, who are called according to his purpose." This is the great assurance of the Christian, namely that everything, be it good or ill, can somehow be made to serve God's purposes.

Often, life can become so comfortable that people become incapable of seeing and understanding the hardships that some must endure. When calamity strikes, it may be a means of making them realize the harder realities of life, and the uncertainty of life itself.

Affliction may be an opportunity to show what is in us. Hudson Taylor was sitting in an inn with a new missionary to China. He filled a glass full of water and then struck the table with his fist. As the water splashed out, he said to the young missionary, "You will be struck by the blows of many sorrows and troubles in China, but remember they will only splash out of you what is in you. Out of some of the blows of trouble splash complaint and bitterness, but out of others joy and victory." We may think of troubles as being like the water test for diamonds. The diamond will continue to gleam, if it is genuine. Just as a strong wind blows down the trees in a forest which have some rottenness in them, but strengthens those that are sound, so calamity will destroy the false or faulty faith of some people, and strengthen and beautify the genuine faith of others.

Calamity should lead to real soul searching. Are there habits of carelessness or sinful indulgence that have brought on trouble? Are there challenges to higher levels of life that affliction brings to us—to patience, courage, a spirit of forgiveness toward those responsible for the misfortune?

If our troubles reveal guilt on our part, then there is an opportunity to repent. To persevere in a wrong course is folly. Just before the great depression in the early thirties, a man who was president of three companies felt that his business demanded more and more of his time, and little by little he withdrew from activity in his church. First, he withdrew from the church board; then, from the men's organization; finally, from attendance at the services. Money became his passion, and work his worship. When the depression came, he was so involved with new development in real estate and expansion of business, that he could not meet taxes and debts. As a result, he lost his wealth and his health. He told me some years after the depression when he was getting on his feet again, "I forgot God, and God forgot me." In his renewed faith and loyalty to God, he found a peace and salvation he would have missed, had not trouble laid its heavy hand upon him. Unfortunately, that is only part of the story. The man's wife was never able to see beyond the loss of worldly possessions. She became bitter toward man and God. She avoided all social intercourse. A sullenness took possession of her. She had placed her trust and found her joy in the things of this world, and when they were lost, she felt that all was lost.

Hard circumstances can often be the making of strong and beautiful character, when they lead to repentance and new dedication. The psalmist says, "A broken and contrite heart, O God, thou wilt not despise." It is wonderful what God can do with a broken heart, if He can get all the pieces. A friend of mine had visited the City Hall in Stockholm, and expressed special delight over the Blue Room. The floor of that Blue Room was made of the left-over pieces of marble from other parts of the building. What was achieved by using the broken pieces was more beautiful than what was achieved with unbroken pieces.

Let us believe that in the plan of God there is a place for both joy and sorrow, both success and failure, but if they are to serve God's purpose they must produce the fruits of repentance, patience, gratitude, or strength.

I BELIEVE IN THE CHURCH

Matthew 16:13-20

IN AN AGE when men have pinned their hopes to so many different political philosophies and leaders, and when they have put their faith in military and economic strength, we could all stand a little buttressing of our faith in the Church of Christ. Wherever Christians gather for worship, they make the confession, "I believe in the Holy Christian Church." They may not always actually say the words, but their very coming together as a group of Christians is a confession of their faith in the church. Nevertheless, it must be admitted that all too often the very people who belong to the church, and who attend worship services in their respective churches, do not show that the church plays a large part in their thinking and living. Do we really believe in the church and, if so, what reasons do we have for our faith?

1. *I Believe in the Church Because Christ Believed in It.*

In spite of the fact that Jesus did not speak much of the church directly, there is much to indicate that He envisioned a fellowship of believers abiding in Him, and continuing that which He had begun. He knew that they would be persecuted, and urged them to remain faithful. He knew that false prophets would arise to confuse people, but promised that the Holy Spirit would guide them into all truth. He knew that the gospel dragnet would gather in

both good and evil, but He insisted that His followers
should not neglect the ingathering of souls. He was fully
aware that the beginnings were as humble as a mustard
seed, but He believed that just as the mustard seed "when
it is sown it grows up and becomes the greatest of all shrubs,
and puts forth large branches, so that the birds of the air
can make nests in its shade," so the peoples of earth would
find refuge in His kingdom. He did not pray only for those
who were His immediate followers, but also for those who
were to believe through their word. He was willing to en-
trust to the church the program of world evangelism. His
followers were to go into all the world, and preach the gospel to the whole creation. They were to make disciples of
all nations, baptizing them into the name of the Father, Son,
and Holy Spirit, and teaching them to observe all that He
had commanded. All this assumed some kind of fellowship
bound together in common faith and purpose, transmitting
His ideals to men everywhere and promoting His way of life.

Christ's words to Peter have been the subject of much
controversy and the basis of much division among those
who call themselves His followers. In the light of all that
Jesus taught about humility and sacrifice and willingness
to do the lowest work of the lowest servant, it is inconceivable that our Lord ever contemplated an organization possessing the pomp, power, and possessions of the Roman
Catholic hierarchy. It was not Peter who was to be the
founding rock of the church but Christ himself. "No other
foundation can anyone lay than that which is laid, which is
Jesus Christ." Paul spoke of Christians as "members of
the household of God, built upon the foundation of the
apostles and prophets, Christ Jesus himself being the chief
cornerstone." Even the words in the original Greek indi-

cate that Peter is not the rock on which the church is to be
built, for in referring to Peter Jesus uses the adjective
"petros," which means "having the qualities of a rock," and
when He speaks of the foundation stone of the church He
uses the noun "petra," which means "rock." It is the confession that Jesus is the Christ, the Son of the living God,
that makes Peter have the qualities of a rock. Whoever
honestly believes and confesses that Jesus is the Christ, the
Son of the living God, is possessed of the qualities of the
rock on which the church is founded. On numerous occasions, Jesus spoke of the need of witness bearing. It was
this host of faithful witness bearers which He envisioned as
comprising His Church. It would be a witness that would
be so strong in its conviction, and so courageous in the
face of opposition, that no power would be able to destroy
it. Such was the faith that Jesus reposed in His Church.

2. *I Believe in the Church Because Christ Is Still in
Vital Association with It.*

Christ promised His disciples that He would be with
them always. His last recorded words were: "Lo, I am
with you always, to the close of the age." Christ instituted
the Sacrament of Holy Communion to assure His followers
that He was still with the church which He had loved, and
for which He had given His life.

Under many figures of speech, the Bible emphasizes
Christ's vital association with His Church. In one of His
last discourses, Jesus said to His disciples, "I am the vine,
you are the branches. He who abides in me, and I in him,
he it is that bears much fruit, for apart from me you can
do nothing." Paul, in writing to the Colossians, says, "He
is the head of the body, the church." He likens the relation

of Christ to His Church to the relation between a husband and wife, and adds, "we are members of his body."

Helen White has written a historical novel of the early history of the Franciscan Order called *A Watch in the Night*. In one of the memorable scenes, three monks are engaged in conversation concerning troubles they are facing, and John of Parma, a monk of St. Francis, says, "I was young, and I thought the heretics must sweep out the whole Church the way they had swept us out. That night with the wind blowing against my back I saw the whole church going down before their violence, and I was afraid. But old Brother Paulo said No. There was nothing to fear. So long as we two there out on the Hillside, naked to the winter night, were faithful sons of Holy Mother Church, it did not matter if all the heretics on earth swept away every stone of every church in the world. And when morning came, and I saw that he was leaving me alone, he bade me remember that if everybody else in the world went over to the heretics, and I stood fast, the church was still firm on earth. And as his eyes swam, he bade me remember that the rest was God's." Always, the faithful followers of Christ can rest on the Lord's promise, "Where two or three are gathered in my name there am I in the midst of them."

The Lord permits His Church to be tested, but He is always with His faithful ones in the furnace of trial. One of the strange phenomena of history is how the church finds secret sources of strength in times of persecution. The church's growth is like that of the sturdy oak, withstanding the bitter winds of adversity, piercing downward through hostile rocks into darkness, and night and day, in sun and shower, continually lifting its arms in prayer.

Many years ago, while a mere child, I was awakened dur-

ing the night and told to look out of the window at a large
fire only a few blocks from our home. The night was very
dark, and the huge blaze only intensified that darkness. A
terrific wintry gale was blowing. The stronger the wind,
the brighter the flames. How like the Church of Christ!
The darker the night of tribulation and the stronger the
gale of persecution, the brighter it shines in the hearts of
its followers, and the swifter it moves forward to its final
destiny. It is impossible to quench that fire which is fed
from the live coals of God's altar in heaven.

3. *I Believe in the Church Because It Is the Agency for
   God's Blessings.*

Blessings do not, as a rule, come by themselves. They
come through means. It signifies little to those dying of
thirst in Death Valley to know that there are snow-fed lakes
in the distant mountains. The water must be piped or carried to the thirsty. The church is the means by which the
water of life is brought to thirsty souls. It means little to
the famine stricken people of the Orient to know that there
are bumper crops in America. Those crops must be brought
to the starving in vessels before they have meaning. The
church is the vessel by which the Bread of Life is brought
to those who hunger in their souls.

It is through the church that the Bible has been compiled,
preserved, translated, printed, distributed, and taught. It
is through the church that men, women and children have
found fellowship of the finest kind—within the individual
congregation and within the church universal. It is through
the church that leadership has been provided in the fight
against paganism, materialism, ignorance, and corruption.
It is through the church that the highest ideals are taught,

and the best way of life is revealed. The church encourages the purest joy. Think of Christmas, Easter, and other festivals of the Church Year. Think of marriage and confirmation. Think of the quiet peace and the deep satisfactions which each recurring Sabbath in the church brings to mankind.

The church mediates the comfort and hope of the gospel, both through personal ministration and institutional activity.

4. *I Believe in the Church Because the Gates of Death Cannot Prevail Against It.*

The church survived the fierce persecutions of the Roman Empire. It survived the great racial movements of the fifth century, conquering the pagan invaders with the Sword of the Spirit. In 410 A.D., when Alaric had sacked Rome and everything seemed lost, Augustine wrote his *City of God*. The church survived the intellectual revolution called the Renaissance, and made it its servant. It survived the efforts of the leaders of the French Revolution to set aside the church and institute the so-called "Age of Reason," as if reason apart from Him who is the truth can have any meaning. It survived the efforts of Nazism to bend it to its diabolical ends. It is resisting the efforts of Communism to annihilate it, and in God's time will rise, Phoenix-like, from the ashes of Communism's destructive fire.

"I believe in the Holy Christian Church" is one of the great affirmations of our Christian faith. Nero didn't believe in the church. Voltaire didn't believe in the church. Lenin didn't believe in the church. Hitler didn't believe in the church. We do not want to be identified with such company. But Jesus believed in the church, and Paul did, and

Augustine did, and Luther did, and Pastor Niemoeller did. Because we choose to stand in that great succession, we shall continue to confess with ever-increasing appreciation and devotion, "I believe in the holy Christian Church."

TWO-MILERS

Matthew 5: 38-42

THOSE FAMILIAR with track meets know that there are several kinds of races, each of which calls for its own special skills and qualities. Some call for a sudden burst of speed for a very short time. Others call for a combination of speed and stamina. It is quite an achievement to be able to run the mile race. It requires a discipline of self and a tenacity of purpose not so rigidly demanded by some of the other track events. The two-mile run, however, is the event that calls for very special qualities. It demands physical stamina, breath control, courage, endurance, and a spirit not called for in any of the other races.

In His Sermon on the Mount, Jesus made a reference to two-milers, but He wasn't thinking about a track meet when He said, "If any one forces you to go one mile, go with him two miles." He uttered the words about the second mile against the background of forced labor common in Syria, when people could be compelled to carry messages or convey soldiers whenever the government demanded it. The incident in our Lord's Passion concerning Simon of Cyrene is an example of that use of authority.

Christianity is often misunderstood as far as its ethics is concerned. Many people think of Christianity as a system of good morals and decency. Justice, respect for human rights, bearing one's share of responsibility, an honest day's work—these are set forth as Christian morality. It is surely

237

expected that Christians should practice all of these things, but Christianity is far more, even in the realm of ethics.

Most Christians, while respecting the rights of others, stand also on their own rights. While willing to assume their share of life's responsibilities and burdens, they are often unwilling to assume someone else's share.

We have been conditioned to thinking of Christianity as a soft and easy religion. It wasn't easy and soft for Jesus. When Jesus said, "My yoke is easy, and my burden is light," He was describing an aspect of Christianity, but not all of Christianity; for Christianity is as hard as it is easy. And if we are to be true Christians, we will have to discover both truths in that paradox.

Probably nothing that Jesus ever said has been harder to accept than His words, "If any one strikes you on the right cheek, turn to him the other also; and if any one would sue you and take your coat, let him have your cloak as well; and if any one forces you to go one mile, go with him two miles." Those injunctions have been called "impractical," "nonsense," "sheer madness." Nevertheless, there the principle stands, pointing a finger in indictment of our weakness, inability, or fear to put it into practice.

The law of the jungle permits unlimited revenge. It was a step forward in the moral development of mankind to place a limit on revenge. Hence the teaching, "an eye for an eye and a tooth for a tooth." We often refer to those words as the guiding principle of a crude and cruel period in the age of mankind, little realizing that they mark a great forward step in men's relations with each other; for they were intended to be a curb on unlimited revenge. If we are honest, we must admit that we are still living in that crude and cruel age of mankind. Jesus asks us to take higher ground. John Burroughs wrote of a hawk being attacked by some crows. Instead of figthing back, the hawk flew to higher altitudes where his tormentors could not follow. Christianity gives this strange ability to live in a higher altitude.

Many people go through life aiming for minimum morality. What is the lowest grade I can get, and get by? How soon can I stop? Have I done my share? How little will it cost me? How little can I put into it? Such are the questions which we too frequently ask. But Jesus said, "Unless your righteousness exceeds that of the scribes and Pharisees, you will never enter the kingdom of heaven." We are thankful for all who do not shirk their duty, who go the first mile of what is expected and demanded of them; but the world owes an inestimable and unpayable debt to those who have done more than their duty, who have exceeded what is rightfully expected of them, who have been two-milers.

People will go the first mile because of compulsion, or expediency, or fear of punishment, or social custom. People go the second mile from higher motives—sympathy, love, devotion to someone else's welfare, gratitude to God.

1. *Life Has Been Made Easier and Happier for Mankind Because of Two-Milers.*

Generally speaking, people dislike doing the things they have to do. Necessity and compulsion rob the daily requirements of life of much of their pleasure. A group of gardening hobbyists, who go through their daily work in anticipation of their evenings and week ends in the garden and who save all they can for new plants and garden equipment, were talking to the gardener of an estate who was surrounded with the beauty of flowers every day. "We envy

you the pleasure of being able to be with flowers all day
long," they said. "You must get a big thrill out of your
work." They were surprised to hear him reply, "It's just
another job." When we think of life in terms of duty, responsibility, requirements, compulsions, then we are apt
to miss the deeper satisfactions of life. It is the glory of the
uncompelled, the voluntary second mile, that adds the dimension of happiness both to our own lives and to the lives
of others.

When people are thinking of their rights, there is often
an element of dissatisfaction in their hearts; for they are
envious of the privileges enjoyed by others, or bitter toward those who may be denying them the full exercise of
their rights. Shylock, insisting on the right to have his
pound of flesh, was not a happy man. The man who fore-
closes on another's property may be satisfying his greed,
but he is not satisfying his better nature.

Jesus taught His followers that they should submit patiently and cheerfully to life's hardships, and that they
should not always insist on their rights. He insisted that it
was wrong to make selfish consideration the basis of conduct. True religion, according to Jesus, is not the keeping
of hard and fast rules. It is a spirit, not a code. "The written code kills, but the Spirit gives life." True Christianity
is not a minimum religion, concerned about getting to heav-
en as cheaply and as easily as possible. It aims at maximum
achievements. It is animated and dominated by love, and
love never asks, "Can I stop here?" "Have I done enough?"
"Isn't that someone else's responsibility?"

When Joseph saw his brothers trying to buy grain in
Egypt because of the famine that had hit their region, he
could have taken revenge on them for having sold him into

slavery, but he had learned that forgiveness gives greater satisfaction than taking revenge. Because of Saul's envy and enmity, David had to live for a time as a hunted creature. On several occasions, David had the opportunity to take Saul's life and be free from being a fugitive, but he would not have been free from an accusing conscience. God had revealed to him that returning good for evil was the better way of life. Booker T. Washington, the great Negro educator, when meekly taking an insult from a white person, said, "I will not let any man reduce my soul to the level of hatred." One of the Doolittle fliers who had been captured and badly mistreated by the Japanese after the raid on Tokyo went back to Japan as a missionary. Three years of imprisonment and torture had not reduced his soul to bitterness and hatred.

The world would not have condemned Joseph for punishing his brothers or David for taking revenge on Saul who was trying to kill him. The world would have understood Booker T. Washington's resentment of an insult or that Doolittle flyer's desire never to have anything more to do with Japanese; but the world finds it difficult to understand the spirit of forgiveness, the readiness to endure insult, the returning of good for evil. Nevertheless, it is because men and women are willing to go the second mile of unselfishness, patience, and forgiving love that many of life's evils are alleviated or remedied.

2. *Mankind Will Reach Still Higher Levels Only Because of the Two-Milers.*

One of the most inspiring parables that Jesus ever uttered was the parable of the good Samaritan. That parable speaks of three classes of people found in every society. There are those who, like the thieves, live at the expense of others. They feel that they are entitled to what others may have. Then there are those who go about their own business like the priest and the Levite. They may not willfully injure others, but they do not feel that it is their responsibility to deny themselves any comfort or money to help others. Finally, there are a few good Samaritans in every society who will take time and expend effort to alleviate need when they find it. Of such is the kingdom of heaven.

The real asset in any social order is not those who do no more and who give no more than their share, but those who go the second mile of generous, unselfish service. We are thankful for all those who do not shirk their duty, who go the first mile of what is expected and demanded of them. However, the world will always owe an unpayable debt to that small but very significant fraction of people who do more than their duty, who go beyond what is rightfully expected of them, who exceed the righteousness of the scribes and Pharisees.

Dr. Grenfell could have retained his medical practice in England instead of going to Labrador. Francis of Assisi could have taken over his father's merchandising. Albert Schweitzer could have remained in his professor's chair instead of going to Lambarene, Africa, as a medical missionary. Elizabeth Fry could have had plenty to do with her large family, and not have taken time to work among the imprisoned. Always, it is this religion of the second mile, the glory of the uncompelled, that adds a crown of glory to humanity.

The challenge to go the second mile, to turn the other cheek, is a challenge to tap new resources of power. Jesus does not mean that through these actions we are to encourage brutality, but He does mean that we are to abstain from anger and revenge. Jesus does not desire that we allow exploitation of the weak to go unchecked, but He does warn against dimming the lustre of Christian character by returning evil for evil. Jesus never meant that we should foster shiftlessness and greed by unwise giving, but He does not want His followers to yield to callousness and lack of pity. What Jesus is asking for is infinite patience, genuine meekness, and boundless kindness—things of which we are generally in short supply. This business of doing only our duty, and standing always on our rights, and having revenge for every wrong done us, is what keeps trouble and strife going. It is only an indication of our perverse and sinful nature. The high and holy moments of our lives are those when we forego revenge and show love for our enemies and go the second, uncompelled mile.

The principle of the second mile can be applied in every area of life—industry, family life, church life, business practices, and international relations; for Christ's call for two-milers is a call for generosity, patience, unselfishness, freedom from pettiness, largeness of vision, and greatness of purpose.

THE HIGHER FELLOWSHIP

Luke 14:12-15

FELLOWSHIP is a beautiful word, but, far more important than that, it is a beautiful experience. The very mention of the word brings back happy memories—a friendly foursome on a golf course, a congenial "bull session" in a college dormitory room, a perfect day on some placid lake with three or four fellow fishermen, an afternoon coffee party with several friends, kinfolk gathered around the dinner table on Thanksgiving, a reunion banquet of one's graduating class. A few minutes of reminiscence, and each one of us could conjure up a long list of such pleasant scenes which would pass in delightful review before our mind.

Jesus never frowned upon fellowship. He enjoyed attending a banquet as much as anyone. He loved to walk through the fields with His disciples. He was happy to be invited to the home of friends like Mary and Martha. In view of Christ's evident enjoyment of fellowship with good friends, it seems strange, indeed, to hear Him saying, "When you give a dinner or a banquet, do not invite your friends or your brothers or your kinsmen or rich neighbors, lest they also invite you in return, and you be repaid." It is impossible to believe that Jesus preached one thing and practiced something quite different. Jesus took for granted that people would be hospitable toward friends and kindred. He felt, however, that pure religion would go beyond such fellowship, for fellowship based only on that which is pleasant and reciprocal is often tinged with selfish motive. There is a higher fellowship based on humanitarianism, unselfishness, and sympathy. Hear the challenge of Jesus: "When you give a feast, invite the poor, the maimed, the lame, the blind, and you will be blessed, because they cannot repay you. You will be repaid at the resurrection of the just." There are some things in life that we should do not because they are fun but because they are right, not because they are expected of us but because they go beyond the call of duty.

This is not to say that there is anything wrong about friendly get-togethers with those who are close to us by reason of blood or interest. We might find a parallel in those words spoken by Jesus to a group of scribes and Pharisees: "You tithe mint and dill and cummin, and have neglected the weightier matters of the law, justice and mercy and faith; these you ought to have done, without neglecting the others," (Matthew 23:23). Likewise, we are to accept Christ's challenge to a higher fellowship without neglecting the ordinary reciprocal fellowships of life.

1. *There Can Be Charity Without Fellowship.*

Long before Jesus taught, the religion of Israel had enjoined charity upon the people. The book of Nehemiah, for example, contains this admonition, "Eat the fat, and drink the sweet, and send portions unto them for whom nothing is prepared," (Nehemiah 8:10). Many of us, enjoying the good things of life, have taken thought of those who are less privileged than we and dropped coins in those containers found so frequently in business places. They bear such names as "Heart Fund," "Red Cross," "Cancer Fund," "March of Dimes," "Retarded Children," "Crippled Children," "Flood Relief." It is wonderful that, amid the complicated situations of our modern world, it is possible through such donations to feed the hungry, clothe the naked and minister to the sick. There must be opportunity for this kind of remote charity for modern Christians; for obviously we cannot be personally present to minister to the diverse needs crying out for help.

Nevertheless, there is a difference between writing a check or dropping a coin and extending a personal invitation to some truly needy person to enter into personal fellowship with us. It is this latter relationship to which Jesus is challenging us.

2. *The Nature of This Higher Fellowship.*

Jesus was often criticized for eating with sinners. Because the Jews often attributed physical infirmities to sin, it may be that the "sinners" referred to were people who suffered from such handicaps as blindness, deafness, and lameness.

What Jesus is urging upon us is the ability to share ourselves with the underprivileged. The giving of money, while good as far as it goes, can never be a substitute for love that gives itself.

Many a church group has discovered a new experience in inviting a group from some other race or a group with some type of infirmity to sit at table with them. Have you ever invited Negroes or tramps or blind people to have dinner with you or to be overnight guests in your home? I can testify that it is not only outgoing charity. It is a reciprocal experience that widens one's horizons and understanding. There are so many artificial barriers that are placed between people. It is our Christian duty to break down as many of them as we can.

How about adopting a blind person as a friend to whom you will go from time to time for the purpose of reading? How about searching out some invalid who would enjoy being pushed around the block from time to time in a wheel chair? How about inviting some poor family who feels left out of everything to a Sunday dinner?

The danger in fellowships of this kind is that an air of patronizing or condescension is apt to creep in and spoil the spirit of the fellowship. Sympathy can never be tainted by arrogance. Fellowship must never be marred by a sense of aloofness. Mutuality, equality, understanding, friendliness— these are the qualities that Jesus wants us to express in our relations with our fellow men.

3. *The Rewards of This Higher Fellowship.*

Is Jesus inconsistent when He says, "You will be blessed because they cannot repay you" and "You will be repaid at the resurrection of the just"? No. In the former sentence, He means that these underprivileged people cannot repay us with money or return banquets. In the latter sentence, Jesus seeks to assure us that one cannot perform unselfish, charitable and friendly acts without receiving some blessing. Perhaps it may not even come in this world. It may be that at the final judgment we shall hear the blessed verdict, "Truly, I say to you, as you did it to one of the least of these my brethren, you did it to me" (Matthew 25:40). Jesus does not want His followers to do things with the thought of reward uppermost in their minds, but at the same time He assures His followers that there is a reward for kindness, unselfishness, and sympathy. That reward is gratitude, love, and divine favor. Are not those rewards better than money, fame, or earthly grandeur?

FOUNDATIONS

Matthew 7: 22-29

FOUNDATIONS are of tremendous importance. Every builder, every educator, every professional man, knows that. However, because foundations are not much in evidence, there are always those who underestimate them. With many people things that are not in the limelight, that do not attract attention, are apt to be despised.

I remember how, as boys, we could quickly erect a shelter out of branches or old boards or pieces of canvas. We needed no foundation, for we were not building for permanence. If, for the moment, it looked like a shelter, we were satisfied. Our reward was the fleeting pleasure of building. I remember also how, as a boy, I often passed a certain spot where a cathedral was being built. Months and years went by before there was any evidence of a superstructure. Where did all the time and energy and material go with so little to show for it all? Into the foundation. Today, as one approaches the city of Omaha from the west, the first building one sees is the cathedral that was erected on that foundation. It was built for permanence, and two hundred years from now it will still rear its proud towers to greet those who approach the city from the west.

This principle of a good foundation applies in the field of learning. I think of two men who sat in the Virginia Assembly shortly before the American Revolution—Thomas Jefferson and Patrick Henry. They had similar opportunities and like ideals. Both had great talents. Every high school youngster, I suppose, has heard of Patrick Henry's famous speech which ended with the words, "Give me liberty or give me death." I often wondered why he played so little a part in the building of our Republic, why he soon became a second-rate figure among the founders of our nation. Recently, in reading a biography of Jefferson, Patrick Henry's colleague in the Virginia Assembly, I discovered a part of the reason. In a day when requirements for admittance to the bar were very low, Patrick Henry was satisfied to fulfill the minimum requirements. He studied law for three months, and was admitted to the bar. Thomas Jefferson wanted a broad and solid foundation, so he studied law for five years before he asked to be admitted to the bar. He believed that history, rhetoric, philosophy, and ethics were as necessary as law, if he were to have a good foundation. That is why all the world has heard of Thomas Jefferson while Patrick Henry's name is remembered chiefly because of one or two flashing phrases from one of his early speeches.

There is always a tendency to trim on foundations in the field of learning. We are apt to give students the subjects that will help them make money or turn out some product or accomplish some specified task, and we call that education. True education must be built on such a broad and solid foundation that people can see life whole. Take an example. A young man has a religious experience and wishes to be ordained into the ministry in order to share that experience with others. He may be somewhat disappointed, at first, to learn that he must go to college for four years and to a theological seminary for three or four more before he can be ordained into the ministry. He discovers that in addition to studying the Bible he must study history, litera-

ture, speech, psychology, philosophy, science, teaching methods, and a dozen other subjects before he is considered fitted for the task he has chosen. Consider the artist also.
Art is more than a matter of mixing colors and having an
eye for form. A good portrait painter must study anatomy,
for example. Furthermore, wide reading gives freshness
and authenticity to the ideas that are put on canvas.

Just as it is necessary to have good foundations for buildings and careers, so is it necessary to have good foundations
for the spiritual temple of character, if we are to build
something that endures and that stands the test of life's
storms.

1. *Jesus Said that Many Build on Insecure Foundations.*

"Every one who hears these words of mine and does not
do them will be like a foolish man who built his house upon
the sand." Most of us have seen buildings built on sand
foundations, but they have been pigstys or chicken coops
or dog houses. At the Chicago World's Fair in 1932, there
were some very attractive buildings built on the sand which
had been dredged out of Lake Michigan. In a year or two,
they were torn down, however. Buildings on sand could
not last.

How did Jesus mean that characters could be built on
sand? He said that failure to apply His teachings to life
was equivalent to building on sand. What are some of the
sandy foundations on which men build their lives?

The person who considers only his own selfish pleasure,
selfish satisfaction, and selfish interests is building on sand.
As we analyze the sins that create our social and personal
problems, that disrupt our economy, that fill our penal institutions, and that spread unhappiness to guilty and inno-

cent alike, we find that selfishness is at the bottom. Forgetfulness of God and inconsiderateness of others are only outward expressions of the basic sin of selfishness. Men lie to benefit themselves. They gratify their fleshly appetites in order to give themselves pleasure. They steal because they think they can thus obtain more gratification of their selfish desires. They harbor racial prejudice because they think they are better than those of other races. They ignore God because they think they are sufficient unto themselves. They gamble because they hope to win and have more to spend on themselves.

Psychiatry is emphasizing what the gospel has always taught, viz., that obsession with self is a sickness unto death. One must get outside of one's self, become interested in something greater than self, if life is to become rich with meaning. Jesus placed high value on personality, which is basically self, but He taught that personality cannot unfold properly until the self responds to something beyond itself— an ideal, a cause, a truth, other beings, the Divine Being. So sure was He of this that He could end His most famous sermon with these words, "Every one who hears these words of mine and does not do them will be like a foolish man who built his house upon the sand; and the rain fell, and the floods came, and the winds blew and beat against that house, and it fell; and great was the fall of it."

2. *Jesus Insisted that the Rock Foundation Which Would Enable Us So to Build as to Weather Life's Storms Was in Hearing and Practicing His Teachings.*

We must approach life's responsibilities and experiences in the light of Jesus' principles. Life brings sunny days and stormy days. We must prepare for all these experiences in our building. A wise builder considers the need of protection against the cold of winter and the heat of summer. His structure must be able to withstand driving rains and strong winds. Therefore it is necessary that the walls be plumb, that the materials be sound, and that the foundation be adequate.

So it is in life. Unless we have built our life according to that plumb line which extends from God to man, and unless we incorporate into our lives the principles of humility, mercy, purity, unselfishness, and brotherhood, we are building lives that will not stand the tests that are sure to come soon or late.

In the parable of the rich fool, Jesus indicated that a course of conduct that ignores the fact of death is foolish. Bygone generations of preachers seemed to believe that the best way to win people for Christianity was by picturing the death agonies of unbelievers rather than by portraying noble lives. We have no desire to bring back that kind of preaching. On the other hand, just as Jesus drew a word picture of what happens to the life that builds on sand, so we must be aware of those storms of life that try men's souls and reveal whether they have built on rock or on sand.

Times of trouble and seasons of sorrow are inevitable. Do they bind us more closely to Him who said, "Call upon me in the day of trouble; I will deliver you, and you shall glorify me"? Or do they fill us with bitterness and despair?

There will be times when unpopularity and persecution may be in direct ratio to our dedication to God's purposes. Can we, at such times, derive comfort and strength from our Lord's beatitude, "Blessed are you when men revile you and persecute you and utter all kinds of evil against you falsely on my account. Rejoice and be glad, for your reward is great in heaven, for so men persecuted the prophets who were before you"?

There will be times when it may appear that compromise with evil and error might make life more comfortable, when betrayal of Christ's principles might bring some fleeting advantage. Do we then remember our Lord's words, "Man does not live by bread alone"? The Book of Daniel tells of one who would not defile himself with the king's delicacies; and Jesus, in speaking of John the Baptist, said, "Those who wear soft raiment are in kings' houses." Comfort and privilege are not solid foundations on which to build the cathedral of character.

In crossing the Platte River in Nebraska, you will go across a bridge one half mile long under which you may see a little stream of water that a child could probably wade across. The builder knew that it was necessary to do more than build a bridge to span that tiny stream. He knew that there would be heavy rains and swelling floods, and he built the bridge accordingly, anticipating the season when the stream would become a roaring torrent, sweeping everything before it in its resistless career. Life itself will bring its torrents of trial and floods of disappointment and disaster. Therefore, we must not build for the balmy days but for the days that try men's souls. That requires a strong and solid foundation. Centuries of human experience attest the truth of Paul's statement, "No other foundation can anyone lay than that which is laid, which is Jesus Christ."

THE GREATNESS OF LITTLE THINGS

Luke 16:10-15

OURS IS AN AGE obsessed with the idea of bigness. We talk about big business, big profits, big wages. We have almost come to the point where a thing has to be big in order to count for anything.

As an antidote to that kind of poison, it ought to be profitable for us to think together about the greatness of little things. Jesus spoke of how effective faith can be, even though it is only the size of a mustard seed. On another occasion, he took a child and set it before his followers saying, "Unless you turn and become like children, you will never enter the kingdom of heaven." In our text for this morning, Jesus says, "He who is faithful in a very little is faithful also in much." I like the way two of our newer translations render that sentence. The Twentieth Century New Testament says, "He who is trustworthy in the smallest matter is trustworthy in a great one also." James Moffatt says, "He who is faithful with a trifle is also faithful with a large trust." From the teachings of Jesus, we learn that He certainly did not despise little things.

1. *Little Things Possess Greatness Because They Are the Essence of Life.*

Take the lives of people generally. They are not made up of great and outstanding experiences, but of commonplaces like study and play, work and worship, eating and sleeping.

It is the arrangement of these little things that makes or mars one's whole life.

If it were not for little things, there would be no great things. The Matterhorn is a tremendous mountain, but it is made up of little mica flakes. The armed might of the allies was a mammoth spectacle, but it was made up of individual men.

Scientists are relying more and more on the microscope; for it brings us closer to the fundamental structure of the universe. And beyond the finiteness of the microscope is the world of atoms and electrons.

We often envy those who become famous, as if their lives had something ours does not have; but everyone's year has 365 days of twenty-four precious hours each, and each one's hour has sixty jewelled minutes in it. The difference lies in the use to which we put these little minutes which God gives us. There is much wisdom in Benjamin Franklin's words: "If thou lovest life, do not squander time; for that is the stuff of which life is made."

Shakespeare's work is a marvel of literature, but his words are the simple words we all know. He learned how to use them. Dr. Paul Scherer had a throat ailment some years ago when the doctor limited him to six words a day, if he were to save his voice. He attributes his mastery of pulpit speech to the necessity of making every word count.

Let us not be overawed by bigness, but let us realize that bigness must always depend on the little things which are the very essence of life.

2. *Little Things Possess Greatness Because They Have a Value of Their Own.*

Take, for example, Christ's estimate of little children. In His day, they were not prized for their own sake, but Jesus showed that they have a value of their own. A parent does not esteem a child because of the future income of that child, but because of what the little child is in itself.

We are told that Paganini charmed thousands with a single string. We would all have more charming personalities if we gave more thought to little things like a smile, a friendly greeting, a kind word, a helpful deed. Remember that Jesus said that if we give a cup of cold water to a little one in His name, we shall not miss our reward.

I have already referred to words as being the essence of a great body of literature, but see how even small words have a significance all their own. Polysyllabic words are not as effective as the little words: faith, hope, love, joy, home, God, life, death, truth. Read the first chapter of John, the Lord's Prayer, the Gettysburg Address. Some of the finest examples of poetry are found in the fourteen line sonnet and the four line quatrain. A number of years ago, I saw a very fine nature film, but after all these years there are only two scenes that I can recall with any vividness. One was a shot of little birds in a nest. The other was a red rose bejewelled with sparkling dew drops. Little things? Yes, but they had a value all their own which was not easily forgotten.

Little lakes are stillest and little farms are best tilled. Little books are read the most and little songs are loved the dearest. Little incidents are often cherished the longest. Little gifts are often treasured the most. I once read of an eye specialist who had a rather worn teddy bear displayed prominently in his office. When a patient expressed curiosity at the presence of a child's teddy bear in a doctor's office, the doctor said, "That is the highest fee I ever received for a case. Years ago, a poor mother brought me her little girl who had gone blind. She could not afford the expensive operation, but I took the case anyway. Every time they visited the office, the little girl was carrying that teddy bear. Nothing in the world seemed to mean so much to her. On the day, when her eyes were finally uncovered and she was able to see again, she looked at her precious teddy bear and then, coming over to me, she placed it in my hand as a token of her gratitude. I have never received a larger fee than that for any case."

3. *Little Things Possess Greatness Because They May Have Great Consequences.*

Early in our reading experience, we came across this little rhyme: "For want of a nail, a shoe was lost; for want of a shoe, a horse was lost; for want of a horse a rider was lost; for want of a rider, a battle was lost; for want of a battle, a kingdom was lost."

Michaelangelo was once asked what he had been doing on a certain statue since the friend's last visit. He replied, "I have retouched this part, polished that, softened this feature, brought out that muscle, given more expression to the lip and more energy to the limb." "But those things are trifles," exclaimed the visitor. "That may be," said Michaelangelo, "but trifles make perfection, and perfection is no trifle."

A lantern kicked over by a cow in Mrs. O'Leary's stable is said to have caused the great Chicago fire. Many times, a spark caused by a short circuit has resulted in a disastrous fire, or a carelessly tossed cigaret has caused a forest fire that deprived the people of much needed lumber.

It was pennies and nickles that built up Wrigley's fortune, and nickles and dimes that built up Woolworth's fortune. The sweepings of the mint floors constitute a fortune every year. Insects and microbes are small but they can be the cause of famines and pestilence. A light pricking of the skin may expose a surgeon to poisoning and death. The Remagen bridge was small, but O, so significant in shortening the end of World War II.

Bethlehem was small, but how large it looms against Berlin and London and New York. "But thou Bethlehem Ephratha, who art little to be among the clans of Judah, from you shall come forth for me one who is to be ruler in Israel."

Jesus taught that trustworthiness in trifles will lead to greater responsibilities. We cannot but be reminded of Lincoln's faithfulness and honesty in little matters.

Jesus taught that judgment will be based on the little things we have done. Little habits of honesty, tidiness, thoughtfulness, purity, and application are not trifles to be lightly esteemed. They have great consequences. They produce good character.

The texts for this day are closely related to the general theme of stewardship. Stewardship is something not merely for the millionaire or for the one with many talents. It is the responsibility of everyone, even though it be that we have been given a single little talent. Let us not forget that in the parable of the talents, Jesus taught that it was the man with the single talent who was condemned because he failed to appreciate the greatness of little things. May none of us be condemned because of our failure to appreciate the greatness of little things.

> Some folks are called to mighty acts
>   That bring them wealth and fame;
> Where men can see their glorious deeds,
>   And all their works proclaim.

Some folks are called to little deeds
  That men know nothing of,
Where only God is there to bless
  The little acts of love.

Be faithful in the little things
  Which you may have to do.
For, be your service great or small,
  The Master watches you.

And when the Lord shall say, "Well done!"
  You'll find that those who best
Have served Him in the little things,
  Share honors with the rest.

LOIS M. LUNDSTROM

THE PERILS OF PROSPERITY

Matthew 11: 20-34

INDIVIDUALS and nations alike yearn for prosperity. People do get tired of the sheer struggle for existence and the perpetual threat of insecurity that hangs overhead like the fabled sword of Damocles. That scramble toward the coveted heights of prosperity is responsible, however, for many temptations and sins. Greed, selfishness, ruthlessness attend the struggle.

There is nothing essentially wrong about desiring prosperity. It would be sheer folly to desire for any people a state of abject poverty with all the frustrated ambitions, filthy slums, and diseased bodies that accompany it. While there is nothing wrong about desiring prosperity, there may be many wrong ways of seeking it.

Let us assume that prosperity has been attained by such legitimate processes as thrift, inventiveness, co-operation, and hard work . What then? The Bible is replete with examples of the perils of prosperity. When Jesus upbraided the cities of Chorazin and Bethsaida, he was talking to the citizenry of two of the more prosperous cities of Palestine. When He referred to Tyre and Sidon, He was speaking of two of the most prosperous cities of western Asia that had come to their doom three centuries earlier. When He mentioned Sodom, He had in mind one of the world's most prosperous cities of the era in which Abraham lived. There was a common denominator about all these cities. It was that prosperity had not been a blessing. It had been fraught with many perils. Long before the days of Jesus, prophets of Israel and Judah had observed and condemned both the unrighteous ways by which prosperity was gained by the upper classes and the indifference to the poor and the debasing luxury which accompanied prosperity.

We are living in an era of unparalleled prosperity. Can we learn anything from the past? Is there any way by which we can avoid the pitfalls and perils of prosperity into which older civilizations fell? To avoid dangers you must understand them. What are the perils of prosperity?

1. *Prosperity Often Produces Envy and Hatred on the Part of Others.*

Few nations have pursued as magnanimous a policy in dealing with other nations as the United States. We sought no territorial concessions in the great wars of the twentieth century. We have granted billions of dollars of aid to friends and former foes alike. Still, we are not trusted. We are not loved. In some quarters we are actually hated.

It is just as true of individuals as of nations that those who are less prosperous are apt to be envious of those who have prospered. Prosperity creates unnatural barriers between people. If the less prosperous do not envy or hate those who are more fortunately situated as far as the world's goods are concerned, they are apt to fawn before those who have prospered. Any normal person would rather be loved and respected than envied and hated.

2. *Prosperity Anaesthetizes People so That They Forget Their Less Prosperous Days and Lose Sympathy with Those Who Never Experience Prosperity.*

The trouble with Dives and Scrooge and Marie Antoinette was that they were unable to put themselves in the position of the poor and hungry multitude. Travelers from our country to the Orient and to Europe come back and tell us that we have no idea how poor the rest of the world is.

While we enjoy expensive cars, good homes, recreational facilities, ample food, and decent clothing, we may forget that millions are hungry, poorly sheltered, inadequately clothed, untouched by the ordinary comforts of life which we have come to regard as necessities. We may be prone to look with disdain upon peoples of other lands as being provincial, but we may be just as provincial in our ignorance of their needs. The economic and social council of the United Nations is doing much to create sympathy for the unprosperous of the world, but there is responsibility resting on us to acquaint ourselves with findings and recommendations. The World Council of Churches is another powerful agency that can keep our eyes open to distress and our ears open to the cry of need and our hands open in Christian charity.

3. *Prosperity Tempts Men to Forget God as the Author and Giver of Every Good and Perfect Gift.*

In the eighth chapter of the Book of Deuteronomy, this very warning is sounded to the people of Israel: "Take heed lest you forget the Lord your God by not keeping his commandments and his ordinances and his statutes, which I command you this day: lest, when you have eaten and are full, and have built goodly houses and live in them, and when your herds and flocks multiply, and your silver and gold is multiplied, and all that you have is multiplied, then your heart be lifted up, and you forget the Lord your God, who brought you out of the land of Egypt, out of the house of bondage, who led you through the great and terrible wilderness . . . Beware lest you say in your heart, 'My power and the might of my hand have gotten me this wealth.' "

Prosperity opens the sluice gates to materialism, to the idolatry of trusting in the things which our hands have made, whether they be coins, buildings, navies, nuclear bombs, or mere gadgets of comfort and pleasure. The prophets of ancient Israel and Judah were devastating in their satire of idol worshipers. They would be no less so today. Something noble has departed from a man's character when he no longer bows before God in gratitude for the blessings of life.

4. *Prosperity Brings with It a Temptation to Debasing Luxury.*

For many of us, Monte Carlo, Las Vegas, and Hollywood conjure up visions of prosperity that has curdled into vice. Those familiar with history cannot forget the last decades in France before the French Revolution or the riotous debauchery of the Roman imperial court. The escapades of the idle rich, as they are brought to light in our scandal-loving magazines, are telling illustrations of the temptation to debasing luxury that comes with prosperity.

We are accustomed to speak of juvenile delinquency and underprivileged children in the same breath, but Police Chief Wm. H. Park of Los Angeles says, "It is the over privileged child who is causing the most trouble today. He has been given so much in the way of material things that he is going haywire looking for new satisfactions."

The corruptions that have ruined one civilization after another were closely linked with prosperity.

5. *Prosperity Engenders a Spiritual Indifference Which Thwarts the Possibility of Repentance.*

It is an old fallacy which believes that sorrow, failure, and poverty are linked with wrongdoing, and that joy, success, and wealth are the rewards of virtue. Those who hold such ideas will never feel that penitence can have any place in the climate of prosperity. Very often, in the experience of mankind, it is the righteous who have suffered and the unrighteous who have prospered.

When prosperity is the result of greedy ambition, dishonesty, and ruthlessness, one can understand how a spiritual callousness is developed that makes repentance well-nigh impossible. Even when prosperity is the result of hard work and thrift and shrewd economy, there is a tendency to look with disdain on those who have not had the diligence and intelligence to succeed. As a result, a spirit of self-righteousness develops, and there is no greater barrier to repentance than self-righteousness. Religious revivals do not originate in the mansions of the well-to-do, or in summer and winter resorts, or among those satisfied with their successes, or in periods of unparalleled prosperity. Plague, war's devastation, depression, calamity—these are the springboards of repentance and revival.

I am not favoring some policy that will destroy our present prosperity, but I am hoping that we will some day learn the lessons of spiritual and secular history and profit by them. By the standards of the first century, Bethsaida, Chorazin and Capernaum were prosperous cities; and that very prosperity seemed to numb their spiritual sensibilities, even as the prosperity of ancient Tyre and Sidon, Sodom and Gomorrah had rendered the inhabitants of those cities indifferent to spiritual values. There are many signs that modern prosperity is having the same effect upon mankind. Let us see in our prosperity both its attendant perils and its challenge to greater avenues of usefulness. Let us be humbly grateful to God for our great measure of prosperity, and regard it as a high trust, a sacred stewardship. So shall prosperity become a continual paeon of praise to God, an inexhaustible larder from which will pour blessings to all those to whom prosperity is a mere dream or idle longing.

GOD'S ARISTOCRACY

Matthew 23:1-12

WHEREVER you have a kingdom, you can expect to find an aristocracy; and that aristocracy is certain to reveal something of the essential strength or weakness of the kingdom. It may, as in the case of France during the reign of Louis XIV, reflect the social apathy, the vanity, and the moral corruption which was soon to plunge France into revolution. Or it may, as in the case of modern Sweden, be marked by a social awareness, an enlightened self-interest, and a true cosmopolitanism, that enables that small nation to make such great contributions toward world fellowship. A nation's aristocracy may be in the realm of the mind as in the case of Greece during the golden age of Pericles. Again, a country's aristocracy might be purely economic and industrial, reflecting the worship of stocks and bonds and machines.

There is a kingdom which is not of this world, but yet is among us. It is the kingdom of God. It has no visible boundaries, no coins, no stamps, no elaborate governmental machinery. Still, it has its aristocracy, to know which will help men to understand the essential nature of that kingdom.

1. *God's Aristocracy Squares Deed with Creed.*

Jesus did not censure the scribes and the Pharisees because of any deficiency in themselves. Jesus accepted the same sacred writings which the scribes and Pharisees accepted. The trouble with the scribes and Pharisees, according to Jesus, was that they did not square deed with creed, they did not practice what they professed and preached.

The world has had more than enough creeds to usher in the golden age, but creeds haven't been enough. Because men and women haven't lived up to noble professions, human life stumbles along in selfishness and pride, in jealousy and hypocrisy. The scribes and Pharisees subscribed to the loftiest creed of their generation, but they failed to square deed with creed. Their religion urged considerateness and helpfulness, yet Jesus observed that these leaders would load burdens *on* others, but would not stoop to lift burdens *for* others. Jesus said of them, "They preach, but do not practice. They bind heavy burdens, hard to bear, and lay them on men's shoulders; but they themselves will not move them with their finger."

Jesus said that He came to seek and to save the lost. See how His life harmonized with that purpose. Paul determined to know nothing but Christ and Him crucified. See how his activity fitted that vow. Luther said that if there were as many devils in the city of Worms as there were tiles on the rooftops, he still would proceed on the journey and bear his witness to the saving power of faith in Christ. See how courageously he carried out that promise.

How about us? As members of the Church of Christ, we have a noble creed. We have committed ourselves to high principles, great truths, and lofty precepts. Do we really believe in God's power, or do we live as if we believe in the dollar's power? Do we really believe in a world-wide brotherhood through Christ or do we show by our attitudes that we feel Negroes, Mexicans, or Japanese are to be barred from that fellowship? Do we really believe that penitence is a condition of forgiveness, or do we often refuse pardon, even though there be genuine repentance?

Some time it would be wholesome for all of us to take two pieces of paper, writing our lofty principles and high ideals on one and our expressed attitudes and daily practices on the other. Assuming that those precepts are right and desirable, the harmony between those two sheets of paper would be a criterion of how worthy we are of being called God's aristocracy.

2. *God's Aristocracy Is Bent on Serving.*

Jesus said, "The Son of man came not to be served but to serve"; "He who is greatest among you shall be your servant." "In the example and exhortation of Christ, God's nobility find their standard of conduct.

Jesus went about doing good. The disciple is not above his master. The parable of the good Samaritan is a constant stimulus and pattern. So great importance did Jesus attach to the serving of mankind that He said we shall be judged by what we have done to the last and least of our fellow men. John Stuart Mill, in his autobiography, stated a conclusion which fits in well with the Biblical view. He found that "those only are happy who have their minds fixed on some object other than their own happiness; on the happiness of others, on the improvement of mankind, even on some art or pursuit, followed not as a means, but as an ideal end. Aiming thus at something else, they find happiness by the way."

Never in human history has there been greater opportunity for rendering service to mankind. The chief difficulty is that the magnitude of what has to be done is so staggering that we are apt to despair before we start. I am reminded of a story which André Maurois, a French writer, tells of how Marshall Lylutey, who conquered Morocco, was riding through the forests of the country when he came to a place where many of the giant cedars had been destroyed by a terrific storm. The Marshal turned to his assistant and said, "You will have to place new cedars here." The man laughed and said that it took two thousand years to grow cedars like those that had been uprooted. "Two thousand years?" said the marshal, "Then we must begin at once." Wherever we look in the world, there is widespread destruction—to property, life, freedom, idealism, moral and spiritual values. If a new world order is ever to be erected above the ruins, then we must begin now. We can start by correcting evils at home. We can start by extending the helping hand to the brethren of our own faith in Europe who have suffered so sorely during these troubled times.

Service demonstrates our sympathy and love. It lightens the burdens that others are bearing. It ennobles the lives of those who serve. It is Christlike. God's aristocracy will be recognized by the type and quality and spirit of their service.

3. *God's Aristocracy Lives Humbly Before God and Men.*

Humility is not a popular virtue. We believe in advertising ourselves. We often go out of our way to seek publicity. But God has always made humility a badge of nobility. Long before the Christian era, the prophet Micah said, "He has showed you, O man, what is good; and what does the Lord require of you but to do justice, and to love kindness, and to walk humbly with your God?" Jesus said, "Whoever humbles himself like this child, he is the greatest in the kingdom of heaven." And again he said, "Whoever humbles himself will be exalted." In the quiet solemnity of the upper room the night before His death, Jesus took a basin and towel and washed the feet of His disciples, giving them an unforgettable example in humility.

The Bible abounds with examples of humility of God's aristocracy—Moses, Gideon, Isaiah, Jeremiah, Paul, John the Baptist.

Augustine, when asked what were the first three steps to heaven, answered, "Humility, humility, humility."

If we ever had the idea that humility is weakness or slavishness, let us discard it. Let us recall not only the great men of God mentioned in Scripture but also the great leaders of the world like Alfred the Great and Lincoln and Pasteur and a host of others whose humility was an outstanding quality in their greatness. John Ruskin made a keen analysis when he said, "I believe the first test of a truly great man is humility."

And now the questions come directly to our own conscience and soul: "Are we among God's Aristocracy? Do our deeds square with our creeds? Are we eager and willing to serve according to our capacity and opportunity? Are we content to walk humbly before our God and fellow men?" If to those searching questions, we can give a sincere "Yes," then we are among "God's Aristocracy."

THE USE OF WORDS

Matthew 5:33-37

MANKIND is unique in all God's creation, not so much because of the ability to feel and think and plan, but because of the ability to express emotions, thoughts, and ideas in words so that others may know them. This expression is not limited to spoken words which are soon lost on the air currents, but it can be conveyed through written words capable of moving people to feeling, thought, and actions many centuries after they were first given expression. Most people do not appreciate the tremendous significance of words, or they would not use them so lightly.

Words are servants. Words are treasures. Words are artillery to batter home ideas. Words are windows that enable us to see into the lives of others. Words can be either the enemy's dagger or the surgeon's knife. Words can be stronger than atom bombs, destroying old superstitions, old cultures, old ways of life with their explosive power.

Words can be of tremendous significance, but they can also be very insignificant. Someone has estimated that the average person speaks about 30,000 words in a day. How trivial and useless most of those words are that fall from many lips! How much better if most of them had never been uttered. On the other hand, how weighty and worthwhile are the words that fall from other lips. Sometimes those who chatter most say the least, while those who speak sparingly speak most wisely. It was probably while thinking of the endless stream of words that are spoken to no purpose or to no good purpose that Jesus uttered the advice, "Let what you say be simply 'Yes' or 'No'; anything more than this comes from evil."

Not all people have the same assortment of words with which to express themselves. Someone has calculated that the average person uses about 3,000 different words. Woodrow Wilson, it is said, had a working vocabulary of 60,000 words. But whether we have a large vocabulary or a small one, the important thing is, "How do we use our words?"

When we consider how words are often used in a profane or lewd or hurtful or dishonest manner, we can realize that the use of words becomes a Christian problem. One book of the Bible, namely Proverbs, devotes much space to the importance and use of words. To read that book with no other object in mind than to glean its message concerning the use of words would be a profitable experience. The Mosaic Law dealt with the misuse of speech. Jesus, too, had some very important things to say about the use of words. The use of words is, therefore, not only something for the literature class to study, but also something for every Christian to consider.

1. *Words Ought to Be Sincere.*

Dishonesty has no place in the Christian life. The Christian business man will remember that in his advertising. The Christian politician will remember it in his campaign promises, and not dismiss them afterwards as "campaign oratory." The Christian author will remember it, and refuse to depend on sensational and dishonest statements that might increase sales. The ordinary Christian will remember it when he is tempted to flatter others or make excuses for himself.

All too often people will say one thing to somebody's face and quite the opposite behind that person's back. Or they will make a confession of loyalty to Christ before an altar, and then proceed to deny Christ during the week. Truth cannot flourish where there is inconsistency.

Words should not be twisted out of their meaning and context. Often, words can be lifted out of a speech or article so that, standing by themselves, they may seem to say the opposite of what the speaker or author was saying. Even the Bible is often sinned against in this respect. The value of words depends on the spirit and context in which they are used.

The world has many false standards, but it abhors a hypocrite. It provides severe penalties for the sin of perjury.

2. *Words Ought to Be Kind.*

It is not enough that words be sincere. They must also be kind. Often, words that are only sincere may hurt because they do not have the added quality of kindness. The importance of speaking kindly is brought out in one of Will Carleton's poems,

> Boys flying kites haul in their white-winged birds
> But you can't do that when you're flying words.
> Careful with fire is good advice we know,
> But careful with words is ten times doubly so.

Much effort is expended in eliminating the physical injuries that may be done to others, but we pay far too little attention to the grievous hurts inflicted by the tongue. James, in his epistle, compares the tongue to the rudder of a boat which can steer the craft into calm or rough waters. Kind or unkind words often determine whether our sailing is in calm or rough waters. James also says, "If any one thinks he is religious, and does not bridle his tongue but deceives his heart, this man's religion is vain." The person who is given to making cutting and sarcastic remarks that hurt people's feelings might well consider what James says about the use of the tongue. There are times when the tongue must lash out against injustice and irreligion, but it is good if we can cultivate the habit of speaking kindly at every opportunity.

3. *Words Ought to Be Reverent.*

Profane language is a sure evidence of a corrupt heart, for, as Jesus said, "Out of the abundance of the heart the mouth speaks." God gave us the gift of speech and, as in the case of all the other blessings He has given us, we ought to appreciate it and use it to His glory. Speech is not to be used lightly. There is a suggestion in the words of Jesus that the taking of oaths had come about because of man's persistent habit of lying. He says, "But I say to you, Do not swear at all, either by heaven, for it is the throne of God, or by the earth, for it is his footstool, or by Jerusalem, for it is the city of the great King. And do not swear by your head, for you cannot make one hair white or black." In other words, swearing changes nothing. If a man is honest and truly fears God, his Yes is sufficient. If a man is dishonest and has no regard for God, his word is worthless however much he may seek to bolster it with oaths.

I knew a man who had been moved by the profane language he heard from so many lips to write a bit of verse about it, have it printed on small cards, and pass out to anyone guilty of profanity. He gave me one of these cards once, not because I had provoked the gift by the use of profane language, however. This is what it said,

It grieves me, friend, to hear my Maker's Name
Thus spoken without reverence or shame.   ,
Be thou a man; thy noble rank maintain;
Appeal to God, but not in words profane;
Scorn to be vulgar or thus impolite;
'Tis neither brave nor wise; 'tis far from right.
You would not speak thus while nearing death;
Reflect—Your Maker now could stop your breath.
For self-respect, for friends you should forbear;
And God in heaven commands, "Thou shalt not swear."

When men learn early to formulate words into prayers, then it is easier to find victory over the temptation to be irreverent in the use of words. Become familiar with the Word of God. Then it will be easy to speak to God and for God. Take active part in the divine worship services. If that is done on Sunday, it will not be so easy on Monday to use those holy words in an irreverent manner.

If we learn the reverent use of words, it becomes easy to use them in the expression of thankfulness. Whining, complaining, griping are forms of irreverence. When we think of God, we think of our unworthiness; and our hearts overflow with gratitude for His unmerited mercy. We might well make the occasional prayer of the pastor in the pulpit our daily morning prayer: "Let the words of my mouth and the meditation of my heart be acceptable in thy sight, O Lord, my rock and my redeemer."

GIVING TO GOD

Mark 12: 41-44

STEWARDSHIP is a beautiful word; it gathers into itself such virtues and graces as faith, unselfishness, generosity, and sense of responsibility. Nevertheless, as far as some people are concerned, there is no subject that is more apt to kill interest than a discussion of the matter of giving.

A story is told about John Wesley and a sermon he once preached on "Money." His first point was: "Make all the money you can." He could see the people nod approval. His second point was: "Save all the money you can." He could see the people's faces light up with satisfaction. His third point was: "Give all the money you can." Immediately, many lost interest. One man is reported to have said to his neighbor, "There, he went and spoiled a good sermon." Yet it was that third point that made it a Christian sermon, that made it a really good sermon.

You will recall that when Jesus told a young man to go and sell all that he had and give the money to the poor, the man went away sorrowful. As in Jesus' day and in Wesley's day, so it is today: when you touch a man's pocketbook, you touch his most sensitive spot. Nevertheless, a man's pocketbook is like a man's conscience. When you have really touched it, you have started a chain reaction that can have mighty and blessed results.

I have read somewhere that one sixth of all the verses in the first three Gospels deal with our material possessions and the use of them. Many of the parables and incidents in the life of Jesus have some kind of relationship to the matter of giving to God. Our text for today is an example. During His last week in Jerusalem, Jesus had gone to the Temple and was sitting in that outer court of the Temple where thirteen chests were placed to receive offerings for sacrifices and other expenses necessary to the functioning of the Temple. Since those chests were in public view, there was nothing to prevent Temple visitors from seeing how much or how little people dropped into them.

As Jesus was sitting there and observing men and women dropping their contributions into the various containers, a poor widow came along and dropped in two small coins—all that she had. Jesus was always able to find teaching opportunities in everything He saw. Calling His disciples to Him, he said to them, "Truly, I say to you, this poor widow has put in more than all those who are contributing to the treasury. For they all contributed out of their abundance; but she out of her poverty has put in everything she had, her whole living."

"She put in everything she had." That is the way to give to God. He has given us everything we possess. It is really His. Therefore, one of our hymns is right when it says, "We give Thee but Thine own, whate'er the gift may be."

It will soon be time for the Every Member Visitation program in our various churches. This story of the widow and her mites is a good springboard for an Every Member Visitation program; for it suggests answers to two very important questions that most people are apt to ask as they face up to the matter of giving to God.

1. *Why Should We Give to God?*

Giving is a necessary consequence of faith and love. James says, "Faith by itself, if it has no works, is dead." If a person really loves someone and believes in that one, can you imagine that he would be sparing and stingy in his giving? When a young man truly loves a young woman, and has faith that she will be the best possible mate through life, he gives her the finest diamond he can afford. When a parent loves his child and believes in the potentialities of that child, he will spare nothing to educate that child for life. All through life we show evidence of faith and love by giving. Should it be less true in our religious life? Can a person really profess faith in Christ and love to God, and then calculate how *little* he can get by with and still maintain some measure of self-respect? Will he not rather think in terms of how *much* he will give?

Giving is a part of worship. The Book of Proverbs urges us to honor the Lord with our substance and with the first fruits of all our produce. When John D. Rockefeller made his first dollar, he gave a dime of it in the offering plate. He honored the Lord with the first fruits of his labor, and he never stopped. He always spoke of his wealth as "God's gold." There are some, no doubt, to whom the announcement of the offering is like static in the radio—something that doesn't belong there. The truth is that the offering is as integral a part of our worship as the sermon, prayers, and hymns. If you study the origins of religion, you always seem to come up against sacrifice in one form or another as the oldest expression of worship. Before man sang hymns of praise or listened to sermons, he conceived of worship as giving.

Giving is a source of blessing. It is obvious that giving can be a source of blessing to others. By supporting the church, we minister to sick and dying, to the burdened and sorrowing, to the struggling and unenlightened, to heathen people and delinquents. Christian charity, unlike the world's brand of charity, is warm, not cold. It builds up self-respect instead of destroying it. It offers an inspiring example to others. Who but God could ever count the souls that have been inspired to noble giving by that poor widow's contribution? The real blessing in giving is to the giver. Niggardly souls will never believe that, but it is so. The Bible says, "Cast your bread upon the waters, for you will find it after many days." Jesus said, "Give, and it will be given to you." "It is more blessed to give than to receive." The truly great have been great givers—of time, strength, means, yes, life itself. Giving blesses the giver by fostering a spirit of unselfishness and a sense of responsibility. Without those qualities of character, no man is truly great.

I said that there are two very important questions that people often ask as they face up to the matter of giving to God. I have suggested a few answers to the question, "Why should we give to God?" The other question is

2. *How Should We Give to God?*

We ought to give gratefully rather than grudgingly. "God loves a cheerful giver." It would not be poor translating to render that verse thus: "God loves a hilarious giver." In other words, we ought to enjoy our giving. We ought to get real pleasure out of it. We ought to feel good inside. Too many people try to make themselves believe that they are giving as they ought to give, but they know in their heart of hearts that they are not and, in consequence, there is always a kind of guilty feeling when people give grudgingly.

We ought to give as it has been given to us. The Bible says, "To whom much is given, of him will much be required." Even the pagan philosopher, Aristotle, recognized this principle when he said, "Liberality is estimated according to a man's substance." The widow woman in the Temple had not been given much as far as worldly goods were concerned and, in a way, she did not give much—just two coins of the smallest denomination. However, the size of our gift is not measured by the amount of our gift but by the amount we have left. In every church there are families in the same giving bracket—let us say five dollars a week; but God does not see any equality in the gift. One may be giving liberally, as God has given. But the other family may be giving only a pittance in proportion to what God has given them. The test is not what we give, but what we keep. The widow woman could have kept one mite. If she had, she would have missed a great blessing. Jesus said of the rich, "They all contributed out of their abundance." You should not treat God's work like you treat a tramp, giving a handout of leftovers from the last meal. "Freely ye have received, freely give" (KJV).

We ought to give regularly. You have all heard of Woolworth and Wrigley. Each of those built a skyscraper. Have you ever considered the testimony of those towers? It is this: when a business can get money from the many in regular, frequent, though small, amounts, there is no limit but the sky to that business. Those two towers erected by Woolworth and Wrigley prove that regular expenditures can be big business. I referred to Rockefeller's gift of a dime out of his first earned dollar, but he repeated out of his next earned dollar, and out of the next. When his income ran into the millions, he was still giving one tenth. Some poor people say that it is all right for the rich to give one tenth, but they can't do it. The rich say that it is all right for the poor to give one tenth, but it is asking too much to expect them to give one tenth. Rockefeller gave one tenth when he was poor, and more than one tenth when he became a multimillionaire. Because he was regular in giving out of his little, it was not difficult to be regular in giving out of his much.

We ought to give trustfully. "Every perfect gift is from above, coming down from the Father of lights with whom there is no variation or shadow due to change." If we recognize the source of our blessings, we should never hesitate to give as we have been blessed, for God's supply is not limited. Let us believe that the Lord will provide, and then stewardship will become a beautiful expression of a living faith.

We ought to give in the knowledge that the Lord sees our giving. Some people never give, unless they know that other people know that they are giving. That kind of giving is not giving to God but to self—to one's own glory, to the gratification of one's own selfish pride. We read in the gospel narrative, "And he sat down opposite the treasury, and watched the multitude putting money into the treasury." When our giving is in the awareness that Christ sees not only the gift but the heart, then giving takes on new dimensions and becomes a vital force in our lives and in the life of the world.

A GRACIOUS INVITATION

Matthew 11:28

THE WORDS of Jesus which are set before us today are among the most inspiring and comforting that Jesus ever uttered. Both art and hymnody have been influenced by them and, in turn, have influenced humanity.

I think of Thorwaldsen's famous statue of the consoling Christ, at the base of which is inscribed the great invitation. You have undoubtedly seen replicas of Thorwaldsen's statue, which represents Christ standing with hands outstretched in welcome. It may be that you have seen it on some altar as you have gathered with other Christians in public worship. It may be that you have seen it in some cemetery as you have stood with bereaved friends in their hour of desolation. In joy and sorrow mankind finds the invitation of the consoling Christ full of comfort and hope.

The great invitation of Christ was in the mind of the Danish painter, Karl Bloch, who painted the original of our altar painting. Childhood and old age, manhood and womanhood, find the invitation of Christ exerting its powerful attraction.

None of us have any idea of how many hymns and solos and anthems have been inspired by Christ's great invitation. Every hymn book contains its share, nearly every choir repertoire has at least one or two anthems stressing the gospel invitation. Countless hearts have been strangely warmed, and many souls have been saved for all eternity, through the mediation of the great invitation carried on the wings of song.

How can we acount for the strange and strong appeal of Christ's great invitation? It must be because of two things: first, because it touches and satisfies a basic need in man; second, because it offers the friendship, companionship, and help of One whom mankind instinctively recognizes as worthy of love and allegiance.

1. *It is an Invitation to the Burdened.*

There are many ways in which people are burdened. Jesus had in mind, primarily, those of His own generation who were struggling to perform all the works of the law, and as a result had nothing but fear that they were never able to please God. Jesus offered men the possibility of entering into a faith relationship with Him. Guilty consciences were granted pardon and peace.

It was this same problem that Luther met in his generation. People were tangled in the coils of an ecclesiastically imposed legalism which they could never satisfy. As a result, consciences were burdened, and souls could find no peace. Luther reminded men and women of the simple teachings of Scripture: believe in Jesus as Savior, and come to Him.

There are other ways in which people are burdened besides the effort to work out their own salvation by observance of all kinds of laws. Sometimes the burdens are the consequence of guilt when the clear commands of God have been violated. I shall never forget the haunting guilt a woman revealed to me many years ago when I was asked to call upon her in a mental institution. More than forty years had passed since the sins of which she spoke, but she could

not forget them. Her mind had become so shattered by
guilt that she seemed unable to comprehend the hope of
Christ's great invitation. In His great invitation Christ
urges all of us to come to Him in humble faith and penitence, and to place our fears and guilt in His outstretched
hands.

Sometimes, the burdens under which men labor and are
heavy-laden are various handicaps and trials that have come
into human experience. In loneliness, illness, and crippling
frustration we need to be made aware of the presence of
Christ and of His sustaining power.

Sometimes the burdens are inflicted by others. Never has
the world been full of so many burdened, unhappy people.
Think of the war-shattered, homeless multitudes of Europe
and Asia who, after more than a decade of peace, are still
weary, emaciated, and insecure. Think of those who have
been shackled by the bonds of Communism, and who can
have no peace and rest as long as that grisly monster stalks
the earth.

Even our prosperous and educated nation is full of mal-
adjusted, tense, and unhappy people. There are many
proofs—the instability of so many homes, the lawlessness
and waywardness of so many youth, the ever-increasing
consumption of alcohol to give a sham and fleeting pleasure,
the incessant strife on the industrial scene, the wide demand
for literature dealing with such themes as, "Living under
Tension" and "Peace of Mind."

It is not a weariness of the body that is reflected in all
these symptoms of disorder, but a weariness of the spirit,
a burdened state of mind, a tossing of the soul that has
found nothing to which it might anchor. Physical fatigue

can often go with health and happiness, but fagged minds and souls are matters of real concern.

Dr. Norman Vincent Peale, whose ministry in New York has brought him close to this matter of burdened minds and spirits, says that the condition can be boiled down to three causes—fear, anger, guilt. The first letters of the three words spell fag. I believe he would be nearer the truth if he made those three words—fear, avarice, and guilt, for it seems to me that the greed of people for money is narcotizing them to the higher values of life and to the satisfaction of rendering real service to mankind.

Against these influences of fear, anger, avarice, and guilt there must be placed the positive qualities of faith, unselfishness, and forgiveness.

It is obvious that since the trouble of mankind is so deep seated, we cannot depend on such palliatives as better housing, higher wages, lower taxes, and better roads. We will not have a better world until we have better people, and we will not have better people until men turn from the quack cures offered by the world, and turn to the great physician who is Jesus Christ. This brings me to the other reason why the great invitation has such a strange and strong appeal.

2. *It Is an Invitation to Come to Christ.*

None greater ever spoke such words. We would be thrilled to receive an invitation from President Eisenhower or from some other great personality of our era. The one who extends this invitation is the Son of God and Savior of mankind. He is more than a good friend or important personage. He is the revelation of a loving God. He could say, "All things have been delivered to me by my Father," "I

and the Father are one." Those who knew Him best found
no gap in what Jesus claimed to be and in what He was.
Those who were closest in spirit to Him could only exclaim:
"Truly, this was the Son of God," "My Lord and my God."
"In him the whole fulness of deity dwells bodily," "very
God of very God."

If, then, it is a divine call that comes to us from One than
whom there is no greater, it deserves consideration and attention, yes, more than that, it deserves acceptance.

None gentler ever called men to himself. We have probably thrilled to some of the famous invitations recorded on
the pages of history. Some, like Judas Maccabaeus in ancient Palestine, and Robert Bruce in Scotland, and William
Tell in Switzerland, have rallied men to the banner of freedom and courage. Some, like Frances Willard, have invited
people to join a crusade. Many leaders have come with se-
ductive promises of wealth, ease, power. Usually, the invitation has been to something beyond the one giving the invitation. But Jesus calls men to himself. He is to be the
goal. In Him is rest and peace and joy.

There has been so much leadership of men that is cold,
ruthless, cruel, fanatic. It has led only to blood, tears, and
death. What a devilish perversion has taken possession of
man that he chooses the arrogant leader to the humble one,
the ruthless leader to the gentle one, the cruel one to the
kind one!

Meekness does not have to be weakness; faith does not
have to be fanaticism; innocence does not have to be ignorance. Only when men experience that total conversion
which changes their ideas of heroes, and alters their standards of value, and readjusts their intuition of character, can

there be an appreciation of what Jesus can mean to the human race. He said, "I am gentle and lowly in heart." How far we need to go to understand that kind of greatness! Apart from a Gandhi, you never hear about its gaining any adherents in the political arena. Certainly, our competitive business world does not encourage such understanding. Television and movies and literature do little to help us understand that kind of greatness. Even in religion, people are too prone to think that greatness dwells in a papal palace, or wears a bishop's robes, or pulls down the biggest salary, or has the greatest number of secretaries.

"Come to me," says Jesus, "and learn of me." When that invitation is accepted, then will humility and meekness and gentleness and lowliness have a place in our vocabularies as synonyms of greatness and honor and glory.

None richer ever promised so much. Consider what fabulous promises have been made by demagogues through history. They have offered gold, luxury, power, honor, splendor, but in the end everything has usually turned to ashes and vapor. Essentially, the reason is found in the fact that those things are not the things that satisfy the deepest cravings of the human heart. Midas with all his gold, Belshazzar with all his luxury, Alexander with all his power, the Agha Khan with all his splendor—none of these could claim that those things were the real riches of life. Possessing those things, there could still be a sense of futility, an experience of heartache, a pretty bauble with a vast emptiness.

Amid the incessant surge of life, man wants calm. In the restless urge to get ahead of others, he wants rest. Under the burden of life with its many problems, he wants a sense of relief.

Once, Walter Pater, the English essayist, was engaged in a conversation with a distinguished literary woman who was an agnostic. Pater had just stated that he believed in Jesus Christ because of His miracles. "Do you believe," asked the woman, "that Jesus made water into wine, walked on the sea, multiplied loaves and fishes?" "I suppose I do," replied Pater, "but I was thinking of His greatest miracle." "And what was that?" she asked. After a moment's silence, Pater answered, "Oh, that He said, 'Come to Me, and I will give you rest.' Millions have gone to Him and have found that rest. That is His greatest miracle."

What Christ offers us is not release from life's burdens, but ability to shoulder them bravely. That is suggested by His words, "Take my yoke upon you." A yoke distributes the burden by sharing it with another. In other words, Christ offers to enter into our life so fully that He shares our burdens.

Life will not be shorn of all distress and disturbance for those who come to Christ, but, in spite of the hard experiences they may have, Christians will find a solid foundation on which to rest, an inward peace of mind amid all the whirl of life. For the one who has truly accepted this gracious invitation of Christ, there will be no unceasing hurrying from one sensation to another that so stamps the unspiritual life. There will be no bitterness and gnawing hatred because the earthly fortunes of others seem for the moment to be better than our own. There will be no harassing anxiety concerning the future, for we know that Christ is our companion all along the road. There will be no spiritual pride or self-righteousness, for we will know that apart from Christ we are nothing, and that what we enjoy of peace and power is by His grace.

No wonder this gracious invitation from the consoling Christ is regarded by many as the greatest passage in the Bible! Thousands upon thousands who have accepted the invitation can testify that there is no emergency in life which, with Him, cannot be boldly met; there is no problem to which He cannot supply the answer; there is no path so difficult or lonely that it cannot be made easier and safer with His leadership; there is no burden so heavy that it will not be lightened when His yoke is accepted.

Listen again to those words coming crystal clear down through all the ages: "Come to Me, all who labor and are heavy-laden, and I will give you rest. Take my yoke upon you, and learn from me; for I am gentle and lowly in heart, and ye will find rest for your souls." Isn't that just what you and I and everybody else needs? Isn't that the balm of Gilead to make the wounded whole, to heal the sin-sick soul?

UNCLOUDED VISION

Matthew 6: 22, 23

TO THE AIR PILOT the expression, "visibility zero," means danger. That same expression was the caption of a recent cartoon designed to encourage safe driving. Two cars were approaching an intersection, but sketched over that intersection as an ominous shadow was the object of a whisky bottle. The subject of that carton, "visibility— zero," was well chosen. There, too, it meant danger. A company manufacturing light bulbs is making a great deal of the need for adequate lighting in homes, schools, and factories, using the slogan, "Sight is precious; light is cheap." I mention these examples to show that our age is becoming more and more aware of the need of unclouded vision when it comes to seeing material objects.

I would not minimize that much needed emphasis, but use it as a steppingstone to a higher and much more needed emphasis, namely, the need of an unclouded vision in discerning spiritual values.

When Jesus said, "If your eye is not sound, your whole body will be full of darkness," He was speaking of that type of person whose visibility is zero when it pertains to the discernment of true values. The Christian ideal is to have an unclouded vision of the abiding truths and genuine values of life. That is what Jesus had in mind when He said, "If your eye is sound, your whole body will be full of light."

It is amazing how some of the smaller organs and glands in our bodies can make or break our whole life. We know what mischief the abnormal functioning of a gland can accomplish. James, in his epistle, says that the tongue, which is such a small member of the body, has an untold power for weal or woe. In the passage which we are considering today, Jesus stresses the consequences of a right or wrong use of the eye. We can never fully appreciate the blessing of unclouded vision, until we realize some important facts connected with our eyes.

1. *What We See Influences Our Life.*

The church has recognized this truth from its earliest days. It has relied on not only what the ear heard through sermon, song, and Scripture. It has depended also on statues, pictures, and symbols to convey truth. Many a person, unable to recall any vivid impression recorded from sermons, can testify to the deep impression that has been made on his life by some statue or altar painting or stained glass windows.

Nathaniel Hawthorne has written an immortal story called "The Great Stone Face." A legend in a certain valley said that some day a man would live whose face would be like the beautiful, strong face which they beheld in the mountain, a face which nature chiseled into the rock. A boy looked often on that face, impressed by its calm, strength, and beauty. When he was old, behold, his face was like the great stone face. What he had seen had influenced his life.

Advertisers are aware of the fact that what people see influences their actions and their life. Their job is to influence taste and habits by what people see. Newspapers have the slogan, "A picture is worth a thousand words."

We think that the movie industry should be under some

kind of control, because movie-goers will be moral or immoral, drinkers or non-drinkers, idealists or crass materialists, according to the message underlying the films presented. We believe Alexander Pope was right when he said,

> Vice is a monster of such hideous mien
> That to be hated needs but to be seen;
> But seen too oft, familiar with her face,
> We first endure, then pity, then embrace.

Therefore it is our Christian duty to look constantly at
that which is pure, beautiful, and elevating, because the
sight of such things will influence our lives for good.

2. *What We See Proclaims What We Are.*

Three men visit Starved Rock or Wisconsin Dells. When
they return, one has chips of rock and talks about how long
it must have required to carve those chasms. Another has
some specimens of mosses, ferns, and flowers. Still another
has pictures of different birds or a new bird call. What
those men saw proclaimed what they were, or at least what
the dominant interest in their lives were.

Many people have visited Paris. What have they gone to
see with the greatest interest—the art treasures of the
Louvre, the architectural grandeur of Notre Dame, Napoleon's tomb, or the Folies Bergere?

The great British preacher, Dr. Joseph Parker, on crossing the ocean, spent much of his time sitting on deck looking out over the limitless expanse of the sea. A fellow
traveler asked Dr. Parker why he was always looking at the
water. "I see nothing there," he said. Dr. Parker replied,
"I see nothing—but God."

If we are true Christians, we will see opportunities for
kindness on every hand. We will see that in every kind of

experience, God is working for good with them that love Him. We will see blessings for which to thank God, rather than misfortunes which lead us to complain.

3. *We See What We Look For.*

Homiletics teachers seldom urge the budding preacher to go to Mother Goose rhymes for sermon material. But even a Mother Goose rhyme can point up a moral. I just said that we see what we look for. That is just what this rhyme says also:

> Pussy cat, pussy cat,
> Where have you been?
> I've been to London
> To look at the queen.
>
> Pussy cat, pussy cat,
> What did you there?
> I frightened a little mouse
> Under her chair.

The cat saw the mouse because it was looking for a mouse. It didn't really desire to see the queen, although that may have been the excuse given for visiting London.

Suppose there is a heavy thunder shower some night. One party will see in it only an inconvenience because some outing had to be canceled. This is what William Stidger saw in such a rain storm:

> I saw God wash the world last night
> With his sweet showers on high,
> And then, when morning came, I saw
> Him hang it out to dry.
>
> He washed each tiny blade of grass
> And every trembling tree;
> He flung his showers against the hill,
> And swept the billowing sea.

The white rose is a cleaner white,
  The red rose is more red,
Since God washed every fragrant face
  And put them all to bed.

There's not a bird; there's not a bee
  That wings along the way
But is a cleaner bird and bee
  Than it was yesterday.

I saw God wash the world last night.
  Ah, would He had washed me
As clean of all my dust and dirt
  As that old white birch tree.*

Then there was John on Patmos beholding, in a vision that he had longed and prayed for, the consummation of the kingdom of God.

In the era that lies ahead, we shall need men and women with unclouded vision.

"God grant us wisdom in these coming days,
  And eyes unsealed, that we clear visions see
Of that new world that He would have us build,
  To Life's ennoblement and His high ministry."

JOHN OXENHAM

*From MASTERPIECES OF RELIGIOUS VERSE. Reprinted by permission of Harper & Brothers.

WHEN CHRIST BECOMES THE SOURCE OF LIFE

John 5:19-21

ONE CANNOT read the Gospel of John without being impressed by the numerous passages that speak of life. Permit me to quote just a few to refresh your memory. In the fourth verse of the first chapter we read, "In him was life, and the life was the light of men." In the sixteenth verse of the third chapter, we have that well-known passage which Luther called the little Bible, "For God so loved the world that he gave his only Son, that whoever believes in him should not perish but have eternal life." In the fourteenth verse of the fourth chapter, we read these words of Jesus to the Samaritan woman, "Whoever drinks of the water that I shall give him will never thirst; the water that I shall give him will become in him a spring of water welling up to eternal life." In the sixth chapter, Jesus is quoted as saying, "I am the bread of life," and "The words that I have spoken to you are spirit and life." In the tenth verse of the tenth chapter, we have the statement by Christ of His mission, "I came that they may have life, and have it abundantly." To Martha, the sister of Lazarus, Jesus said, "I am the resurrection and the life; he who believes in me, though he die, yet shall he live, and whoever lives and believes in me shall never die." In the third verse of the seventeenth chapter, the chapter generally known as Christ's high priestly prayer, we read, "This is eternal life, that they know thee the only true God, and Jesus Christ whom thou hast sent." In the thirty-first verse of the twentieth chapter, the author of the gospel gives his reason for writing it in these words, "These are written that you may believe that Jesus is the Christ, the Son of God, and that believing you may have life in his name."

It is evident throughout that the life of which the Gospel of John has so much to say is not mere existence. Existence is terminated by death, but the life referred to in John's Gospel is life that knows no death—eternal life.

Furthermore, it is significant that this rich and abundant life is always regarded as having its source and substance in Jesus Christ. Nothing that is out of touch with Christ is vibrantly alive. Christ is the true vine, and those not united with Him are dead branches.

One of the typical passages in the Gospel of John concerning Christ as the source of life is found in our text, "As the Father raises the dead and gives them life, so also the Son gives life to whom he will."

How can we recognize this life that has its source in Christ?

1. *When Christ Becomes the Source of Life, There Is Peace.*

There is peace in the soul. Sin has a way of tormenting the conscience as well as the flesh. It arouses a sense of guilt which in turn creates an uneasiness and restlessness. This experience of soul tension is no unfamiliar experience to any of us, for "all have sinned and done that which is evil in the sight of God." Not all, however, have found the peace of forgiveness. "Blessed is he whose transgression is forgiven, whose sin is covered," said the psalmist. Paul had discovered this secret of soul peace. Though he had sinned greatly, he was able to confess, "Since we are justified by faith, we have peace with God through our Lord Jesus Christ." This is what Jesus was talking about in the upper room when He said to His disciples, "Peace I leave with you; my peace I give to you; not as the world gives do I give to you." Everyone who, in penitence and faith, has turned to Christ has found a relaxing of life's tensions and the ineffable experience of soul peace.

There is peace in a person's disposition when Christ becomes the source of life. A follower of Jesus does not go about with a chip on his shoulder, looking for a fight. He has put on the sandals of peace. As far as in him lies, he lives at peace with all men. He is free from most of those bad manners that generate strife. He possesses the knack of pouring oil on troubled waters. When we have found the peace that comes through Christ, it is surprising how much more patient and understanding we become toward others.

It must follow that in proportion as many individuals find the inner peace that reconciles them with God and with their fellow men, evidences will be found in the industrial and international life of the world. Commitment to Christ is a commitment to a way of life, a way of life that is marked not only by reverence and honesty and purity, but by sympathy with the underprivileged, opposition to social abuses, and a spirit of brotherhood toward those of different races and cultures. For many years, Chile and Argentina had carried on intermittent warfare, but they finally decided to discontinue the struggle which accomplished nothing, and as a testimony to the Christ whose followers they claimed to be, they fashioned a huge statue of Christ out of bronze cannons which had been melted down. This statue was placed on one of the Andes mountain peaks which mark the boundary between Chile and Argentina. On its base is inscribed these words, "Sooner shall these mountains crumble to dust than Chile and Argentina wage war on each other." Where the spirit of Christ is regnant, peace prevails.

2. *When Christ Becomes the Source of Life, Life Becomes Creative.*

In Christ all necessary and constructive work is freed from drudgery. A Community Chest advertisement carried a picture of a little girl carrying a child. Beneath the picture was the caption, "He's not heavy; he's my brother." Much of the drudgery or pleasure in life is largely a matter of attitude. Two students may be taking the same subject. One regards it as a means by which he may be able to build a bridge or perform a life-saving operation, and rejoices in his study. The other thinks of it as a necessary evil toward obtaining a degree, and loathes every minute he devotes to it. Christ glorified the common task, and we often refer to Him as the Carpenter of Galilee. Pagans may look down upon manual labor, but not those who have found in Christ the source of their life.

Christianity has created institutions like hospitals and free schools. It has placed new values upon personality so that slaves, children, the mentally ill, and those of other races are seen in a new light. Christianity has created new forms of architecture, art, and music. It has fostered new economic ventures of sharing. It is constantly discovering new ways of caring for the unfortunate, for the aged, for the sick, for the unemployed.

When Christ comes into life, one's calling becomes creative. See what George Washington Carver brought to the chemical laboratory. See what James Friederich brought to the motion picture industry when he started making religious pictures for church use. See what Charles Wells has done with his ability to draw, making cartoons with a social and religious message. We could go on and on mentioning such personalities as Golden Rule Nash in the field of business, Martha Berry in the field of education, Bucky O'Connor in the field of sports. Their work became a means of making lives rather than making a living.

When Christ comes into one's life, even suffering becomes creative. We think immediately of those two Christian women—Fanny Crosby, the hymnist, and Grace Noll Crowell, the poet.

When Christ comes into life, new outlets are created for people's capacities. The frivolous, the ne'er-do-well, the drunkard, and the miser find a new direction for their lives.

3. *When Christ Becomes the Source of Life, Life Becomes Joyous.*

Much that the world calls pleasure is only camouflage. In parts of the Orient, tombs are whitewashed, and gleam beautifully in the sunlight, but they house decay and death within. So it is with bright lights and laughter and worldly pleasure; there is often emptiness, and guilt, and sorrow beneath the surface.

To Christ all life was radiant with joy—the laughter of children, the unselfishness of motherhood, the carefreeness of the birds, the establishment of a home, a dinner for friends, a walk through the fields. Some people can't find joy in anything.

Jesus said, "These things have I spoken to you, that my joy may be in you, and that your joy may be full."

What religion has released such fullness of harmony as

Christianity? We think of its hymns, chants, oratorios, and cantatas. What religions have given such festivals of sheer joy that might compare to Christmas and Easter and Thanksgiving?

4. *When Christ Becomes the Source of Life, It Is Endless.*

There is much concern, in our day, about the possibility of an atomic war that could destroy civilization. It is well founded. We ought to do all within our power to preserve the values of life that have taken centuries to develop. Life is a sacred thing, and should not be placed in jeopardy.

However, this earthly existence is not all of life. We humans are sometimes humbled when we stand in the presence of one of those great redwoods of California that was already old when Columbus discovered America. We seem so little before the majestic grandeur of the Grand Canyon. If a piece of rock would fall off and hit us we would be crushed, but ten thousand years from now the walls of the canyon would stand as imposing as they stood ten thousand years ago.

But we are immortal. The oldest trees will eventually die out, never to live again. The stone walls of the Grand Canyon will crumble to dust in time, but we, because we are spiritual beings, born again through Jesus Christ, redeemed by his blood and clothed with immortality, will live forever.

Because Christ lives, we too shall live. That is our invincible hope. May the peace, power, and joy of this eternal life which is ours through faith in Christ be a bulwark against the evil which we meet on every side and a leaven for righteousness in a world under judgment.

THE FOUNDATIONS OF FREEDOM

John 8:31-36

FEW WORDS in our language stir men's hearts and fire their wills as much as the word "freedom." At the same time, there are few words concerning which there is more confusion. Freedom has been associated with right of assembly, the right of trial by one's equals, the privilege of having a voice in selecting one's political leaders, the right to choose the kind of work one wishes to do, the privilege of selecting one's own mate, liberty to choose one's own religious faith, freedom to choose one's place of residence. Usually, men think of freedom within a political framework, but real freedom goes deeper and further than that. There must be strong and sure foundations for freedom, and they are not political or economic, but spiritual.

The world does not realize or appreciate what a liberating force Christianity has been. The more man has resisted or rejected Christianity, the more the blight of some kind of slavery has settled upon him. The more man has been receptive to the truth, power, and spirit of Christ, the more life has been freed from those fears, frustrations, and follies that impoverish and imperil life.

It is no accident that where freedom has been most enjoyed, Christianity has been a dominant influence; and that where freedom has been limited, Christianity has been limited also. If the essence of freedom is spiritual, then Scripture should shed much light on both the nature and the foundations of freedom.

1. *Freedom Must Rest on Truth.*

Jesus said, "The truth will make you free." He went so far as to claim that He was the truth. The truth that Jesus revealed dealt with a few fundamental realities—God, man, redemption, eternal life. There are many areas in which we desire to possess more truth, but concerning which Jesus was silent. Generally, those areas are secondary. Jesus dealt with the primary areas of life; for He knew that secondary truth has little significance or worth if we have not come to the primary truth. For example, what good does it do to be able to know so much scientific truth that we can split atoms, if we have not discovered the truth about life that enables us to harness that power for good rather than for annihilation of life and civilization? Or what good does it do to be able to discover such truths in the realm of areonautics that we can make non-stop flights from Tokyo to Chicago in less than a day, if we have not discovered the deeper truth that enables us to be good neighbors?

We are apt to confuse truth with facts. There is a difference. A person may know all the facts about Jesus' life, and still not appreciate the truth of living the Christian life. He may know much about Scripture, but still miss its message. Robert Ingersoll and many infidels like him have known the Bible well enough to find fault with inconsistencies and inaccuracies, but they never grasp the real truth of Scripture.

Never has education enabled more people to acquaint themselves with more facts, but never has there been so little understanding of truth, so much confusion, such twisted philosophies of life. Propaganda is a much used word in our day. It may handle facts in such a way as to distort truth. There are forces in the world that cannot tolerate unadulterated truth. They have something to gain by distorting truth. Take, for example, an incident in the life of the great Swedish botanist, Linnaeus. While visiting in Hamburg, Germany, he was shown a seven-headed hydra, reported to be part of the loot brought back by Crusaders five centuries before. Objecting to the idea that God would have given such a lowly creature seven brains, Linnaeus managed to obtain an opportunity to give the specimen a critical examination. When he discovered that the hydra consisted of seven heads of weasels which, with two clawed feet, had been skilfully fastened together, he incurred the wrath of the Mayor and Corporation of the town who had planned to cash in on the hoax. He found it wise to leave Hamburg because those in authority did not want the truth. There are people today who do not want to accept the truth which accompanies such facts as that there is no difference between Negro and white blood. The strength of Nazism and Communism alike lay in the concealment or distortion of facts, so that truth was barred.

Some have ignorantly assumed that the quest for truth leads away from Christ. On the contrary, truth brings men into relationship with Christ, for He is the truth. You cannot have truth apart from personality. You can have facts, but it is the understanding and harmonization and interpretation of facts that make truth. That requires personality. It requires more than that. Truth consists of facts in their total relationship to the universe. Individual acts may be right or wrong, but it is truth that stamps them with their proper designation. The facts of atomic energy may consist of the possibility of atomic fission, the need of atomic piles, the supply of uranium, and such things; but the truth is that we have laid hold on cosmic power, that we are stewards of it, that we must use it to glorify God and ameliorate the conditions of earth, or it will be our ruination. This brings us to a recognition of what Christ meant when He said, "I am the truth." Without His personality and spirit in our life, slavery of one kind or another will make real freedom impossible.

2. *Freedom Must Rest on Christian Discipleship.*

This is a tremendous claim to make, but it is the claim Jesus himself made. He said, "If you continue in my word, you are truly my disciples, and you will know the truth, and the truth will make you free." He also said, "If the Son makes you free, you will be free indeed." Paul discovered how true Christ's words were, for he testified to the Corinthians, "Where the Spirit of the Lord is, there is freedom." And to the Romans, he wrote of "the glorious liberty of the children of God."

Jesus never agitated against physical or political slavery, but He planted principles that doomed slavery. Paul was a slave to the Mosiac Law, but was set free when he learned that the righteous live by faith. Philemon was a slave to a system which embraced slavery, and Onesimus was a slave in that system, but when both became disciples of Christ, they became brothers and found a new freedom.

Fellowship with Christ is the road to freedom, for freedom is a thing of the spirit far more than of the body. Christians have often been in cramped situations, and have yet experienced freedom. Paul in his prison, chained to a Roman soldier, was more free than Nero who kept him there; for Nero was slave to his lusts. John Bunyan, sitting in prison writing "Pilgrim's Progress," was more free than his jailers. Pastor Niemoeller, helping his fellow prisoners to know Christ, was more free than the Nazi tyrants who lived in continuous fear of assassination. It is this sense of moral freedom that Christ gives. To delight in doing the things that please God is the glory of Christian discipleship.

3. *Freedom Must Rest on Righteousness.*

What a true conception of slavery Jesus expressed when He said, "Every one who commits sin is a slave to sin." There are slaves to be found all about us—slaves to drink, slaves to lust, slaves to greed, slaves to superstition and fear and prejudice. Try to persuade one of these slaves to cast off his shackles, and you will discover how strong are the chains that bind him. There is only One who can speak, with authority and comfort, the words, "Your sins are forgiven." Christ has shown in countless lives His power to forgive, cleanse, and redeem those who have been held in the clutches of some vile habit. There are many in every Christian congregation who must confess that they have been kept from enslaving vices not because of their own desire or will, but because of the all-encompassing grace of Christ. The more one sins, the more one adds strands to the cables that confine. The more one seeks to do the will of God, the more one develops the muscles of righteous living.

Freedom from sin must never be understood as freedom to sin. It is a perversion of the mercy of God through Christ to think that forgiveness is nothing more than erasing a slate, so that we can draw more ugly caricatures. To be forgiven only that we may go back to sinful practices with fresh ardor is no part of Christian doctrine. Forgiveness deepens our hatred of sin; it draws us closer to our Savior who died for sin; it cleanses us of unholy love for sin; it empowers us to fight against sin; it obligates us to follow Christ in righteous living.

All too many people think of righteousness as morality

in purely personal relationships. Righteousness, as a basis
for freedom, must involve group morality. It involves justice for all, irrespective of color or class. It respects personality for itself, whether it is the personality of an educated person or an uneducated person, of a white man or a
colored man, of a rich individual or a poor one. Righteousness will have nothing to do with exploitation. The Christian will not practice exploitation nor will he sanction it in
others. Social righteousness is a great expansion of the
Golden Rule.

Righteousness is the freedom to do right, to love truth, to
love our neighbor as ourself. This freedom Christ confers
upon His followers.

An unknown poet was seeing very clearly when he penned
these lines:

> I am not strong till Thou hast clasped my hand,
> I am not fit till by Thy side I stand.
> I am not brave till Thou hast come to me;
> Till Thou hast bound me fast, I am not free.

THE THING LACKING

Mark 10:17-27

A YOUNG MAN came to Jesus one day, asking what he had to do to inherit eternal life. Jesus referred him to the Commandments, and, with a gleam of pride, the young man said that he had observed them from his youth. Now it isn't every person who can make such a claim as that, and Jesus loved this young man for his moral character and religious zeal. Nevertheless, Jesus read the man's soul as an open book, and saw that something was lacking. When Jesus said, "You lack one thing," the young man probably expected Jesus to call attention to some trivial fault that could be easily remedied, but when Jesus added, "Go sell what you have, and give it to the poor, and you will have treasure in heaven; and come, follow me," he was crestfallen. With a heavy heart, he turned away from Jesus, for what Jesus demanded was a greater price than he was willing to pay.

To think of those words of Jesus as an indictment on the holding of property, or as a universal command to dispose of wealth and live in poverty, is to miss the point. Jesus was a physician of souls, and adapted each prescription to the patient's needs. Zaccheus, Joseph of Arimathea, and Nicodemus were men of means as well as this young man, but Jesus never asked them to give away their possessions. Zaccheus, Joseph of Arimathea and Nicodemus possessed wealth, but wealth possessed this young man. There is a great difference between possessing wealth and being possessed by wealth. In all his zeal for the Law, the young man had never been able to forget that he was rich and respectable, and this attitude fostered a spirit of self-righteousness and smug complacency. What should have been regarded as blessings from God became barriers. What should have been accepted as an invitation became an impediment.

There are few portions of Scripture that more vividly demonstrate the inadequacy of outward morality to save man's soul. If any here are laboring under the impression that respectable living is sufficient for salvation, let them stand beside the respectable, moral young ruler, and hear with him the words of Jesus, "You lack one thing."

What are the elements that make up the thing that is lacking?

1. *The Young Man Lacked a True Understanding of God's Law.*

Righteousness is more than refraining from deeds forbidden by God's law. It is more than outward obedience to its commands. The Pharisees and scribes were good citizens and noted for their many virtues, yet Jesus said, "Unless your righteousness exceeds that of the scribes and Pharisees, you will never enter the kingdom of heaven." Jesus was not criticizing the scribes and Pharisees for observing the letter of the law. He was condemning their failure to obey its spirit. Rigidly refraining from the grosser expressions of sin, they did not examine themselves as to the secret motives and impulses. This was probably what was wrong with the rich young ruler. His deeds were better than the motives for the deed.

All of us have done good from unworthy motives. God does not see those good deeds as good deeds. He sees the unworthy, selfish motives that prompted the deeds. Some people are decent because they are afraid of the social consequences of being indecent. Some people are generous because they enjoy the praise and prestige that generosity brings to them. Some are outwardly moral because they have been spared great temptations. When we read of legislators or government officials who have accepted large bribes for special privileges, are we sure we could have withstood the temptation, had we been in that position?

Read the Sermon on the Mount, and see what absolute perfection Jesus says the law demands. Abstaining from murder does not fulfill the command, "You shall not kill." Jesus places hate, contempt, and anger along with actual murder as a violation of the commandment, "You shall not kill." In speaking of the command, "You shall not commit adultery," Jesus points out that marital infidelity is not the only way of breaking that commandment. Impure thoughts, lascivious desires, sensual looks are also sins against the commandment. All through the list of commandments, Jesus would have men understand that obedience to God's will must involve thoughts, desires, and purposes, as well as words and deeds. Keeping God's law is a matter of the spirit and not only of the letter. A true understanding of God's law involves affirmation as well as negation. It calls for adventure as well as restraint.

In the light of such a high conception of God's law, the model citizen must stand with the thief and murderer and pray, "God, be merciful to me a sinner." True righteousness must begin with a deep sense of sinfulness.

2. *The Young Man Lacked a True Understanding of Salvation.*

The rich young ruler thought that he could win eternal life by doing something. Salvation is not something man earns but something God gives. The beautiful character of a true Christian is not his method of securing salvation, but rather the fruit and proof of his salvation. A few random passages from Scripture will illustrate this important truth. "By grace you have been saved through faith; and this is not your own doing, it is the gift of God." "A man is justified by faith apart from works of law." "Without faith it is impossible to please [God]."

Whatever a man may be, whatever natural sweetness of disposition he may possess, whatever decent life he may lead, cannot serve as a substitute for faith. There is but one door to eternal life, and that is faith in Jesus Christ. We sing

> " 'Tis not by works of righteousness
>   Which our own hands have done;
> But we are saved by sovereign grace,
>   By faith in God's own Son."

One of the hardest lessons we have to learn is that salvation is God's gift, not man's wages. Therefore, when those who minimize faith and who base their hope of eternal life on their own good character say, "We are just as good as most church members, perhaps even better," we can only tell them what Jesus told Nicodemus, "Unless one is born anew, he cannot see the kingdom of God."

In emphasizing the Scriptural teaching that faith is the key that unlocks the door to eternal life, a word of warning to those who might confuse intellectual assent with living faith is needed. We are saved by faith alone, but the faith that saves is never alone. James probably knew some who conceived of faith as an easy assent which released them from all responsibility. He challenged his readers with these words, "Show me your faith apart from your works, and I by my works will show you my faith." "Faith by itself, if it has no works, is dead," said he. James does not say, "Works without faith will save." Character does not produce saving faith; saving faith produces Christlike character.

3. *The Young Man Lacked a True Knowledge of Jesus.*

I think it is significant that it was not as Savior but as Good Master or Teacher that the young man addressed Jesus. There are many who see in Jesus only one of superior sanctity, or a man with a strange insight into spiritual problems, or a wise teacher. That is spiritual myopia. It is like the nearsighted person, seeing only a man where he ought to see his father.

Jesus is the incarnation of God, the source of abundant life, the Redeemer of mankind. We do not see Him clearly if we recognize only "the poet of Galilee," "the carpenter of Nazareth," "a man of genius," or "comrade of the downtrodden." He may be all that, but it is something far more than that which makes Him the good shepherd, the bread of life, the water of life, the way to the Father. He is life's great necessity, the soul's richest treasure, the sinner's only hope. We never have sufficient knowledge of Jesus until we understand something of what He meant when He said, "I am the vine, you are the branches. He who abides in me, and I in him, he it is that bears much fruit, for apart from me you can do nothing."

4. *The Young Man Lacked a True Understanding of Stewardship.*

Christian stewardship is the placing of our all to the highest conceivable use. It means willingness to sacrifice and to cast our lot with Christ in an absolute and unconditional surrender. It is a giving to God and a giving to man, not as the price of our salvation, but as the proof of it.

Stewardship is faith in action. It is Christian love proving itself in self-denial and self-sharing. "If any man would come after me," said Jesus, "let him deny himself and take up his cross daily and follow me." In the light of this challenge, whoever declines to perform a Christian duty because it conflicts with personal pleasure or comfort is not a faithful follower of Jesus. That was what was lacking in the rich young ruler. He did not want to follow Christ for fear it would conflict with his established mode of living. He preferred his gold to God.

There are two famous paintings of the rich young ruler. Hoffman paints him wearing a jaunty cloak and floating plume. George Fredrick Watts shows the sorrowful Christ and the young man on the vanishing road. One who saw Watts' picture said to the artist, "This is not a picture of the rich young ruler. All you can see of him is his back." The artist replied, "That is all there is of the rich young ruler; just his back." He turned his back on Christ. Are there any in this audience who see themselves in that picture of a man going down a vanishing road?

While mighty earthquakes rock the world's foundation
    And chaos threatens empires and their kings,
While men of strength lie stricken in the wreckage,
    And men of wisdom cease their utterings,
While darkness menaces man's puny striving,
    And newborn terror haunts the land and sea,
Still walks a lonely Peasant by a lakeside
    And calls to His disciples, "Follow Me."
Thomas Curtis Clark.

WHY CHRISTIANITY LIVES

John 7:40-52

THERE is nothing that draws people together in spiritual fellowship like a religious festival. Witness the popularity of our Christmas, Easter, or Good Friday services. In the strict meaning of festival, we would not classify Good Friday with Christmas and Easter, but in the sense that a festival commemorates some important religious event we can justify the association of Good Friday with Christmas and Easter. In the days of Jesus, religious festivals were occasions when people came together in Jerusalem from near and far. Even though people lived hundreds of miles from the city of their Temple, they would endeavor to get to Jerusalem for at least an occasional observance of one of the great Jewish festivals. It was during such a celebration that we find Jesus and His disciples in Jerusalem and in the Temple.

This particular festival was the Feast of Tabernacles which was held in October to mark the completion of the harvest of fruit, oil, and wine. It was an eight day festival, and people dwelt in lightly constructed booths as a reminder of the temporary dwellings in which their ancestors lived during the wanderings in the wilderness. Processions, sacrifices, lights, and music made the festival a truly gala occasion for all who were in Jerusalem during the celebration.

It was natural that Jesus would seek to give spiritual nourishment to people whose willingness to journey long distances to a religious festival testified to their spiritual hunger. The leaders, however, resented the attention which the people gave to Jesus, and sent officers to arrest Him. We can imagine the consternation of the religious leaders when the officers who had been sent to arrest Jesus returned empty handed. When asked why they did not bring Jesus with them, they gave a surprising excuse. They did not say, "We could not find Him." They did not say, "His followers were so numerous that we would have been unable to lay hands on Him." Instead of such excuses, their excuse was, "No man ever spoke like this man!" Was there ever a higher tribute to the power of words? These men were under orders from their superiors. They were armed. Yet, they were so charmed by the utterances of Jesus that they forgot their reason for coming, or they felt the unreasonableness of the orders which had been given to them.

Others had spoken before Jesus, but their words have lost much of the power they once had. Plato, Aristotle, Confucius, Zoroaster, and Buddha had all spoken, but their words do not have the power that the words of Jesus have. Philosophies and religions come and go, but the words of Jesus live on, and therefore Christianity lives on. Christianity lives on because Jesus said things that were both new and true.

What were some of the things that Jesus talked about that give reason for the excuse of the officers, "No man ever spoke like this man"? To realize the uniqueness of Jesus' teachings will enable us to see why Christianity lives on, and why it will continue to live on, in spite of opposition and persecution.

1. *Jesus Spoke of God as a Loving Father.*

There are many ways in which men think of God. He is Creator, or, as the philosophers may prefer to say, "the

First Cause" or "the Prime Mover." He is the Great Spirit, as the American Indian calls Him. He is the Almighty, the Eternal. We may cower before Him as a Judge whose judgments are altogether righteous, or we may bow before Him as "One altogether Other," to use an expression from Karl Barth. All these ways of thinking of God are true and valid, but they do not elicit the full response of man's soul. It is not until man can think of God as a loving Father that religion becomes the vital reality that can transform humanity.

It was this knowledge of God that Jesus held before men. At the age of twelve, on a visit to Jerusalem, Jesus spoke of God as His "Father." In His Sermon on the Mount He said, "If you then, who are evil, know how to give good gifts to your children, how much more will your Father who is in heaven give good things to those who ask him?" Also in that sermon, Jesus said, "Look at the birds of the air; they neither sow nor reap nor gather into barns, and yet your heavenly Father feeds them. Are you not of more value than they?" In the parable of the prodigal son, Jesus revealed a loving Father suffering with His erring children and rejoicing over their repentance. In Gethsemane, He prayed, "My Father, if it be possible, let this cup pass from me; nevertheless, not as I will, but as thou wilt." And finally, as He breathed His last breath on the cross, He prayed, "Father, into Thy hands I commit my spirit!"

The great prayer which Jesus taught to His disciples begins with the words, "Our Father." On the occasion of the Feast of the Tabernacles which offers the setting for our text today, Jesus spoke to the people about God as Father, but the evangelist reports, "They did not understand that he spoke to them of the Father."

Men still fail to understand the depths of meaning involved in thinking of God as Father, but Christianity cannot die as long as it has these words of Jesus about God as a loving Father. No man ever spoke of God like this.

2. *Jesus Spoke of Each Personality as of Infinite Worth.*

Man is always faced with movements in history which tend to submerge personality. On that particular visit to the Temple, Jesus had been speaking about the change that would come into the individual who believed in Him. He said, "He who believes in me, as the scripture has said, 'Out of his heart shall flow rivers of living water.'" The religious leaders, on the other hand, regarded the people with contempt. When they learned that many were listening respectfully to what Jesus had to say, they said, "This crowd, who do not know the law, are accursed." Nicodemus defended Jesus against hasty judgment. He had once gone to Jesus by night, and had seen for himself how ready Jesus was to respect each individual. This is a frontier on which modern man is threatened today, for totalitarian movements like Communism have no respect for the individual.

Too often individuals, by their instability, greed, and wickedness, add weight to the arguments of those who would submerge personality. Jesus, however, always believed that man could be redeemed. To Him, nothing is capable of such high achievement as human personality, and He gave His life in that conviction and for that objective.

As we read the Gospels, we find that Jesus was always coming to the defense and rescue of the individual. Every type of personality came within the range of His concern— the child, some social outcast like Zaccheus, a poor widow, a leper, the blind Bartimaeus, the fallen woman, the wayward Samaritan woman at Jacob's well, the sincere seeker Nicodemus, the penitent thief.

When Jesus gave a vivid word picture of the judgment, we observe that the reward of heaven and the retribution of hell depended on how men's faith had prompted them to act toward individual persons—clothing the naked, feeding the hungry, ministering to the sick, visiting the imprisoned.

Jesus taught that personality was so sacred that it was worthy of enduring after death. Some religions teach that personality will be merged with the divine nature as drops of water with the ocean, and thus lose all personality or identity. Not so Jesus. Even the last, the least, and the lost have been able to hope since Jesus spoke; for He placed a new value upon each human personality—a value that was sealed on the cross with the giving of His own life.

No man ever spoke like He did about the worth and sacredness of the human personality. That is another reason why Christianity lives on.

3. *Jesus Spoke of an Ideal Society—the Kingdom of God.*

Others, before and since the time of Jesus, have dreamed and spoken of the ideal human society; but Jesus portrayed it in such appealing descriptions and in such challenging fashion that as long as men have any capacity to long and strive for a better world, they will find their chart and compass in the words that Jesus spoke.

In this kingdom, love transcends force, giving is a finer goal than getting, humility and purity of character are surer marks of greatness than wealth or intellectual brilliance, and spiritual values are more important than material values. In the Old Testament times, men were given those stirring word pictures of the ideal kingdom as preserved in the Book of Isaiah. Even in the pagan world before the days of Jesus, Plato described what he thought would be an ideal republic. In our own era, men like H. G. Wells and James Hilton have given reins to their imagination and pictured what, to their minds, would be an ideal kingdom. But as we read these wistful descriptions, we cannot escape the conviction that something very vital is lacking. Without Christ and the spirit that He brings to mankind, the ideal kingdom will ever remain only an ideal. Christ taught us to pray always for the ideal kingdom. He showed us what manner of men we must become to dwell in that kingdom. No man ever spoke so appealingly and challengingly about the ideal human society as did Jesus. That is another reason why Christianity lives.

4. *Jesus Spoke of Himself as the One Through Whom All Life's Highest Hopes May Be Fulfilled.*

The controversy mentioned in our text had been occasioned by Jesus' claiming that He had the living water. "If any one thirst, let him come to me and drink. He who believes in me, as the scripture has said, 'Out of his heart shall flow rivers of living water.'"

This was not the only occasion when Jesus had spoken confidently and authoritatively of himself as to what He was and what He could mean to mankind. We recall those other claims: "I am the bread of Life," "I am the good shepherd," "I am the way, the truth, and the life," "I am the resurrection and the life." It is true that many have made tremendous claims for themselves, but their character and deeds have refuted their claims. In the case of Jesus, it is different. His spotless life, His broad sympathies, His matchless wisdom, His revelation of the character of God, His victory over sin and death have all verified His claims. Not only because of what Jesus said, but because of what He is, Christianity lives. As long as we hold to Him we have the bread of life and the water of life. As long as we follow Him, we are on the way that leads to the Father. As long as we believe in Him we have everlasting life. There should be no doubt in the minds of Christians that with such a Lord and Savior Christianity will live on until that time when it is consummated in glory and "the Lamb in the midst of the throne will be their shepherd, and he will guide them to springs of living water; and God will wipe away every tear from their eyes."

SINFUL STEWARDS

Matthew 21:33-46

FEW NATIONS in history have had such a consciousness of divine mission as ancient Israel. She was to live for God, not for herself. It was only as Israel was faithful to her responsibility of preserving faith in the true God that she had any special justification for existence. However, it is a matter of historical record that time and again the Jewish people and their leaders forgot their mission.

The closing days of Jesus' life reveal just such a glaring lapse, especially on the part of Israel's leaders. In those final controversies which Jesus had with the Jewish leaders, we can see how earnestly He tried to reawaken in them an intelligent appreciation of Israel's place in the cosmic plan of God. It was to emphasize the fact of Israel's unfaithful stewardship of privileges and opportunities that Jesus told the parable of the wicked husbandmen.

It strikes us immediately as an improbable story, but it is because of that fact that it arouses such interest. Jesus wanted to show the Jews that they were behaving toward God worse than the most treacherous tenant; for no tenant would behave so notoriously toward his landlord as Israel behaved toward God. Furthermore, Jesus wanted to show the Jews how good and patient God was; for no landlord would exercise such forbearance toward sinful stewards as God had done toward Israel.

The parable, therefore, presents a sharp contrast between the character of God and the character of His stewards.

1. *Look at the Picture of God Which It Presents.*

Jesus taught that God is good. He richly endows His people. "There was a householder who planted a vineyard." How simply Jesus reminds the nation that they must trace the origin of every blessing to God.

The comparison of the kingdom of God to a vineyard runs throughout the Old Testament. In Psalm 80:14-15, the Psalmist exclaims, "Turn again, O God of hosts! Look down from heaven, and see; have regard for this vine, the stock which thy right hand planted." Jesus must certainly have had in mind as He spoke the parable that earlier parable of Isaiah in the first seven verses of the fifth chapter of that wonderful Book of Isaiah, for some of the very expressions Jesus used had been used by Isaiah. Isaiah's own words are a clue to the understanding of the parable: "For the vineyard of the Lord of hosts is the house of Israel, and the men of Judah are his pleasant planting; and he looked for justice, but behold, bloodshed; for righteousness, but behold, a cry!" Ezekiel, also, had used the figure of the vineyard in referring to Israel. "Your mother was like a vine in a vineyard transplanted by the water, fruitful and full of branches by reason of abundant water." In one of his sermons, Hosea said, "Israel is a luxuriant vine that yields its fruit."

Of this vineyard which is Israel, Jesus said the householder set a hedge around it. Jesus was not given to allegories, but the allegory is quite evident here. God had given Israel a certain protection and isolation through the Law, the Sabbath, and the many ceremonies to be observed. The reference to digging a winepress was a reminder of the blessings of joy and prosperity granted by God to His people. Then Jesus added, "He built a tower." It was from the tower that watch was kept, so that thieves coming to steal the grapes would be discovered. The mention of a tower ought to have been suggestive to the people of God's special care and revelation.

Privilege always entails responsibility. That is what Jesus was trying to emphasize when He said, "He sent his servants to the tenants, to get his fruit." God is not indifferent to what use man makes of his blessings and resources. Jesus pictures God as expectantly waiting for returns from the vineyard He had planted and entrusted to Israel.

Furthermore, God is patient and persistent. When the tenants of the vineyard took the servants sent to get the fruit, and beat one, killed another, and stoned another, the misdeeds were met with patience and forbearance. God's anger did not flare up at the first offense. We are reminded of that story of an infidel who was trying to prove the non-existence of God. Dramatically, he pulled out his watch and said, "If there is a God, I will give him one minute to strike me dead." The audience waited through the minute which seemed interminable. Finally, someone rose and asked, "Does the little man think he can exhaust the patience of Almighty God in one minute?"

Not only is the God pictured in the parable as good and patient and persistent. He is unselfish. Even though the servants have been mistreated and rejected, the householder sends his own son, fully aware of the risk that is being taken. God does not easily give up man. We should never cease to thank Him for that.

2. *Look at the Picture of Sinful Stewards Which the Parable Presents.*

In what was literally a last appeal, Jesus was reminding the Jewish leaders that they had been and were defrauding God of that to which He was entitled. However, if we, after these many centuries, confine ourselves to the historical situation alone, we will miss much of the meaning of this parable. To see the scribes and priests and Pharisees of Jesus' day as sinful stewards is not enough. That might result in a fatal complacency and self-righteousness as far as we are concerned.

This parable covers the whole range of man's responsibility to God. There is a sense in which you and I have succeeded to the place of trust and responsibility once held by those to whom Jesus was speaking during that last fateful week. Our self-will and self-interest are antagonistic to God's will as truly as was the self-will and self-interest of the Jews in Jesus' day.

There is not one of us who has not been made the steward of some opportunity, privilege, or talent. Consider our privileges of the open Bible and open churches, Christian homes, Christian ideals, Christian influences. Have we made the most of them?

This parable emphasizes the fact that no one receives a charge without a challenge to fulfill it faithfully. Every privilege is connected with a corresponding responsibility. We may not be free to choose the resources God sees fit to bestow upon us, but we are free to make the best or worst of them. We are not free to choose our native or peculiar talent, but we are free to double the talent or bury it.

Wherever one reveals to you an opportunity to do good, wherever one points to a wrong which you can help to right or an evil which you can help to remove, wherever one shows a service that you can render or a truth that you can champion, there is a servant of God come to receive the fruit of His vineyard. Are not such messengers coming to us daily?

This parable should stimulate sincere soul searching. Before the tribunal of our own conscience we should see what poor stewards we have been of that which God has committed to us and pronounce the sentence on ourselves, "We have been unprofitable servants." Out of the valley of repentance flow the refreshing streams of high and noble resolution.

3. *Look at the Picture of the Smitten Son Which the Parable Presents.*

When one servant after another had been sent to receive the fruits of the vineyard, and had received only brutal treatment as a result, the householder sent his own son. What a prophecy of impending events Jesus gave when He said, "They took him and cast him out of the vineyard, and killed him." Elijah, Isaiah, and John the Baptist had been servants, but Jesus did not classify himself with the servants. He was the Son. The fact that no one seemed to grasp the import of our Lord's words reveals to what extent they had accustomed themselves to sin and unbelief.

The parable of the wicked husbandmen is a very short parable, but just as a small mirror can reflect a whole landscape so this parable gives us a picture of God, a picture of sinful stewardship, and a picture of the smitten Son. God grant that we may not be as dull to understand and as ready to reject its message as those to whom Jesus first related this parable. Rather, may the parable speak to us of God, of duty, of redemptive love.

IT WAS WINTER

John 10:22-30

ALL PEOPLE can look back over their national history and thrill at the recital of exploits of their ancestors, and thank God for gracious deliverances. The Jewish people had much to remember, and they observed certain festivals for the recollection of high points in their history. Such a celebration was the Feast of Dedication which commemorated the purification of the Temple by Judas Maccabaeus after its desecration by Antiochus Epiphanes. Antiochus Epiphanes of Syria had waged war against the Jews from 168 to 165 B.C. Among his atrocities was the sacrificing of swine on the altar in the Temple. When Judas Maccabaeus and his followers finally drove out the invader, one of the first acts was to rededicate the Temple to the worship of Jehovah. Ever since, the Jews have celebrated that dedication by holding a feast in the middle of December.

Jesus rejoiced in the history of His people, and was often found in Jerusalem for the observance of such great occasions as the Feast of Tabernacles, the Feast of Passover, and the Feast of Dedication. Our text relates the happenings in connection with our Lord's presence in the Temple for the Feast of Dedication. It was winter in a very literal sense. Jesus was walking in one of the porticoes of the Temple, no doubt pondering the historical and spiritual significance of the celebration. He probably thought of how war brings out the beast in mankind, as it had done in the case of Antiochus Epiphanes. But He could not but recall how war may bring out the heroic in man as it had done in the case of Judas Maccabaeus. The Feast of Dedication, observed in the middle of December, reminded the Jews of those wintry days when a cruel tyrant was attempting to wipe out their religion. It must have been a truly spiritual thanksgiving festival for the Jews as they celebrated the restoration of free worship in the tradition of their forefathers.

The Roman Winter

It was winter not only in a literal sense but in a political sense also. The cold power of Roman rule had swept over Palestine like a blizzard. It irked and humiliated the Jews to have to pay taxes to representatives of a foreign power. It made them cold and sullen to have a Roman procurator's palace only a stone's throw from their Temple. They longed for the springtime of a resurgent nationalism, such as that which had rallied to the banners of Judas Maccabaeus. They eagerly awaited a Messiah to lead an insurrection against Roman rule. It was this longing and desire that may have prompted the question put to Jesus, "How long will you keep us in suspense? If you are the Christ, tell us plainly."

Roman ideas, vices, and customs were moving in upon the people like a great glacier. So benumbed were the spirits of some of the people becoming that they almost failed to feel their loss of freedom, as is indicated by their statement to Jesus at an earlier visit to the Temple, "We have never been in bondage to anyone." It is always tragic when people protest that they are free when all the time a terrible tyranny is holding them in its power and benumbing their judgment. You may have heard some slave of alcohol make the boast, "I can quit any time." Spiritual freezing, like physical freezing, deceives its victims with a certain kind of drowsiness.

Most significant of all, it was winter in a spiritual sense. In spite of all the truth of which they as a nation were the repository, the Jews missed much of its real meaning. Religious life had frozen into hard and cold formalism. Christ had come as the fulfillment of their Messianic prophecies, but they would not believe Him. They rejected Him who alone could bring spring to their wintry souls. Legalism, self-righteousness, pride, hatred were everywhere present. The vision of a world-wide brotherhood of living in peace and love, and engaged in a common quest for truth, had been lost. When unbelief and cold formalism sweep over a people it is winter indeed; for spiritual aspiration is benumbed and religious expression becomes frozen into lifeless forms.

Yes, it was winter, but the Source of Life was there in spite of the deadness, and the true Light was shining in spite of the coldness, and spring was not far away—if they had only known. Jesus said to them, "My sheep hear my voice, and I know them, and they follow me; and I give them eternal life, and they shall never perish," but they did not hear His voice and they did not follow Him. As a result, there was winter in their souls.

It Is Winter Still

If I were to stop at this point, you might go home enlightened a little about a certain situation long ago, but with very little light for the situation at hand. Let us change the tense of our sermon subject from "It was winter" to "It is winter."

It is winter in a literal sense. Cold weather is already

here. People are going to suffer grievously during this winter which is just beginning. Particularly in Europe, the approach of winter is something to dread. Even this long after World War II a shelter problem exists for millions of people. Then, too, there is the matter of clothing and food—both of which are scarce and inadequate. Many say, "Let them work out their own salvation," but you have to have adequate clothing and food to work, and you have to have the feeling that the work will not be in vain. It is going to be a hard winter for many people, but Christ is still walking in our temples, touching worshipers with the spirit of sympathy, brotherhood, and self-sacrifice. Through Lutheran World Action and Lutheran World Relief and through similar agencies in other denominations, food, clothing, medicine, Bibles and other aids will be furnished. And we have faith that it will be more than a prolonging of their sufferings, that it will be the prelude to spring.

It is winter in a political sense. Press and radio are constantly telling us about the cold war. When one nation resents the help that another nation is giving a war-ridden people, there is only one word to describe it—cold-heartedness. When the warmth of sympathy and friendly co-operation gives way to fear, suspicion, and selfishness, winter has set in. Just as Palestine was no longer free in Jesus' day, so there are many nations no longer free today. The pathos of it is that this is true after we fought a war to guarantee four fundamental freedoms for mankind. A dull despair has settled down upon millions of people, like the despair that settles down upon a snow-bound community when no hope of relief seems to be in sight.

It is winter in a spiritual sense. All through the Second World War, ministers and educators and statesmen were reminding the people that winning the war would be futile, if we did not win the peace. If we would not rise above materialism, selfishness, and vindictiveness, we would only sow the seeds of another more terrible war. In spite of the object lesson of the dangers of greed and reliance on force, we have gone our unspiritual ways. Vices are continually gaining a stronger foothold in our national life,—graft, racketeering, gambling, alcoholism, willful limitation of production in the face of world need. Most sinister of all is the widespread ignorance of, and indifference to, that which alone can redeem, regenerate, and revitalize modern life, namely, the Gospel of Christ.

It was in winter that the Temple was rededicated, bringing a new springtime to man's spiritual life. It was in the political and spiritual winter of Pilate's and Caiphas' rules that Jesus walked in the Temple, bringing the promise of a new springtime to mankind. The poet Shelley, in one of his poems, asks, "If winter comes, can spring be far behind?"

As far as our present problem is concerned, it depends on several conditions. There will have to be a larger measure of spiritual receptivity. Jesus said, as He walked in the portico of Solomon, "My sheep hear my voice." We need to listen to His voice by more reading of our Bibles, by more faithful and frequent attendance at worship services. Jesus asks unhesitating obedience. He said of those whom He called His sheep, "They follow me." It may not always be easy to follow where Jesus leads, but we have seen enough of the consequences of sin and war to know that it is far from easy to follow where blind leaders lead. Christians do not follow their Master in a spirit of stoical resignation to some grim doom, but in a spirit of joyful anticipation of a heavenly destiny. They have the Lord's promise spoken at that Feast of Dedication, "I give them eternal life, and they shall never perish, and no one shall snatch them out of my hand."

It may be winter, but spring is never far behind when there is spiritual receptivity to Christ's words, unhesitating obedience to His commands, and a sure confidence in His promise of eternal life.

THREE ASPECTS OF THE CHRISTIAN LIFE

Mark 4:21-25

THIS BUSINESS of being a Christian is not nearly as simple a matter as might at first appear. Many people confuse becoming a Christian with being a Christian. It isn't hard to become a Christian, but it is hard to be a Christian. Ask the politician, the business man, the labor leader, the operator of a hotel, the publisher of a paper, the young person facing the alluring temptations of the world. They will admit that honesty, purity, and courage are often compromised because of expediency, party loyalty, popularity, and profit. There are many aspects of the Christian life, and easy answers to the many problems which face a thinking and sincere Christian are not always possible. Merely to recognize the problem is not to solve it. Diagnosis without therapeutics is far from being a cure.

There are three aspects of the Christian life mentioned in today's text which can contribute toward answering many questions that come up in the experience of a Christian.

1. *There Must Be Spiritual Receptivity.*

Jesus said, "If any man has ears to hear, let him hear." One may certainly question the sincerity of anyone's professed Christianity, if that person indicates no desire to learn what Christianity offers and demands. There is no other avenue through which God makes His will known than the Word of God. Therefore, it is an essential part of the Christian life to expose one's self to that Word through churchgoing and Bible reading.

Jesus said, "Take heed what you hear." There was never a time in the history of the world marked by such a miraculous extension of the hearing power. Through radio and television, we can hear sidewalk gossip from every part of the world. We can hear friends and loved ones across the continent merely by lifting our telephone receivers and calling a certain number. By means of radar, we can hear the signals emitted by a radio transmitter on a space satellite. When we reflect upon our hearing power, there comes to mind the exclamation of little Red Riding Hood to the wolf masquerading as her grandmother, "What big ears you've got, Grandma!"

In view of the great mass of sounds to which we are constantly exposed, we ought to pay special attention to our Lord's counsel, "Take heed what you hear." With a constant increase in the sounds and voices to which we may listen, there comes a greater need for selectivity. There are many who listen only to the sensational or shocking or shoddy. Truth does not satisfy their perverted appetites. Just as a drunkard is not interested in wholesome food, being satisfied with nothing less than strong drink, so many people are not interested in the Bread of Life. They prefer the highly seasoned but detrimental diet of materialism and unbelief. The Apostle Paul spoke of those who had "itching ears." They wanted to hear the new rather than the true. They were more interested in what appealed to their senses than in what appealed to their souls.

Alongside our Lord's counsel to "take heed what you hear" we might add this counsel, "Take heed *how* you hear." We ought to listen discerningly. Everything is not of equal value. Of what use is it to spend our time listening to that which is worthless or harmful? We ought to listen thoughtfully. We have heard of those for whom words go in one ear and out another. If we have exercised selectivity in our hearing, then the words we hear deserve thoughtful consideration. We should not dismiss them lightly. Furthermore, if we exercise selectivity, we shall want to listen hungrily. And above all, we must listen reverently. Many miss a blessing because they lack the spirit of reverence. When the spirit of reverence passes from a person's life, all the channels of receptivity are clogged.

2. *There Must Be a Radiation of Our Christianity.*

Jesus asked, "Is a lamp brought in to be put under a bushel, or under a bed, and not on a stand?" In His sermon on the mount, Jesus said, "Let your light so shine before men, that they may see your good works and give glory to your Father who is in heaven." In other words, the Christian is not to be a terminal but a transmittor.

I heard of a young, professing Christian who worked for some time in a lumber camp noted for its profane and godless lumberjacks. When he returned from the season's work, friends asked, "What did they do to you when they found out you were a Christian?" "They never found out," he said. That man had put his light under a bushel, if he really had any light in the first place.

There is a common expression that is often used by people. It is "You can't prove it by me." That ought never be said by a Christian concerning Christianity, for a Christian ought to be living proof of the joy, peace, goodness, and kindness which are basic ingredients of the Christian life.

Perhaps we do wrong in talking so much about full-time Christian service when we are recruiting for the ministry or mission field. We should never create the impression that a merchant or factory worker or salesman or politician can be only a part-time Christian. Any true Christian, whatever his walk in life, should think of himself as being in full-time Christian service, because he ought to be a Christian all the time. It might be considerably harder for a barber or salesman or politician or labor leader to be a Christian all the time than for a minister or missionary.

By fairness in all our dealings, by honesty and integrity, by humility and helpfulness, by courage and compassion and consideration of others' rights, we ought to let our light shine before men.

This week marks the climax of stewardship emphasis in our congregation. This is an area of life where we can be luminous Christians; for when we recognize that God is the giver of our time, talents, and treasures, and when we gladly return a proportion of these blessings in the extension of His kingdom, life becomes truly radiant.

Many people have been bothered by the words of our Lord which are quoted in four places with slight variations, "For there is nothing hid, except to be made manifest; nor is anything secret, except to come to light." Obviously, Christianity is utterly divorced from those mystery religions which were so common in Jesus' day. These religions taught that their initiates had some wisdom that the uninitiated could never possess. The gospel is intended to be shared. Lack of faith and insight and Christian experience may make it seem that Christianity is obscure or hidden, but it will ultimately be made known to and through those who open their minds and hearts to the regenerating and sanctifying power of the gospel. The truth that is in Christ was never intended to be a secret possessed by a select circle. It was meant to be translated into human lives. It was meant to shape itself in the events of history.

3. *There Must Be Growth.*

There is another statement of Jesus in this text that has perplexed many people. "To him who has will more be given; and from him who has not, even what he has will be taken away." Unthinking man asks, "Is that fair? Should it not be the other way around—that from him who has shall be taken away and to him who has not shall be given?"

Think a little deeper, and you will see the truth of Jesus' words. John Dewey enunciated a simple truth that has been a guiding principle in modern education: "We learn by doing." John Dewey failed to grasp much of Jesus' teaching, but in this statement he was merely saying what Jesus had said long before.

The fishes in Mammoth Cave, Kentucky, have lost their eyes by not using them. The hawk, on the other hand, has developed phenomenal vision by constant use of its eyes. We have seen jugglers perform feats that seemed well-nigh impossible. They gained the skill by adding to what they had. We may have lost certain abilities (e.g., the ability to memorize long passages). Because we did not develop that ability, it was taken from us. Toward the end of his life, Charles Darwin regretted that he had lost his ability to appreciate music and poetry. He had devoted himself so exclusively to the examination of scientific data, that the aesthetic side of his life atrophied. It was taken from him.

So it is in the spiritual realm. We shall grow spiritually only if we use the light that we have. If we wait until we know all truth and have all light, we shall lose the little truth and the little light we already possess. It is a dangerous thing, therefore, to neglect the exercise of our spiritual powers. Like muscles left unused, they quickly become flabby and useless.

When we think of this addition to our life in proportion as we make use of our powers, we find that the growth will be in three directions. There will be downward growth— sending roots deep into the Word of God, deep into the history of the kingdom's development, deep into a knowledge of the human heart and its motives and emotions. There will be upward growth—up to the stature of Christ in Christian idealism, never satisfied with minimum essentials; up to a vision of the great mercy of God; up above our pathetic trust in science and political platforms to the grace of God; up to the eternal throne that will endure when the hurry and scurry of life is a forgotten memory. There will be outward growth—out of our comfortable complacency with things as they are; out of our provincialism that leaves so much room for racial prejudice; out of our selfishness that sees no need but our own, and that in a false light.

As I stated at the beginning of my sermon, there are no easy and pat answers for the many problems that face the serious and sincere Christian. I think you will agree, however, that if these three aspects of Christian life of which I have been speaking are not neglected, that if we maintain spiritual receptivity, and endeavor to share or radiate our Christianity, and add constantly to that which we already have, we shall be amazed at how many of the problems of life have come much closer to solution.

JESUS AND THE TEMPLE TAX INCIDENT

Mattew 17:24-27

IN EVERY saying and action of Christ, we can detect some true reflection of His character. At first glance, this temple tax incident seems rather unimportant. When people come across it in their Bible reading, they are apt to pass on quickly into the next chapter without pausing for reflection as to its significance. It is not a popular text for sermons, and when it is used it is often twisted to serve as a starting point for a sermon on loyalty to civil government, although there is no reference in the text to civil government. The only evangelist who has preserved an account of the incident is Matthew, and he no doubt does so because, having been a tax collector, anything involving tax matters or money matters would naturally catch his interest.

In spite of the comparatively small attention the incident has received, we find, on careful scrutiny, that it serves as a frame for setting forth several of our Lord's characteristics. A small pool can reflect the amplitude of sky, clouds, and sun. A small cameo can bring out details of facial expression with remarkable clearness. Likewise, this little episode in our Lord's life accentuates some of the divine and human qualities of His character.

1. *We See Something of the Lowliness of Christ.*

When the collectors of the temple tax at Capernaum asked Peter if his Master was in the habit of paying the annual assessment which was levied on every male Jew over nineteen years of age, Peter unhesitatingly replied in the affirmative. When Peter came into the house, Jesus asked him from whom the world's monarchs levied tribute, from their sons or from others. Peter replied, "From others." He meant that the family of the king was exempt from taxation. In our Lord's reply, "Then the sons are free," there is a delicate suggestion of the divine sonship of Jesus. Then, Jesus went on to say, "However, not to give offense to them, go to the sea and cast a hook, and take the first fish that comes up, and when you open its mouth you will find a shekel; take that and give it to them for me and for yourself." In other words, Jesus was saying that though He was Lord of the Temple, and therefore above the tax, He was willing to submit to the tax in order not to cause offense.

Much of the trouble that comes into life comes because somebody is standing upon his dignity or insisting upon his rights. Orientals are not the only people in this world who are afraid of losing face. Here Jesus set an example in being willing to step down and submit to something, although He certainly could have stood on His dignity, or insisted on His rights. How beautifully His former words, "I am meek and lowly in heart" find fulfillment here. As Paul said, "Though he was rich, yet for your sake he became poor, so that by his poverty you might become rich."

Christ's whole life was distinguished by lowliness. At twelve He went home to Nazareth with Joseph and Mary and "was obedient to them." In Gethsemane, He prayed, "Not my will, but thine, be done."

"Learn of me," said Jesus. And one thing that we ought to study far more diligently than we have so far is the lesson of lowliness and obedience to constituted authority.

2. *We See Something of the Loyalty of Christ.*

When Jesus went down with Joseph and Mary to be subject to them, He was loyal to His home. When He said, "Render to Caesar the things that are Caesar's," He was loyal to earthly government. In His payment of the temple tax, we see Him loyal to His Church.

Consider the Church of Jesus' day! From the high priest down to the scribes, there was a tendency toward some serious moral or spiritual shortcoming. Lust for power, desire for wealth, love of titles, indifference toward the needy, prejudice, etc.—these were the faults that Jesus beheld. And yet, Jesus loved the Temple; He often lingered in its courts; He willingly contributed towards its support.

There is something bigger in life than personal likes and dislikes. David was loyal to Saul, although Saul sought his life. Moses was loyal to his nation even when the people were plotting rebellion against him. Ruth was loyal to Naomi, though it meant hardship and loneliness. Likewise, Jesus was loyal to the Temple, because it was bigger than its unworthy servants. Loyalty and pettiness cannot dwell together in the same soul.

Jesus knew that man could not live by bread alone. Worship was as necessary to humanity's true welfare as food. In the Temple, He had conversed with the elders about the law. There He had gone to be with those whose thoughts, like His, dwelt on spiritual things. There He had gone to witness the sacrifices. Those temple doors were avenues to God, and Jesus would be loyal to the divine institution, no matter how many evidences of human frailty He found among those who were serving as stewards of the manifold mysteries of God.

All this is especially pertinent as a congregation pledges

its financial support to the church for the coming year. From the baptismal font to the deathbed, from the Sunday school to the Christian college, from the marriage altar to the family pew, from the orphanage to the old people's home, from our first reading of some Bible story book to our last reading of some favored hymn or Bible passage—the church touches life at a thousand points. Petty and short-sighted, indeed, is anyone who will allow some flaw in the grand structure to blind him to its great claim upon one's loyalty.

3. *We See Something of the Power of Christ.*

Jesus told Peter that if he did a certain thing a miracle would take place. The actual miracle of Peter's finding a coin in a fish's mouth is not recorded, but there is no reason to suppose that it did not take place. There would have been no object in relating it, if it had not taken place. And the miraculous element, consistent with the teaching of the narrative, causes the lordship of Christ to stand out.

Archbishop Trench says: "Here, as so often in the life of our Lord, the depth of His poverty and humiliation is lighted up by a gleam of His glory; while by the manner of His payment, He reasserted the true dignity of His person, which else by the payment itself was in danger of being obscured and compromised in the eyes of some. The miracle, then, was, like all His other miracles, to supply a real need. It was not for himself; it was a sign for others."

Let us never forget, however, that Christ's power is always manifested before us wherever He imparts something of His own lowliness of spirit and loyalty to God and His kingdom into lives that would otherwise be arrogant and lawless. These miracles of Christ can be experienced by any who truly desire to know the power of Christ.

KNOTHOLE TO ETERNITY

Luke 20:27-40

IF YOU have ever watched a baseball game through a
hole in the fence, you have discovered that even the partial view afforded by the knothole can still furnish some
satisfaction and thrills. That knothole view intensifies the
desire that some time you will be able to be inside the park
and enjoy a full and adequate experience of what previously has been only partial.

Many people have expressed wishes that there was fuller
and clearer knowledge concerning eternity. They assume
that, because we do not know all there is to know, we can
know nothing about eternity with any degree of certainty.
That is not true; for Scripture sheds a good deal of light on
the subject of eternity.

Jesus spoke of the glory He had had with the Father from
the beginning. He spoke of the kingdom of heaven as emi-
nently worthy of all the sacrifices and labors which might
be the prerequisites for entrance. Everything we know
about Jesus suggests that He could have given an exact
blueprint of heaven, had He chosen to do so. But it would
have been as incomprehensible to us as the formula for
atomic energy. Instead, Jesus gave only brief glimpses of
what might be found beyond the horizon of earthly life. He
felt that the full light of heaven would be too dazzling for
the eyes of mortals. He felt that our earth-bound conceptions would prevent our understanding all He might wish
to reveal. As He himself said, "You cannot bear them now."

What Jesus did might be compared to our leading a child
to a knothole in the fence surrounding some athletic field,

341

and giving him a partial but nonetheless true and satisfying view of the big drama taking place on the other side of the fence.

The text before us gives us one of these knothole views of eternity. It certainly is not a photographic view. We could wish for further information. Nevertheless, let us see how adequate a view of eternity Jesus has given us and to what extent it meets our hopes and needs.

1. *Life Goes on Beyond the Grave.*

Jesus never doubted the fact of immortality. For Him, life was an ongoing pilgrimage, and death was only one of the milestones on the way. Then, as now, however, there were those who persisted in denying that life went on beyond the grave. In Jesus' day the unbelievers were the Sadducees. They comprised one of the Jewish parties, and they refused to accept any of the Sacred Scriptures of the Jews, except the first five books of the Bible which are called the Pentateuch. Since the idea of immortality or resurrection is not set forth as a definite teaching in those books, they felt they were justified in denying that life goes on beyond the grave. In denying the doctrine of the resurrection, it was logical for them to deny the idea of any heaven or hell; for if there was no life beyond the grave, there could be neither salvation nor damnation. If there is neither salvation nor damnation, there is no virtue in morality and no evil in immorality. In short, one can find no meaning to life. There is no purpose in living.

One day, when some Sadducees tried to argue with Jesus about resurrection, they told a story about a woman who had been married, successively, to seven brothers. In accordance with the levirate marriage law set forth in the twenty-fifth chapter of Deuteronomy, if a man died without

heirs, the dead husband's brother should marry the widow.
The story related by the Sadducees was no doubt invented
for the sake of argument. The question which they put to
Jesus, and which they felt would make the doctrine of resurrection seem ridiculous, was this, "In the resurrection,
therefore, whose wife will the woman be? For the seven
had her as wife."

Often, when people hurled questions at Jesus, they turned
out to be boomerangs. Instead of catching Jesus in a trap,
He would trap them by a simple argument or question. In
this case, He threw the question out of court with the simple
statement that in the age of the resurrection there will be
no marriage. Then He went on to quote an incident from
their own sacred books of how Moses, at the burning bush,
called the Lord the God of Abraham and the God of Isaac
and the God of Jacob. He was saying, in effect, that Abraham and Isaac and Jacob were still alive in a true sense,
even though they had passed through the portals of death
centuries before.

It is faith in the ongoing process of life that gives it value
and beauty. This life has purpose when we believe in the
resurrection, and the purpose is to live so that we may be
"accounted worthy to attain to that age and to the resurrection from the dead." Such truth is not only something to
live by, but also something we should be ready to die for.
A long line of martyrs can attest to that fact. Our highest
hopes inspire that faith in us. Christ's own teachings and
His resurrection and ascension give us all the proof we need.

2. *There Is an Absence of Earthly Standards in the
World to Come.*

Some religions have taught a belief in the world beyond
death, but have thought of it as a continuance of this earth-

ly life. It is for this reason that the ancient Egyptians buried chariots and weapons and utensils with the dead; that Assyrians buried wives and servants with the masters who died; that Indians buried bows and arrows with departed braves; that Mohammedans thought of eternal life as a continuous banquet attended by beautiful maidens. It is no such conception of the life beyond the grave that Jesus presents to us. He says, "Those who are accounted worthy to attain to that age and to the resurrection from the dead neither marry nor are given in marriage." He speaks of the redeemed as "equal to the angels" and "sons of the resurrection" and "sons of God." There is a new relationship, implying the submergence of the earthly family idea, and the emergence of the divine family idea. Marriage is only for this world where there is death, and consequently the need for the perpetuation of the race. There is no marriage relationship in heaven because there is no death.

Jesus does not deny that we shall recognize one another, but He does teach that sex, race, and class distinctions, as we know them, will vanish. There is no room for family exclusiveness or any other kind of exclusiveness in heaven. We shall rejoice not only in reunion with those of closest kin to us, but we shall rejoice in fellowship with all the saints of all the ages. The love in heaven will be inclusive, not exclusive. There will be a purer life and a diviner satisfaction than this life can ever know.

3. *There Should Be More Emphasis on Earth on the Things That Abide Forever.*

While Jesus taught that many experiences associated with earthly life such as pain, sorrow, and death will be done away in that life beyond the grave, He did reveal that spiritual values recognized on earth will have fuller meaning in heaven. In speaking of the redeemed as "equal to the angels," Jesus implied that glory and nearness to God would mark the life of the redeemed. In one of His pictures of the last judgment, He showed that sympathy for the unfortunate would have value before the judgment throne. Paul, in his matchless thirteenth chapter of First Corinthians, said that faith, hope, and love would abide forever.

How cheap and puny are such things as popularity, power, pleasure, and possessions when placed against kindness, goodness, unselfishness, and truth! How poor Dives was when he passed through the door of death in spite of all his wealth! How rich was Lazarus in spite of his rags and sores! Seek first God's kingdom and His righteousness.

As we draw toward the close of the Church Year, our thoughts are directed toward death and judgment only that they may be channeled to that which lies beyond. These last Sundays of the Church Year challenge our faith and hope as few Sundays in the calendar do.

All of us have felt at times that we wish God had given mankind a fuller knowledge of that life which lies beyond the grave. We have been permitted to look through a knothole into eternity, and what we have seen is hope inspiring. We can believe that nothing is too great or too good to be true. This is a universe of boundless possibilities. If the energy of an atom has such tremendous possibilities as we now recognize, who is stupid or stubborn enough to deny that the human soul, God's crown of creation, has even more infinite possibilities of life and power?

Thinking along these lines will naturally result in a greater hatred of sin and falsehood, for these things can deprive us of the most enduring and precious values in the world. Our thinking will also result in a greater love for Christ who is the way, the truth, and the life. Let us not engage in the worship services that mark the close of the Church Year with the feeling that there is something morbid about them. Let us rather feel that we are laying hold on the secret for which God gave life to mankind, namely to glorify Him and enjoy Him forever. Let us appreciate the knothole-view of eternity that the Scripture lessons give us.

WILL TROUBLES NEVER CEASE?

Matthew 24: 1-14

THERE are times when, in spite of all our efforts to control the forces of disruption and destruction, we fail so miserably that, in desperation, we ask, "Will troubles never cease?" Often, when in spite of honest effort and every conceivable precaution, we meet with disappointment and failure and frustration, it is hard not to ask the question, "Will troubles never cease?" So eager are men and women to find the answer to that question that they consult all types of fortune tellers in the hope of finding a satisfactory answer.

Somehow, we never get accustomed to trouble. For ourselves and for our world, we hope that the time will come when troubles will cease. There is an innate hope in the heart of humanity that looks forward to a golden age, and that hope is a constant spur to efforts aiming toward the conquest of everything that contributes to the recurring predicaments in which people are always finding themselves. Fortunately, hope springs eternal in the human breast. Men are always finding new programs, new leaders, new techniques to which they might pin their hopes, but there is a strange irony in the fact that those things in which man often puts his faith and hope are apt to be the very things that prove his undoing.

When the machine age dawned, it heralded the breakdown of slavery; but instead of a better life coming to mankind, a new slavery and insecurity came into the world. The

347

farmers of many western states plowed under thousands of acres of virgin soil in order to raise wheat, and they felt that a new era of prosperity was ushered in; but when drought was followed by winds, the rich farms became a dust bowl. We created atom bombs to break the threat of Japanese imperialism, but today the world is more insecure than ever because of this terrible power that has been developed. A recent news release carried the disheartening information that the new antibiotics in the penicillin family which we thought might eliminate the scourge of germ-induced diseases are losing their vaunted power, and by statistical records are proving less potent in conquering disease than a few years ago. Are we compelled to believe, then, that troubles will never cease?

Scripture is insistent on one thing as far as the solution of our social problems is concerned, and that is that mere human power will never enable man to achieve the golden age, and certainly the verdict of history confirms that. How pathetic and puny, then, must be the effervescent activism of those who will have nothing to do with the Church of Christ, but who devote themselves so energetically to civic and uplift programs that may sometimes have the form of godliness but deny the power thereof! Christians, at least, should have learned by this time not to expect the cessation of life's troubles as a result of the wisdom and efforts of non-Christians.

Did Jesus have anything to say as to whether we can hope to reach a point in civilization where troubles cease to exist? That depends largely on how you interpret His teaching regarding the kingdom of God. Generally speaking, Jesus is more optimistic about the inner life of human character and the future life of eternal glory than He is of the present social order. In the parable of the tares, for example, Jesus seems to indicate that the perplexing presence of evil will continue to vex mankind to the end of time.

While Jesus does not teach the possibility of perfection on this earth, it should be mentioned that He does not deny the possibility of betterment. All His teaching is a call to repentance and higher living, a challenge to the dedication of all we are to following Him. However small a minority give heed to Christ, the world is to that extent made better.

Some of our Lord's clearest insights into the future were expressed during the last week of His life. In our text for this day, Jesus said something which bears on the question, "Will troubles never cease?"

1. *In Some Respects, Christ's Words Were Anything but Encouraging.*

During our Lord's last week in Jerusalem, He and the disciples were leaving the Temple when someone in the group directed attention to the impressive buildings. Jesus, however, was not tremendously impressed by stones and outward grandeur. His response was, "I say to you, there will not be left here one stone upon another, that will not be thrown down." Jesus foresaw the havoc which the nationalistic spirit of the Zealots would precipitate. We have seen in our own day the troubles that come because of narrow nationalism.

Jesus knew that a pagan society would not welcome His followers and His teaching. There would be persistent attempts to abolish the church. It was to prepare His disciples for the terrible testings ahead that Jesus said, "Then they will deliver you up to tribulation, and put you to death; and you will be hated by all nations for my name's sake."

Jesus realized that troubles come from within as well as from without. "Many will come in my name, saying, 'I am the Christ,' and they will lead many astray." Every movement and every institution finds that it must reckon with deviation from the principles that brought it into being. Loyalty and enthusiasm cannot always be maintained on a high level. Jesus said of a period in the future, "Most men's love will grow cold." "Many will fall away."

There is nothing in the sayings of Jesus to indicate that the church will ever be anything but the Church Militant on earth, always struggling with problems, always fighting against something sinful and sinister.

Jesus stated that political disturbances would keep the international scene confused. "And you will hear of wars and rumors of wars; see that you are not alarmed; for this must take place, but the end is not yet. For nation will rise against nation, and kingdom against kingdom." This does not mean that we should throw up our hands in despair and attempt nothing. In fact, Jesus urged His followers to have faith and hope. His injunction to have faith is found in the words, "See that you are not alarmed." His invitation to hope is reflected in the the words, "The end is not yet."

Jesus indicated also that public catastrophes would continue to disturb man's complacency and security. "There will be famines and earthquakes in various places." We may learn to raise two ears of corn where one grew before, and thus make the need of famine obsolete, but, as counteracting influences, we may have economic bungling that plows under the corn, or strikes on the part of workers which cripple the distribution of food, or wars which blast away the irrigation dams.

2. *Although Christ Paints a Rather Gloomy Picture, His Words Are Not Lacking in Encouragement.*

In the midst of a narration of dire predictions, Jesus said, "This is but the beginning of the sufferings." It would be a better and more faithful translation to say, "These things are the beginning of birth pains." That puts an entirely different meaning into the statement. The beginning of sufferings may be preliminary to disaster and death. The beginning of birth pains suggests the ushering in of new life. Jesus was using an expression which the rabbis used for the sufferings and woes which were to precede the Messiah, only He applied it to the coming of the Messianic age. There is a difference between trouble and travail. One may be the prelude to some tragic finale; the other is the preface to a new life. It is in this latter sense that Jesus bade His followers regard the trials of life, especially the trials that come as a result of noble purpose, high endeavor, and unflinching loyalty. Martyrdom, sacrifice, loneliness, persecution—these are troublous and tragic experiences, to be sure, but Jesus bids us think of them as birth pains to larger and fuller life, here or hereafter.

"This gospel of the kingdom will be preached throughout the whole world, as a testimony to all nations." You and I have some responsibility, if that prophecy is to be fulfilled. Nevertheless, how reassuring to know that in spite of barriers and difficulties, the achievement of world-wide evangelization is a possible goal. Jesus did not say that all men would accept the gospel, but He did envision the time when all would have the chance to accept. We talk about the underprivileged as being those who lack material advantages. Jesus recognized the need of material blessings, but in His eyes the real underprivileged were those who have never heard of God's power, justice, mercy, and salvation in Christ.

Before the establishment of Christ's kingdom in all its glory, there will be need of patient perseverance on the part of Christ's followers. Jesus said, "He who endures to the end will be saved." Christians will always need patience, courage, faith, and hope, but in the end the salvation will more than balance the troubles.

We could sum up the teachings of Christ concerning the windup of history in this way: If troubles cease in this lifetime, it will not be because of man's merit or accomplishment, but because of God's mercy and power. If we remain true to our Lord, come what may, troubles are sure to cease in the kingdom of glory, and when that has come it will make all past troubles seem as mere trifles.

Found on the body of an unidentified Australian who died in the first World War were these lines scrawled on a piece of notepaper:

> Ye that have faith to look with fearless eyes
> Beyond the tragedy of a world at strife
> And know that out of death and night
> Shall rise the dawn of ampler life,
> Rejoice, whatever anguish rend the heart,
> That God has given you a priceless dower
> To live in these great times and have your part
> In freedom's crowning hour,
> That ye may tell your sons, who see the light
> High in the heavens, their heritage to take,
> I saw the powers of darkness put to flight,
> I saw the morning break.

That soldier was too optimistic about war as a means of ushering in freedom and light. Wars often bring new slaveries and new darkness, especially to the conquered. He did understand, however, that tribulation was the price and preface to a new life.

Will troubles never cease? No, not in this world. Nevertheless, the dangers and tribulations that are borne in a spirit of love and faith can be the birthpains of a new and better age in which righteousness and peace may dwell.

THE UNEXPECTED COMING OF THE SON OF MAN

Matthew 24:35-44

A DISTURBED age creates two attitudes. One segment of the population is apt to feel that civilization is heading for a crack-up, and that doom and destruction are the inevitable outcome. Another segment of the population may look on the brighter side, and feel that everything will turn out for the better. Jesus lived in a disturbed age. His people had been conquered. A rule by brute force prevailed throughout the world. Clashing philosophies created an atmosphere of confusion. One of two alternatives must be in the process of shaping up. People believed that either the world civilization must come to its end in some disastrous debacle, or God must intervene to save it and change it.

1. *Jesus Recognized the Fact of Divine Judgments in History.*

In many of the preserved discourses of Jesus, there is evidence that He was fully aware of the impending crisis of human civilization. He seems to have mingled prophecies of hope with predictions of doom. He did not remove himself from the human situation and the dangers confronting humanity. He placed himself in the center of the maelstrom of events. He claimed that the final outcome would be determined in relationship to Him. The world could not get rid of Him. He would always appear either in judgment or in blessing.

Just how to interpret the teaching of Jesus regarding apocalyptic events is uncertain. Obviously, He did not believe that human history would go on and on forever. There would be a climax to history; the curtain would come down on the pageant of civilization. Because Jesus identified himself so completely with this climactic event, the church began to speak of Christ's second advent. True Christians are interested in the so-called second advent of Christ just as devout, earnest Jews were expectantly awaiting His first coming. Unfortunately, the whole area of Christ's teaching concerning the future has been exploited by false sects to satisfy morbid curiosity or to arouse fanatical zeal. These rabid religionists have brought the doctrine of the second coming of Christ into disrepute. As a result, many sincere Christians are badly confused, and others who are equally sincere dismiss the whole body of teaching on the subject with a shrug of the shoulders.

2. *The Difficulty of Interpreting Christ's Apocalyptic Sayings.*

We must bear in mind that the Gospels which preserve the teachings of Jesus were written a generation or two after the words were originally spoken. During those forty or fifty years, some of our Lord's sayings had been forgotten. Others had been understood in the light of events that had happened during those intervening years, rather than in the light of events that were still to take place in the future. Still others, spoken in the language of symbolism or poetry, were passed on in the language of literalism and prose. As a result, we are faced with an aspect of our Lord's teaching where roads are not clearly laid out, and where paths are sometimes overgrown with the underbrush of man's opinions. For example, it is fairly clear that Jesus spoke both of the destruction of the Temple and of a final judgment upon the world. However, His words on these subjects are placed together in the gospel record in such a way that they might be construed as being one and the same event.

Many of us have approached a mountain range where it seemed as if two peaks were close together and of similar size, but as we drew nearer we discovered that the first peak was much smaller than the second and that the second and larger peak was still many, many miles ahead. Take another illustration. To the naked eye, two stars may seem to be so close to each other that they appear as one. Upon looking through a small telescope, we see that they are two separate stars which seem to be close together. However, when they are viewed through a much larger telescope, and when astronomical knowledge and mathematical calculations are applied to the subject, it is found that those two stars which seemed at first to be one star are in reality millions of light years apart. These illustrations may help us to understand some of the teachings of Jesus. With prophetic perspective, He may have spoken of the fall of Jerusalem and of the final judgment in the same discourse, but men, with their finite understanding, may have regarded the two events as identical, or at least as two events happening close to each other.

The manner in which the followers of Jesus misunderstood and misinterpreted His sayings regarding the judgments of God has found its way into the gospel narratives. For example, in our text, Jesus is quoted in verse 34 as saying, "This generation will not pass away till all these things take place," and in verse 36 as saying, "But of that day and hour no one knows, not even the angels of heaven, nor the Son, but the Father only." How could Jesus be so sure of the nearness of the end of the age and still insist that neither He nor anyone else knew when it would take place? There are various explanations. One is that, in the former instance, Jesus was talking about the destruction of Jerusalem and, in the latter instance, He was talking of the end of the world. Another interpretation is that verse 34 is Matthew's personal belief, and verse 36 is what Jesus actually said.

The Bible itself bears record that the early Christians interpreted Christ's sayings of His coming again as an event to be fulfilled in their lifetime. They greeted each other with the words, "Our Lord, come!" and "The Lord is at hand." The mischief wrought by the expectation of Christ's return in that first century is reflected in Paul's letters to the Thessalonians, for in Thessalonica there were Christians who neglected their daily responsibilities in order to await the immediate coming of Christ. Even though Paul himself believed that Christ's coming was not far off in time, his counsel to the Thessalonians was wise and sane. Christians are to await Christ's coming, not in a spirit of restless, excited feverishness, but by the humble, faithful performance of their daily responsibilities in full assurance that they are always in the Lord's keeping.

It is important to remember that Jesus conceived of His coming again in different ways—in blessing as at Pentecost when He conferred the Holy Spirit on His followers, and in judgment as at the destruction of Jerusalem. It might be more in accord with Scripture to speak not of Christ's second coming, but of His coming again for He does come again and again in judgment or in blessing.

There is probably no area of Christian doctrine where we ought to be more humble and undogmatic than in this area of Christ's coming again. If charity is a Christian virtue, and none can deny that it is, then we might well practice it here.

3. *Jesus Urged Men to Be Prepared for the Unexpected in Life.*

There have been times when men have felt that life would go on and on in an endless spiral, and that each gyration would find mankind on a higher level. They have felt that this upward trend was the result of man's own genius and effort. Jesus recognized the presence of demonic forces in the world which could pervert man's genius and thwart man's efforts, and He recognized the presence of divine power which could overrule man's ambitions. There would be judgments or climaxes in history which men could not predict nor prevent. Some of these might be in the immediate future; others would be far in the future.

The important thing in regard to all divine judgments is to avoid such spiritual carelessness and such absorption in purely worldly concerns as prevailed in Noah's generation, so that one is not totally unprepared for God's invasion of history. Christ's concern was that in every generation His followers would anticipate His fuller coming, and be prepared to receive Him.

Why should we want to read the scroll of history yet to be written? If we knew it in advance, we would be deprived of the courage, dedication, and zeal that come through faith. It is enough to know that God is supreme and that His will is done. Our responsibility is clear, namely, that we seek to know His will, and strive to do it. "Watch, therefore, for you do not know on what day your Lord is coming."

THE DRAMA OF THE DRAGNET

Matthew 13: 47-50

A LL THINGS must eventually come to an end. Today, our Church Year comes to its end. It is fitting on this last Sunday of the Church Year, that Christians turn their thoughts to the end of all things and to the final judgment which will accompany it.

For many, that thinking will be tinged with dark fears and forebodings. It may even strike terror in their hearts. For others, it will only seem to be the natural denouement toward which history and revelation move. The judgment means different things to different people. It is at once both warning and hope, both threat and promise. It should certainly be a sobering thought to everyone.

We cannot look at life's heights and depths without feeling the necessity of some form of divine judgment. We cannot read the Scriptures without realizing that they bring a powerful testimony to the certainty and reality of judgment. A number of our Lord's parables were told to teach something about the judgment. Ordinary intelligence suggests that divine justice would be something less than just if good and evil were to weigh the same in the eternal balances. Divine love would be a strange love indeed if it saw no difference between fidelity and faithlessness, purity and obscenity, honesty and dishonesty. If God is to be true to His nature, He must discriminate between the innocent victim of torture and the cruel, guilty torturer.

Judgment is an inescapable doctrine of Christianity. If

359

sin is not to be condemned, then the cross of Christ has no
solace for us. If judgment is to be erased from Christian
thinking, many of the most powerful pronouncements of
Jesus must be stricken from the gospel narrative. Still more
would have to be deleted, for if there is no judgment, why
should there be salvation? If there is a heaven to be saved
for, it is logical that there must be some kind of hell to be
saved *from.*

Jesus was much concerned about saving men *from* something as well as *to* something. His teaching concerning judgment is confined to no isolated and ambiguous utterance. He
reiterated His teaching on the judgment at different times
to different people under different figures of speech. To
farmers, He spoke of gathering the tares for burning, and
saving the wheat. To fishermen, He spoke of the separation
of good fish from the bad after the dragnet had gathered in
both kinds. If He had spoken to Texas cowboys, it would
probably be under the figure of the fall roundup. If He had
preached to a convention of bankers, He would probably
have spoken of discerning and discarding the counterfeits.
Jesus was terribly intent on making plain and vital the
truth that life is not without responsibility and liability and
accountability.

One of the parables by which Jesus sought to illuminate
the fact of final judgment is the one we know as the parable
of the dragnet. As He spoke of the separation of the goats
from the sheep when addressing the shepherds of Judah, so
He spoke of separating the bad fish from the good fish when
talking to the fishermen of Galilee. There is a tremendous
sweep to this parable of the dragnet, for it embraces the
task and nature of the church as well as the final results.

Every person who was listening to Jesus that day had

stood on the shores of Galilee and had seen the fishermen haul up their huge dragnets, nets that were so large that they had to be pulled through the water by boats, so deep that their leaded weights sometimes swept the very floor of the sea. As those nets had been pulled up on the beach, they had seen the writhing mass of large fish and small fish, edible fish and fish that were not edible. Then they had seen the fishermen sit down and separate the good fish from the bad, sending the good fish to market, and discarding the undesirable ones. In using this familiar scene as an illustration, Jesus was describing both the growth and the consummation of the kingdom of God.

1. *Jesus Recognized That His Church Would Have Hard Work in Carrying Out Its Mission.*

No worthy endeavor can succeed without equipment and effort. Jesus spoke of a net, of boats, of men, of hard work. Anyone acquainted with the work of the church knows that a well-equipped plant and well-trained personnel are essential, if a good job is to be done. I attended a Negro church once where there were no hymnals. The people knew the hymns or spirituals by heart. How impoverished worship service must be, however, if the worshipers are limited to a handful of memorized hymns. I understand that in some European countries the churches are not heated; but how many people will worship Sunday after Sunday in a chilly church? We want ample literature for our Sunday schools, well-heated and well-lighted plants that satisfy the aesthetic nature as well as the spiritual nature. We want good music that exalts. We want adequate facilities for all our activities. The church has always had too little with which to tackle too much. Yet, there have always been those who have expected results without cost or effort. Members who never lift a finger to do a single one of the multitudinous tasks that require doing are often the first to criticize lack of results.

Christ has called all of us to be fishers of men. Into the gospel dragnet we may bring young and old, rich and poor, learned and ignorant. The child at play can invite a playmate to Sunday school. The man at work can speak of the church to a fellow workman. The woman at a social gathering can encourage her unchurched friend to accompany her to church next Sunday. The student can speak to a friend about the need of Sunday worship. Thus the dragnet gathers in all kinds. Everyone of us can have a part not only in the work of winning others, but also in the joy of seeing the spiritual unfolding of another personality.

2. *Jesus Was Aware That There Would Be Diversity Within the Church.*

Just as a dragnet catches those fish near the surface as well as those near the bottom, so the fishers of the kingdom reach high and low, rich and poor, learned and ignorant. In the very first century of the Christian era, the gospel dragnet gathered in scholars like Nicodemus and Saul of Tarsus, a physician named Luke, a lawyer called Zenas, officers of the Roman army like Cornelius, and women with leadership qualities like Lydia, but it also reached down into the depths of the social order and rescued slaves like Onesimus and outcasts like the crippled beggar at the gate of the Temple called Beautiful. As at the first Christmas, wise men and lowly and unkempt shepherds have found their King and Savior in Christ.

Jesus spoke of the dragnet gathering in fish of every kind.

There are varieties of Christian experience, and one of the tragedies of Christendom is the oft-recurring tendency to expect all professing Christians to conform to one type of experience and expression. The diversity is not only in size and quality of the good, but in the presence of both good and evil in the same net. Judas, Demas, Ananias, and Sapphira were in the same apostolic Christian Church with Lydia, Dorcas, Barnabas, and Philemon. Jesus did not anticipate that His Church would be a pure church composed only of perfect Christians. There would be people with different attitudes, ideals, cultures, and moral attainments. We have a long way to go in recognizing this fact. The day will no doubt come when the Church of Christ will be far more ecumenical in spirit than it is at the present time, having in its hymnal, for example, songs that are indigenous to the people of all continents. Why should people of Scandinavian extraction sing only hymns of Scandinavian, German, or English composition? Why not sing hymns composed by Japanese, Indians, Hungarians, Brazilians, and Africans? Why should ecclesiastic symbolism be correct if it comes out of Greek or Italian background, and incorrect if it comes out of Chinese or Persian or Russian? What makes sixteenth or twelfth century expressions of religious feeling more sacrosanct than twentieth century expressions?

In some respects, the point of the parable seems to be that there is room for great diversity within the church. There is a deeper lesson still, however. It reminds us that only that is important in all our work which will stand the test in the final judgment.

3. *Jesus Taught That There Will Be a Final Judgment.*

There are some people to whom the idea of a final judgment is unpopular and unpalatable. They close their eyes to the injustices of this world. They forget and reject the Biblical pronouncement, "It is appointed for men to die once, and after that comes judgment."

If good and evil, righteousness and wickedness come to the same end and receive the same final evaluation, God would prove to be morally indifferent—and, therefore, something less than God. But God is not morally indifferent. All Scripture testifies to that. He does not look with like favor upon virtue and vice, upon faith and disbelief.

Of all the doctrines of Christianity, none has so profoundly stirred the soul of mankind as the doctrine of judgment. Like Felix to whom Paul preached, many since then have trembled, as ambassadors of God have reasoned with them of righteousness, self-control, and judgment to come. Who can measure the effect of Dante's Inferno or Michaelangelo's Last Judgment? All New England felt the impact of Jonathan Edwards' famous sermon, "Sinners in the Hands of an Angry God." It is not only the fiery evangelists who preach on the theme of judgment. All faithful preachers who rightly divide the Word of God speak, from time to time, on the fact of accountability to God and the consequent fact of final judgment.

Deep in its soul, humanity senses the justice of divine judgment upon sin, and whenever a great spiritual revival has swept over a people with its healing and rejuvenating power, the doctrine of judgment has been an important factor.

In that great separation at the final judgment, in which group will we be? The opportunity is ours to know God's will. The privilege is ours of accepting God's grace in Christ. The responsibility is ours to abide in Christ. We must see to it now that we will be in the right group in the great separation which is the final judgment.

It is not the will of God that anyone be lost. In divine mercy, God sent His Son into the world to save the world. Paul stated it clearly when he said, "The saying is sure and worthy of full acceptance, that Christ Jesus came into the world to save sinners." As one reads and listens to the gospel message, it begins to dawn upon the soul that there is a greater sin than breaking God's commandments, and that is breaking God's heart by spurning His mercy.

HAS CHRISTIANITY A FUTURE?

Matthew 13:31-33

VARIOUS theologians have found the main emphasis of Christ's teaching in different places. Some find it in the doctrine of the Cross; some in the emphasis on the spirituality of religion over against its outward expressions of ritual and sacrifice; still others find it in His repeated utterances concerning the kingdom of God.

Perhaps we do wrong to set one emphasis over against another, for as we examine them carefully we find that they are different movements in the same grand symphony of God's plan of salvation for mankind.

It is certainly true that one great theme of our Lord's preaching was the kingdom of God or kingdom of heaven. Its nature, its subjects, its future—these were the basic ideas of our Lord's discourses on the kingdom of God. Jesus urged His disciples to pray for the coming of the kingdom, and He commanded them to proclaim its coming. When we consider all that Jesus had to say about the kingdom of heaven in His public discourses and in His private conversations, we conclude that He felt that the kingdom of God or kingdom of heaven was so great a theme that it could never be covered by one sermon, or reduced to one simple definition.

When Jesus told His disciples that the kingdom of heaven was like a sower who went out to sow seed, most of which never returned any harvest, and when He told them that the kingdom of heaven was like a field in which tares grew along with the wheat, they must have been somewhat discouraged. The knowledge that there would be more or less failure, and that there would be opposition to the kingdom of heaven, was not exactly inspiring news. But Jesus wanted His disciples to be realists. They were not to imagine things that were not so.

Nevertheless, Jesus wanted His disciples to be optimistic as well as realistic. He wanted them to believe in the final victory of the kingdom of heaven. We have seen many setbacks to Christianity in our generation. In whole nations, atheistic governments have placed every kind of obstacle to the spread of the kingdom of heaven. Churches have, in many instances, been turned into warehouses or museums. Where churches remain open, preaching is often forbidden, and the worship is confined to prayer and liturgy. The working arms of Christianity to which we are accustomed, such as Bible societies, Bible schools, organizations of men, women, and young people for mutual Christian development, are outlawed or discouraged. Even in lands where religion is enjoying momentary popularity, one may wonder at times how deep and strong the roots of Christian faith really are. Experience has shown that materialistic prosperity has often been a threat to spiritual life, and many wonder whether the era of prosperity which we are entering may cause people to feel that God is not necessary for a rich life. The question arises in many minds: "Has Christianity a future?"

Jesus has answered this question. In the parables of the mustard seed and the leaven, He assured His followers that the kingdom of heaven will make both visible and invisible growth. Let us take a close look at these easily overlooked parables.

1. *The Parable of the Mustard Seed Assures Us That Insignificant Beginnings Are Not Necessarily an Embarrassment.*

It was not long ago that we celebrated Christmas, and knelt in spirit before the manger of the Babe of Bethlehem. How could the citizens of Bethlehem have guessed that that child would be the greatest preacher and miracle worker of all time, yes more, that He would reveal God to man and bring man to God? Nazareth was a village of dubious reputation, and when Nathanael was told that Jesus had lived in Nazareth for most of His life, he asked, "Can anything good come out of Nazareth?" It was only a small basket of loaves and fishes that a lad had, but with them Jesus was able to satisfy the hunger of five thousand. There was nothing very impressive about the Mayflower and its cargo, yet it was the beginning of a great nation with great religious principles woven into the fabric of its national life. There was a log cabin in Kentucky, inferior to many log cabins, but in it was born one who was to become the president of our nation and the emancipator of a race.

Despise not the day of small beginnings! All great movements begin as small things, as insignificant things. Instead of being embarrassed by small and insignificant beginnings, we should glory in them. Mighty oaks from small acorns grow.

There are some additional thoughts suggested by our Lord's use of the mustard seed for this parable of hope. While the mustard seed is not the smallest of seeds, it was the smallest seed sown by the sower of that day, and when people wished to emphasize smallness, they would say "small as a grain of mustard seed." Nevertheless, small as was the mustard seed, it was not without worth in antiquity.

It was supposed to have medicinal virtues. Perhaps Jesus used the mustard seed as an illustration because He not only wanted to point out the growth, but also the healing qualities His Church would have for the ills of the sin-sick world. Then, too, the seed is not used until it has been bruised, and Christianity would not perform its healing mission until Christ had been bruised on Calvary, and the missionaries of Christianity persecuted in every possible way.

The mustard seed was sown by a man. There was design or purpose in its being sown. Likewise, the church is not an accident. It is in God's scheme of redemption. In the rich soil and long growing season of hot climates, the tiny mustard seed grows into a sizable shrub. Flocks of birds light upon its branches and find food and shelter. So does the kingdom of God offer shelter and nourishment for the souls of men. From despised beginnings, it has become a force overcoming sinful practices, exalting the simple virtues of kindness, sympathy and honesty, alleviating suffering and misery, and bringing men and women into a living relationship with God.

2. *The Parable of the Leaven Reminds Us That Dynamic Forces Often Operate Silently and Invisibly.*

Our generation has been startled by the tremendous detonation of the atomic bomb. Through the use of radio, it has literally been heard around the world. But consider the secret working of the idea that gave it birth. Not until the blasts at Hiroshima and Nagasaki did the world realize that it was in the making. Yet, secretly and unostentatiously, in many laboratories and factories, the bomb was being manufactured. Who can measure the force of an idea? If this tremendous power of shattered atoms is to be used for constructive rather than destructive purposes, it will be because of the still greater power of ideas, silently and unobtrusively shaping men's ideals and wills.

The kingdom of God works through ideas—concepts of love, salvation and worship, ideals of justice, righteousness and mercy, awareness of evil and recognition of the need of repentance, religious convictions, and high hopes. There is seldom any fanfare as ideas enter human lives to begin their work, nor is there any melodrama in their working. The leaven was taken from outside and put into the measures of meal. Likewise, Christianity is not of this world, not a discovery or invention of man. It is ideas breaking into time from eternity, into human life from God's divine life.

Jesus probably attached no significance to the number of measures of meal into which the leaven was placed. That was probably the customary amount of an average bake day, the capacity of the oven. If we feel there must be some significance to the number of measures of meal, let it symbolize the three-fold nature of man's life—physical, mental, and spiritual; for the leaven of Christianity must influence every area of man's life. The spiritual side of life cannot be touched without a corresponding influence being exerted on the way man works and lives and on what he reads and sings. Leaven is like our yeast. It is a living organism. It is life. That is what God's Word is. That is what the kingdom of heaven is. It is a new kind of life supplanting the old, not by any sudden and violent revolution, but by unobtrusive and silent processes changing a life here and there, until whole measures or areas of life reveal the effects of that mysterious influence.

Coming back to the question to which our thinking has

been directed, "Has Christianity a future?" we find that these parables give an unqualified affirmative answer. Christianity does have a bright future as well as a glorious past. However, God depends on us to plant the seed and spread the leaven. Let us work at the kingdom tasks while it is day, assured that He who has begun a good work in us will continue it until the day of Christ, when every knee shall bow and every tongue confess that He is Lord.

THE DESCENT FROM THE MOUNT OF TRANSFIGURATION

Matthew 17: 9-13

A S THE days of our Lord's earthly ministry drew to an end, an event transpired the purpose of which was to prepare and strengthen both Jesus and His disciples for the terrible furnace of trial through which they were soon to pass. On a mountain in Galilee whither Jesus and His disciples had gone for meditation and prayer, Jesus was transfigured before them, so that His face shone as the sun, and His garments became white as the light.

The disciples, gazing in rapt attention at their transfigured Master, saw two figures appear and enter into conversation with Jesus. They were Moses and Elijah, and the subject of conversation was the approaching death of Jesus in Jerusalem. It was an amazing testimony to the centrality of Calvary in history. Those who had died in faith and those who were living in faith stood on common ground before the fact of Christ's atoning death. Like a spindle on which is thrust the records of yesterday, the plans for today, and the memorandums for tomorrow, so the Cross pins man's history and hopes together, uniting past, present, and future into an intelligible whole.

What a thrilling sight it must have been! No wonder Peter exclaimed, "It is good for us to be here." Human language is impoverished when it seeks words with which to describe the supernal, ineffable experience. What a proof text it would have been for those disciples, Peter, James, and John, as they sought to convince their friends and foes that Jesus was the Messiah! Yet, as they descended from the mountain with the glow of that miraculous scene still burning in their souls, Jesus said to the Apostles: "Tell no one the vision, until the Son of man is raised from the dead."

Why should Jesus give such a command? Why should He prevent the disciples from sharing the lofty feelings and convictions that were theirs as they gazed entranced upon that scene, a scene such as no other mortals had ever been privileged to see? There are at least three reasons.

1. *To Have Talked About It Would Have Dissipated the Effect of It.*

After great spiritual experiences, it is well to think them through, to ponder, reconstruct, and relive them, so that they may be firmly fixed in our souls. Not until they have become a part of us should we feel prepared to share our great experiences. After all, we have a right to share only that which is indisputably ours. After His baptism and the assuring voice of the Father, "This is my beloved Son, with whom I am well pleased," Jesus went into the wilderness to spend forty days in fasting and meditation, before He ventured forth on His public ministry. Nor did Paul begin to preach immediately after his conversion on the road to Damascus. He went down into Arabia to ponder its meaning and challenge.

A spiritual experience has little value standing alone. It is only as it is woven into the fabric of our daily conduct that it takes on meaning. Unless it is intertwined with the fiber of our motives, energies, affections, and hopes, it makes no valid contribution to the fullness of our life. A great vision is not to be regarded as a fortunate topic for conversation; it should be a dynamic force by which our weakness is transformed into strength, by which our stumbling blocks are turned into steppingstones, by which the barren areas of our life are so irrigated and enriched that a large fruitage of righteousness and Christian service is inevitable.

After Paul had that vision in which he saw a man saying, "Come over to Macedonia and help us," he did not go and tell them that vision, for the vision by itself would have done them no good. Instead, he helped those Macedonians to be free from the thrall of heathenism by preaching Christ as the Savior from sin and the hope of everlasting life. After Augustine heard the voice to take up the Scriptures and read, and in compliance with the command read an appeal to forsake his immoral life and put on the Lord Jesus Christ, he did not go about telling that experience to everyone. He translated it into a sanctified life by the power of God's grace. So it has been with every great spiritual experience, whether it be in the lives of the outstanding servants of God, or in your life and mine. If it has been a valid vision, it has been fused with everything in us, and like certain alloys made strong because of an added element, so we have become stronger spiritually because of what these spiritual experiences have wrought in our life.

Lest some be discouraged by this talk of visions, and say in all sincere sadness, "I have had no such exalted experience," I wish to explain that it is not the astounding features that make a vision valid, but the sanity and the practicality of it that justify it and give it worth. I doubt that there is anyone here who at some point in the worship service, has not felt as if some hymn stanza, some sentence in the liturgy, some Scripture passage, some utterance from the pulpit, has been for that individual alone—not because the minister intended it, but because the Spirit of God intended it. Perhaps the love of God has dawned upon your soul with such a splendor as you never saw it before, and you can hardly keep back your tears of joy and gratitude. Perhaps a path of duty and opportunity has beckoned and, following it, you have seen that it was God's gift to you. Perhaps you have felt the sustaining presence of Christ in some trial when you have prayed for help. These are but examples of spiritual experiences that ought to be a part of our religious life. Live up to that vision; hearken to that voice.

Those disciples and our Lord himself were strengthened by their mountaintop experience. They didn't need to talk about it. It spoke through their deepened faith and their heightened joy. If we take our mountaintop experiences with us into life, if we carry Sunday worship with us into the tasks and temptations of the week, others will soon know that something has touched us and blessed us.

2. *To Have Revealed That Vision Would Have Torn It from Its Context.*

"Tell no one the vision, until the Son of man is raised from the dead." Jesus did not place a wholesale prohibition upon the disciples. It was a conditional prohibition—"Until the Son of man is raised from the dead." Why could they relate that experience after the resurrection but not before? Evidently the resurrection is the key to an understanding of it. Recall who appeared to Jesus—Moses and Elijah, saints long passed from this earthly life to the life beyond. The whole miraculous scene pointed to the glory of the redeemed in the life after death. It revealed Jesus as the fulfillment of the hopes of the living and the dead; for the conversation pertained to Christ's approaching death in atonement for man's sin and as the price of his redemption.

The vision could not stand alone. It was incomplete without the Resurrection. Therefore, it could accomplish little good apart from the fact which supported it and which it supported. Not until after that first Easter did the full radiance of the Transfiguration scene burst upon the disciples. Then it was that they saw that Christ, and Christ alone, lights up the life beyond the grave. There is no darkness, no weeping, no sorrow where the glorified Christ reigns. The Jewish conception of the life beyond the grave was one of gloom and inertia. Jesus changed that conception to one of light and activity for the children of God.

3. *To Have Told It Might Have Encouraged False Ideas and Fanaticism.*

Messianic yearnings are apt to assume strange and distorted expressions in any age. False and fanatical ideas of the coming of the Messiah prevailed in Jesus' generation, and every generation since has been prone to grasp at unwholesome and unworthy conceptions of the millennial reign. It was to forestall such a development, probably, that Jesus enjoined silence until the course of events would shed light upon its real significance.

In the prophecy of Malachi there are found these words: "Remember the law of my servant Moses, the statutes and ordinances that I commanded him at Horeb for all Israel. Behold, I will send you Elijah the prophet before the great and terrible day of the Lord comes." Was this mountain vision the fulfillment of those words? Jesus said No. Referring to John the Baptist, He said that Elijah had already come. He did not mean that any reincarnation had taken place. He meant that the spirit of Elijah was the same as that of John—a spirit of fearless, faithful preaching of the Word of God. He was saying, in effect, that God would visit no judgment on men, unless through God-inspired preaching they had had an opportunity to repent. If any perish in God's judgment, it must then be their own fault.

There is a sense in which it can be said that all preachers of repentance are forerunners of the Messiah's reign in human life, like Elijah and John. God's Word does not fail. That, however, does not justify a false literalism. See how close to that error the disciples came until Jesus corrected them by placing a deeper, spiritual interpretation upon Malachi's prophecy. There is a type of mind that is always ready to believe that the most impossible and unlikely interpretation which can be placed on a passage must be true. Another example of false literalism that led to grave error was the interpretation of Jesus as the King of the Jews. Because He had no crown, no palace, no army as other kings had, the Jews could not see anything kingly about Him.

Let us read our Bibles intelligently and not superstitiously. A false literalism in interpreting Scripture has been a ball and chain on mankind. It has justified cruelty in the name of religion; it has hindered scientific discovery; it has brought schism into the Church of Christ; it has defended the institution of slavery. Let us learn of Jesus to beware of false literalism that can only foster fanaticism and error. Let us not tithe mint and cumin, as the Pharisees did, and forget the weightier matters of God's Word. Let us be as familiar as possible with the Bible, even as Jesus was, and from its hallowed pages will come voices and visions for us, rebuking, comforting, transforming, and strengthening us.

HEAREST THOU THE CHILDREN'S VOICES?

Matthew 21:14-17

ST. MICHAEL'S DAY is the day in the Church Year when Christians think of angels and children. Somehow it is easy to put the two together. It is comforting to learn, as we do in the epistle for the day, that there are spiritual hosts fighting on the side of goodness and purity and truth. It is challenging to learn, as we do in the gospels for the day, that we have the responsibility of training the younger generation, so that they also may fight on the side of goodness and truth.

The cruel and tragic events that took place in Jerusalem during the last week of our Lord's earthly life are lightened here and there by some occasional gleam of praise, sympathy, or faith. News had spread that Jesus was in the court of the Temple, and soon blind and lame people were gathered about Him, seeking deliverance from their physical handicaps. "And he healed them," we are told. As a result of those miracles, all who were present were amazed. There were some boys present, who, like Jesus at the age of twelve, were there for their first obligatory attendance at the Passover. These boys, on seeing the miracles performed by Jesus, broke into the chant which had been sung the day before by their elders as Jesus entered Jerusalem, "Hosanna to the Son of David!" The priests and the scribes resented the homage being paid to Jesus, and desired Jesus himself to curb the demonstration. They said to Him, "Do you hear what these are saying?"

We have all heard the saying, "Children should be seen and not heard." Nevertheless, we would do well to listen to the voices of children more than we do. I would like to lift those words of the scribes and the priests out of their original setting, and give them a much wider application. Think of the children of the world in these troubled times. "Do you hear what these are saying?"

1. *There Are the Voices of Those Crying for Freedom to Unfold Their God-given Possibilities.*

We think of the physically handicapped. There is no more beautiful and touching chapter in the story of Christian enterprise than the ministry to the physically handicapped. Have you ever been to an institution like Bethphage in central Nebraska? Have you seen the children with their various deformities and handicaps? They must lift their voices in hosannas of praise to Jesus who has inspired the ministry of love and sympathy which they receive. Deep in the soul of every human being is the desire to be loved, to be remembered, to be understood. Even when there cannot be physical release, there can be spiritual release, and every Christian institution that ministers to the unfortunate can point to those who are happy in heart and free in soul because of the sympathy and love they have found.

We think of those fettered not by physical handicaps but by racial prejudice. We have seen what has happened in Little Rock and other southern communities. Children who have been yearning for an education have, for years, been given poor teachers and poor facilities. When, at last, federal courts decreed that in the interests of justice and public welfare, they were entitled to the same education as that received by white children, prejudice and hatred stood in their way. There were people who wanted to silence the voices of these children crying for an education. The tragedy was not that federal troops had to intervene to guarantee those children the right to attend high school. The real tragedy is that so many people will not accept the principles of justice and fair play.

We think of the hungry and cold children of so many areas in our disturbed world. There are agencies through which their voices are brought to us. One of the chief agencies is that of Lutheran World Relief. The clothing, medicine, and food which are supplied through this agency must surely cause many children to join their voices to those in the Temple who sang, "Hosanna to the Son of David!"

We think of the children in our own midst who desire to draw near to Jesus. A child needs more than clothes and food and schooling. A child needs Christ, needs the faith and moral idealism and unselfishness that Christ gives. How can any parent worthy of the name withhold that boon from their children?

2. *There Are the Voices of Those Children Who Have Been Kept from Christ.*

"Do you hear what these are saying?" There is no praise of God or Christ upon their lips. Even as children they have learned only blasphemous use of divine names. Even in the lowest grades of our schools, it is not uncommon to find children whose home influence is so undesirable and godless that these children become a problem by reason of their profanity.

What these children are saying underneath their profane speech is, "We are not as guilty as our elders." Those who have to deal with the problem of delinquency tell us that it is not a problem of juvenile delinquency but of parental delinquency. There is much we elders can do for children. We owe them a good example. We can give them every encouragement toward a noble life. We can show interest in their school work, their programs, their recitals. We can pray for them. We can encourage them to attend Sunday school and junior choir and Luther League.

When children are allowed to grow up in un-Christian homes, surrounded by un-Christian influences, it is only a question of time before they become a menace to the peace, health, and safety of their community. We are shocked at the crimes being committed by youngsters. Even though the situation is relieved a little by the fact that such youngsters are a decided minority, the pathos of the matter is that it is such a noticeable group that judges, writers, and others view the problem with grave concern.

When people bring children into the world, they have the responsibility before God to train up those children in the way they should go. It is more than responsibility. It is wonderful opportunity and high privilege. This brings me to the most beautiful scene of all.

3. *There Are the Voices of Those Who Have Had the Advantage of Religious Training.*

They are filled with a spirit of true joy. Christian training ought never be a gloomy thing. It should touch the emotions of joy for children. On Rally Day, and at Christmas and Easter programs, one is given a feeling of exaltation when one hears the glad enthusiasm with which the children praise God. They recognize the saving power of God. It is a wonderful thing for children to learn to believe in God and see Him at work in the world. They realize instinctively that this world must be God's world. They are attracted to Jesus. He is the kind of friend they want, and He wants them. Long ago, when some elders tried to monopolize Jesus and prevent the children from coming to Him, Jesus said, "Let the children come to me, do not hinder them; for to such belongs the kingdom of God."

Man is so constituted that he wants a hero, a master, someone to follow and emulate. That mankind has often demonstrated that it is like foolish sheep following false shepherds is a matter of historical record. We need not go beyond our own generation. Mussolini, Hitler, Stalin, and a host of lesser false shepherds have lured millions to their physical and spiritual destruction by reason of false promises and deceptive appearances. Jesus possesses the qualities man really wants—strength of purpose, sincerity of motive, courage of conviction, sympathetic understanding, moral grandeur, unselfish spirit. Children are naturally drawn to such a personality as steel filings are drawn to a magnet.

Let us not withhold from our children that which is their right and joy, namely, a buoyant faith in Him who is the light of the world and the light of man. Parents have a definite responsibility to nourish children's faith and to tune their hearts to worship through the religious spirit of the home. They should be allies of the Sunday school, not stumbling blocks which Sunday school training must overcome. Let us not, like some long ago, resent the voices of the children in the Temple of God. The corporate worship of a congregation is for all—men and women, young and old. There are men who feel that it is sufficient if the women attend church while they putter with household chores. There are grownups who feel that only they can benefit by the service of worship, so they allow their children to go home, or run the streets, while they are at church. Let us learn the value of the family pew. There is nothing finer on a Sunday morning than to see father, mother, and children sitting together in the same pew, worshiping the same Lord and Savior, singing the same "Hosanna to the son of David!"

GOD'S SOIL

Matthew 6:20-26

IN THE heart and mind of the average person, four goals loom large as the fulfillment of human ambition and effort. They are the acquisition of earthly riches, the joy of continuous feasting, the thrill of worldly pleasures, and the fame of an enviable reputation. Give people these things and they think they will be happy and contented. Or will they?

Jesus did not think so. He said, "Woe to you that are rich, for you have your consolation. Woe to you that are full now, for you shall hunger. Woe to you that laugh now, for you shall mourn and weep. Woe to you, when all men speak well of you, for so their fathers did to the false prophets."

The wealthy Wall Street broker going out for a glass of milk to still the gnawing pain of his ulcers, the people who throw enough in their garbage cans every day to keep a refugee family alive, the giddy crowd that nightly makes the round of gambling casinos and night clubs, the egotist who never tires of seeing his name and picture in the papers—are these life's fortunate ones?

The trouble with riches is that they often spoil a man's relations with his fellow men, they may seriously deteriorate a person's character, and they often displace God as an object of trust. The trouble with constant feasting is that it dulls, enervates, and soon leaves men hungry again— hungry not only for food, but for some permanently satisfying experience. The trouble with worldly pleasures lies in the fact that, like drugs, they break down self-control, demand increased doses, and only add to life's nervous tensions and problems. The trouble with fame is that it is mostly froth and bubble, it is such a transient thing, it is built on shifting sands. God finds meager harvests from the soil of riches, pleasure, and fame. Or perhaps we should say that the devil, being envious of God's harvest prospects, always sows abundant tares in such soil.

God's soil is of another kind. Because it seems so sterile, the devil often feels that there would be no purpose in sowing tares in it, and so he, the arch deceiver, deceives himself. Thus it comes about that the soil from which God raises richest harvests of faith, love, righteousness, and hope is that which, in the eyes of most men, seems most unpromising.

1. *Poverty.*

"Blessed are you poor, for yours is the kingdom of God." In pronouncing that benediction, Jesus was not blessing poverty as such; for there is no blessing in overcrowded tenements, in unsanitary living conditions, and in low living standards. Poverty, rather than opening men's eyes to God's kingdom, may be conducive to apathy, drunkenness, and immorality. Jesus was speaking to His disciples, to those who followed Him and listened to Him. The fact that they had to work hard for a living saved them from the temptation of idleness. The fact that they never knew whether they would have food to eat on the morrow led them to depend on God. They were never encased in the hard shell of self-sufficiency.

For over a thousand years, certain orders of Roman Catholic Christianity have been pledged to poverty, and from some of them have come strong and radiant personalities like Francis of 'Assisi. One often wonders if great leaders like Abraham Lincoln and Booker T. Washington could have grown in any other soil than poverty.

The difficulty of earning a livelihood calls for everyday heroism. With none of the allurements of wealth to distract them, the poor have a soil condition in which they can find happiness within themselves rather than in outward luxuries. Jesus said, "The kingdom of God is within you."

2. *Hunger.*

"Blessed are you that hunger now, for you shall be satisfied." How could Jesus who must have seen the dull eyes of starving men and the bloated stomachs of starving children speak such words? Did he envision an upsurge of sympathy in men that would result in such a sharing of food that none should know hunger? Or was he thinking only of a deeper hunger in mankind?

One might say that all history is the record of hunger— hunger for land, hunger for power, hunger for fame, hunger for food, hunger for truth, hunger for freedom. Take the hunger of man's soul and mind and body away, and you have stagnation. Those who hunger are possessed of a tremendous driving power.

As I pointed out in connection with the previous beatitude, Jesus was talking to His followers. He was not thinking of the insatiable craving for power and possessions that drives man to cruel deeds at times. He was thinking of those who followed Him because they were hungry for truth. He had in mind those who were in harmony with himself because they hungered for something of that goodness and holiness which they recognized in Him. Such hunger will be satisfied, not because of the driving power toward realization which the hunger creates, but because of the receptiveness of spirit which exists. When men are willing to receive, God gives. The virgin Mary in her song said, "He has filled the hungry with good things." She was quoting from Psalm 107, "He satisfies him who is thirsty, and the hungry he fills with good things." God's children have always been able to make that discovery.

Johan Bojer in *The Great Hunger* shows how hunger for knowledge and riches and fame drives a man on, but lacks the power to bring permanent satisfaction, and that it is only through spiritual hunger that man finds true satisfaction.

There certainly are times when emptiness rather than fullness proves to be the soil in which God can produce rich harvests.

3. *Sorrow.*

"Blessed are you that weep now, for you shall laugh." To whom do these words bring no message? Nothing is more universal than the experience of sorrow. A woman whose son was dead once came to Buddha hoping that he might in some way restore her little one to life again. Buddha told her to take a bowl and go round the city and beg a peppercorn from each house in which some close relative had not died, and he promised to restore her child when she brought back the bowl full of peppercorns. When the woman returned at nightfall, there was not a peppercorn in her bowl. Thus she learned the universality of sorrow, and was exhorted to endure what all must suffer.

Jesus knew full well the universality of sorrow, but He had a better message than an exhortation to endurance. He said it could be a blessed experience rather than a bitter one. There are some things we learn best when sorrow is our teacher—tenderness, sympathy, gentleness, understanding. It is only as we know sorrow that we can truly know the fullness of God's comfort and healing.

To develop a photograph, the negative must be taken into a dark room where the image will gradually reveal itself; and it is a simple matter of experience that as far as human character is concerned the image of Christ is developed best in the dark room.

While thinking of the ministry of sorrow to fuller life, we must recognize that Jesus did not exclude sorrow for sin as a prelude to joy. Read the story of the prodigal son who did not know the joy of welcome, the ring, the best robe, the feast until he had been a sinner mourning his sin. Read the story of those two women who knelt in shame before Jesus—the adulteress and the one who washed His feet with her tears—and we see again how comfort cannot come until there has been sorrow. Or read the story of the penitent thief on the cross. Had he not experienced the wracking pain of crucifixion, he might never have found the joy of salvation. In every congregation, there are those who are closer to Christ because in some dark hour the true Light shone into their lives. Sorrow can truly be fertile soil for God's rich harvests.

4. Persecution.

"Blessed are you when men hate you, and when they exclude you and revile you, and cast out your name as evil, on account of the Son of man! Rejoice in that day, and leap for joy, for behold, your reward is great in heaven; for so their fathers did to the prophets."

In a godless world, hatred and persecution are the inevitable results of faithfulness to God. Sometimes it may be only ridicule or ostracism or criticism; again it may be imprisonment, exile, or horrible suffering and death. Whatever form the persecution takes, it becomes a test of faith. It may come to children playing on the playground, when they refuse to join in some naughty prank. It may come to teen-agers in high school, when they refuse to compromise their Christian ideals on dates. It may come to the workman who will have no part in "soldiering" on the job.

Christ calls for moral courage and uncompromising loyalty. He foresaw the price that many would have to pay, but He also foretold the ultimate reward. The epistle for All Saints' Day speaks of a multitude which no man can number clothed in white robes and with palms in their hands, standing before the throne of God and of the Lamb. They are those who have come out of the great tribulation. Out of such soil does God garner His sheaves. The chapter of the roll call of the heroes of faith is not yet closed. There is room in it for your name and mine.